Writing the New World

Utopianism and Communitarianism
Lyman Tower Sargent and Gregory Claeys
Series Editors

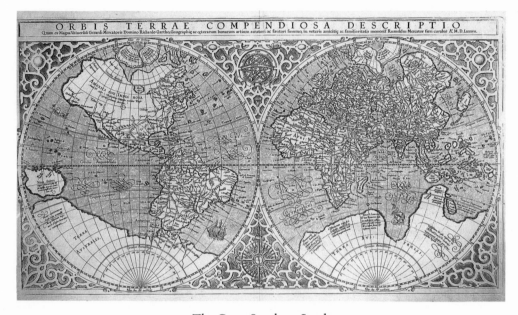

The Great Southern Land

Writing the New World

Imaginary Voyages and Utopias
of the Great Southern Land

~~~~~~~~~~

DAVID FAUSETT

SYRACUSE UNIVERSITY PRESS

First Edition 1993
93 94 95 96 97 98 99   6 5 4 3 2 1

The paper used in this publication meets the minimum requirements of American National Standard for Information Sciences—Permanence of Paper for Printed Library Materials, ANSI Z39.48-1984. ∞™

Library of Congress Cataloging-in-Publication Data

Fausett, David.
    Writing the new world : imaginary voyages and utopias of the great southern land / David John Fausett.
        p.   cm. — (Utopianism and communitarianism)
    Based on the author's thesis (Ph.D., Ecole des hautes études en sciences sociales, Paris, 1988).
    Includes bibliographical references and index.
    ISBN 0-8156-2585-5. — ISBN 0-8156-2586-3 (pbk.)
    1. Voyages, Imaginary.   I. Title.   II. Series.
G560.F25   1994
809.3'9372—dc20   93-28555

Manufactured in the United States of America

Contents

David Fausett was born in New Zealand in 1950 and has studied there and in the United States and Europe. His doctoral work on semiotics and literature at the Ecole des Hautes Etudes en Sciences Sociales, Paris, was completed in 1988 and forms the basis of this book.

Illustrations

Preface

The subject of this book may be unfamiliar to some, and my approach to it may seem even more so. The topic does not fall squarely into an academic discipline. It is a history, but one embodied in literature — a form that writers often used to discuss history and social theory before the nineteenth century. As such, however, it may throw some light on modern issues of historiography. Again, the ideas discussed are sociological or even theological, whereas the scenes within which they are played out tend to refer to the primitivism that was a forerunner of ethnography. The process of discovery and exploration that lay behind such scenes and speculations takes one at times into the realms of geography, nautical technology, or the history of trade and economics.

Although one cannot, today, claim expertise in all these areas, it remains a fact that knowledge, in the ages under consideration, was not compartmentalized in the manner familiar today — that to appreciate earlier forms of it one must be prepared to stand well back from the canvas. So it is with early ideas about the physical world and its role in shaping human social, spiritual, and intellectual life. The worldview of pre-Enlightenment folk was precisely that — a view of themselves through their relationship with the world and the wider cosmos. One can now appreciate it only by a conscious effort to recuperate such modes of thinking. In this book I attempt such an approach to the relationship between Europe's discovery of the New World and the literature that it inspired.

Some surprisingly close links have emerged from the study. At times they may be difficult to accept; one cannot decisively know, for example, what were the mutual influences between seventeenth-century cases of shipwreck and marooning and the sudden rise of a literature based on that theme. But by traversing the mental landscape a little and assembling the evidence that exists, it becomes possible to at least examine the question. In recent years both history and literary theory have become increasingly sensitive to the context of discourse, and it is hoped that the "global" context studied here can contribute to that perspective.

I am grateful to many who have taken an interest in this work, which began as a doctoral thesis at the Ecole des Hautes Etudes en Sciences Sociales under the supervision of Professor Louis Marin. The Australia-New Zealand Studies Center at Pennsylvania State University enabled me to spend the summer of 1989 at their Pattee Library, whose staff were most helpful. A Newberry Library fellowship allowed me to spend another valuable summer in 1991 at the Hermon Dunlap Smith Center for the History of Cartography, whom I thank for help with the illustrations (one of which was kindly provided by the Huntington Library). I hope the book is worthy of the help that mentors, family, friends, and librarians have contributed to its production. All translations not otherwise attributed are mine.

David Fausett

Auckland and elsewhere
July 1988–July 1993

Writing the New World

CHAPTER ONE

What Was Utopia?

In this book I examine a mode of utopian writing that was common in earlier times and closely bound with patterns of travel and human geography. It has given way to other forms, such as futurism, science fiction, social planning, or feminist utopias, that are not specifically grounded in this way. My aim is to assess what modern ways of writing about society, whether fictional or nonfictional, owe to that earlier mode, how the latter functioned as a vehicle for speculative thought, and whether a history of such ideas might, if treated as an evolving process of writing about the world, provide a useful perspective on wider problems of social theory.

It has, accordingly, three main facets: (1) a study of the basis for such writing in cosmology or geography and their growth as sciences; (2) a definition of utopia; (3) a close analysis of the difference between modern and earlier modes of such writing — of the cultural semiotics they embodied. The latter is outlined in the conclusion; the first two facets are elements of the method adopted on the way to that conclusion.

Fiction and Geography

Utopian societies before the nineteenth century were often set in unknown regions to the south of the Old World, especially in the legendary Great Southern Land. They developed an ancient link between fiction and places that, before they became empirically known, were literally "u-topian."[1] Growing familiarity with the Far East and the Americas turned the focus to *terra australis incognita,* which continued to provide a rich source of imagery. In the end this last earthly un-

1

known would be lost with James Cook's exploration of the Antarctic latitudes in 1772–1775. Its demise coincided with that of utopian writing in its original (geospatial) sense.[2] The relationship between these developments, and between writing and geography generally, is here traced through a history of the austral theme, especially as it was used by rationalist thinkers in the seventeenth century. It was one pivotal to both literary and intellectual history and had more to do with questions of truth and cultural difference than with utopian idealism. It was born of the skepticism with which travelers' tales were received. These were a source of literary inspiration because they were never simple, value-free reports of an individual's experience but were ideologically loaded, implicated in a collective identity and belief-system. The exotic, whether as fact or fiction, exposes an allegorical loading that is common to all discourse. The history and theory of it bear, therefore, on that of cultural and semiotic processes generally.

Austral fiction was exemplary in this regard historically as well as theoretically. Ancient Greeks had deduced that there must be a vast landmass to the south but found reasons to suppose that it was either inaccessible, uninhabitable, or peopled by monsters. Such factors resulted in the fabulous tone of reports by Marco Polo and other travelers in medieval times. An allegorical relationship with the world's "other half" (as seen, for example, in the King Neptune ceremony at the crossing of the equator in which the captain is dunked in a ritual inversion of social roles) stemmed from the earliest ages of travel.[3]

With Renaissance moves to exploit the riches of the East it gained new relevance, especially as commercial or state secrecy, rather than merely physical obstacles, came to dominate the issue. Portuguese exploration beyond the Spice Islands early in the sixteenth century is difficult to reconstruct, so effective was their policy of secrecy. Similar factors resulted in the persistence of a purely imaginary austral continent on the otherwise good maps from later in the century. Such problems were not unique to the southern oceans but were aggravated by their vast distances and rigors, by the difficulty of calculating longitude in early times, and by the rich spoils (whether real or imagined) to be had by overcoming such obstacles.

When the first documented visits to Australia resulted from Dutch activity in the seventeenth century, these were again shrouded in secrecy. Inroads into the myth of a southern continent were made by the middle of the century, but then the topic lapsed for a further century and more. During this time it flourished as a literary theme, an enigma that symbolized the growing contrast between mythical and empirical knowledge. These each had, too, a political bearing in an age fraught with persecution and populist revolution. The former was equated with the dogma and chicanery with which state and church connived to prop up the remnants of feudal society, the latter, with the power to unmask it and sweep it away.

Hence, the significance imaginary voyages and encounters with unknown societies had for earlier ages — they contained a grain of truth that could be construed or constructed in various ways by a writer or reader. They exposed a fact-fiction problem that can no more be denied at the level of cultural formations than at the individual level where (as Freud showed) there is no pure fantasy; any thought, behavior, or dream is based on prior experience, however deeply buried. The critical task in each case is to define what knowledge of the "unknown" region was available at the time; how it affected the work; and what impact the latter, in turn, had on perceptions and ideas in its time.

Europe's commercial expansion and exploration, especially as it approached its antipodean limits, formed the background to its exotic literature. This was a fitful process, leading broadly to geographical knowledge and realistic description, and was most clearly manifested in fiction about the regions that remained unknown the longest. Authors of such writings used the topic of exploration as a narrative basis while at another level they inquired into the effects it was having on social ideology — effects that heralded an age of enlightenment and revolution. their works, too, would finally be overtaken by history and supplanted by scientific descriptions of the natural and social worlds.[4]

The eighteenth century was the heyday of such literature in numerical terms, producing the spate of works epitomized by *Robinson Crusoe* and *Gulliver's Travels*. But the popularity of themes of maritime adventure had largely been established by a set of works spanning the four decades from 1668 to 1708. They, and the prior tradition they built on, form the object of the study presented here. Again, seventeenth-century English political utopias are significant in the genealogy of modern fiction and social theory but are examined here only insofar as they show the basis of all such writing in human geographies.

This approach is made from various angles: sociological, epistemological (as a problem of distinguishing fact from fiction), and literary (as a phase in the evolution of the modern novel). In each of these ways, the austral enigma lent itself to the critical or analytical function and gave rise to new kinds of literary and social realism. Thus, it transcends both its regional and its literary interest.

Such works were often announced as "philosophical novels" and usually had a preface emphasizing the truth of the story. To appreciate this ploy, and why a novel should pretend to be philosophical, it is necessary to view them against a background of political censorship or, more generally, of a premodern conceptual horizon—that of the closed society. The claim of veracity was a thinly veiled play on truth itself. It was not merely a boastful indifference to it, an indulgence in fantasy, as it might now seem. It had a more positive significance for ages saturated with communitarian ideals and allegorical styles of discourse. The unverifiability of distant events and places was exploited as a way of "dislocating" uncritical acceptance of the status quo and lent itself to polemical purposes, particularly under repressive regimes such as the France of Louis XIV.

While at one level these novels addressed problems of the latter order, at another level they embodied the closed society's opening onto a wider world—its confrontation with history. This was a process bearing in turn on language. Statements about the world always imply an element of cultural relativity, however small—a gap that reflects the presence of a knowing community and is exploited as a marker of its identity. Truth and meaning obliquely refer to this semantic "matrix," or collective subject. Exotism, in describing a world beyond that circle, engages a problem that one critic has called the "inexpressibility topos." A traveler who has witnessed another world reports things that may either depend on or evade known truths, but "both strategies fend off an essential problem of travel writing: the traveler's medium is language, and the language he uses has evolved as an envelope specific to its region and culture. It has no words for what is alien."[5]

The foregoing defines the problem in approaching a form of writing closely related to the travel account and originally derived from it. For that abstract (en)closure—the semiotic matrix, the envelope of the letter—was what the classical utopia portrayed. It gave imaginary form to something that, although traditionally held to be the highest good, was inexorably dissolved by history. It was a relay in the march from

1. The archaic notion of a southern continent in Macrobius's fifth-century *Commentary of Scipio's Dream. Courtesy the Newberry Library.*

a world of myth or "local truth" to one of referential objectivity, one that would arise as a result of the globalization of the social world. The latter, thus, had a downside as well as an upside. It is pivotal both to the history of utopian writing itself and to any meaningful approach to it today.

Utopia and History

Such writing referred, beyond processes of discovery and cultural "knowledge" (in the biblical sense as well as the scientific), to truth itself and its social foundations. One is less concerned here with the political ideas embodied in utopias than with the latter as a rhetorical form — one effective in earlier ages but no longer in modern times. The study focuses on the conjunction, during explorations of the austral unknown, of a residually utopian history and an increasingly realist form of utopia — a double paradox that made the genre as a whole, and the austral theme in particular, an ideal crucible in which to experiment with ideas about society. Real reports were normally viewed with skepticism, whereas fictional ones were often so artfully contrived that they were received as real. The two modes of discourse and reception overlapped as long as the places referred to remained empirically unknown.

But the progressive separation of fact from fiction or allegory would eventually raise empiricism into an end in itself, displacing myth in favor of today's dichotomized, dismembered forms of knowledge. Such was the impact on early thought of a sudden broadening of worldly horizons. A historiographical approach is, therefore, needed if one is to re-create the conditions of knowledge of a bygone era. This implies, too, a position on the vexed issue of defining *utopia*. A distinction is made here between "utopianism" in the modern sense (of an active, future-oriented, usually political idealism) and a more contemplative earlier form that examined ideals or propositions speculatively.[6] There, tropical abundance might be a metaphor for wealth, or equatorial uniformity for egalitarianism; an antipodean "world upside-down" might signify a revolution in moral values, and so forth.

The term *utopism* is used for this type of writing,[7] by contrast with the utopianism that, in the *Oxford Dictionary*'s words, is "characteristic of an ardent but unpractical reformer." The classical mind, ever locating

6

or seeking its ideals in the past, saw the speculative function as a basically conservative one,[8] and its utopias were implicated in that aim. Weaving a text from the tension between the real and the ideal, between travelers' reports and the ideas of cosmologists or geographers, they held up images of other worlds to the real one as distorting mirrors. To realize a model was not usually the issue (societies were not made in those times, but lived) nor was prediction of the future. The message lay in an aping of travel reports and their allegorical implications. Ambivalence with regard to cultural values and an abstractive (rather than programmatic) interest in social models characterized the classical utopia. It even tended toward self-parody, and from ancient times partook of a style known as Menippean satire, which combined moralistic and parodic or ironizing tendencies.

Modern criticism tends to misjudge its significance by falling prey to various kinds of anachronism. Individualistic concerns with a hero and his adventures (or even with psychoanalyzing the author)[9] obscure its communitarian focus and reflect forces that were, at the time, only beginning to dominate society. They would find expression in the castaway "Robinsonade"—the progression toward which took place within the series of works examined here, as noted. This does not mean, however, that late classical utopias have no interest other than as forerunners of the Robinsonade or that they can be adequately understood through it. They built on earlier traditions and had a radicality that reflected the deformations these were undergoing with the world's globalization.

By turning pretentions to know the truth inside out, they offered an "ideological critique of ideology."[10] Their motivations were of an order that matches neither the Robinson image of industrial humanity as a *homo œconomicus* nor modern socialism as a distribution of material wealth. The latter was, before the rise of industrial society, only one among other concerns that were more abstract. Although it is true that a political economy was at least implicit in early utopias, it formed only part of a broader set of provisions illustrating the imaginary society. A distortion is introduced by making it central.[11]

Another way to view the early utopia is as a forerunner of science fiction. Darko Suvin sees the sixteenth and seventeenth centuries as one of the "great whirlpools of history," generating a type of literature "as opposed to supernatural or metaphysical estrangement as it is to naturalism or empiricism."[12] Yet, there was at the time no science, in the modern sense, to fictionalize. Such works can, at the most, be regarded as a prescience or "pre-science" of later cultural developments. The tension identified by Suvin makes sense in terms of traditional modes of writing about the world, not of modern ones transcending its bounds through technological fantasy.

Modern literary categories tend to anachronistic if applied to classical utopism. Such writing was marginal in its own time and discussed, if at all, by reference to the works of Plato and More. Only in the eighteenth century did seventeenth-century English political works come to be thought of as utopias, and their heuristic function, although recognized, was little theorized. Nor was much distinction made until the nineteenth century between utopias, Robinsonades, and imaginary voyages. There was (and still is) little agreement about which of these ingredients were necessary or how they related to each other.[13]

A solution may lie in recognizing that any of them may be present and that one's task is less to classify a work in terms of such criteria than to define its relationship with the historical conditions of its production. None of the possible approaches (literary, political, geographical, theological, psychological) alone offers an explanatory model that encompasses the variety, evolution, and downfall of utopian writing. A purely literary one is inadequate because utopia was always marginal to literature, as much involved with ethnography or with politico-economic or religious theory as with literary aims. The other approaches, too, impose their distorting grids. The writing in question was the product of an ethos that did not make such distinctions and was relatively passive in its relationship with social history.

Nor is authorial intention a reliable criterion as critics have noted in discussing the various types of utopia (eutopias, dystopias, satire, aspirations to social control, religious millennia, pastoral Arcadias, "Lands of Cockayne," or ideal commonwealths).[14] Even peripheral forms, such as the medieval empire of Prester John, shared "a utopian need: the specificity of a formal framework, and not of a cultural given. Of a function, therefore, not an intention."[15] In literary utopias the problem is exacerbated by the fact that the concept of utopia has become inextricably linked with intentional communities and, for nonspecialists today, has no other meaning. In theoretical terms, this attitude translates into a "hope-principle"[16]—one that more might today subscribe to if it were able to offer a credible analytical basis for such optimism.

Categories such as those mentioned are useful, but no such "essence of utopia" can be agreed upon. The historicist approach adopted here has no such preconceptions but is based on certain fundamental postulates: that the concept originally referred to geospatial configurations and their cultural significance; that a distinction must be made between modern and earlier modes of such writing and of its societal referent; and that its formal or rhetorical qualities need to be distinguished from its use in a directly political way, as a tract.

The writing in question reflects the embedment of any society (real or imaginary) in a historical and geographical context. In narrative terms this means that a utopia is inseparable from the imaginary voyage to it, and the terms *voyage-utopia* or *utopian novel* are used to keep that relationship in view. Social ideals, too, are referred to a wider explanatory paradigm: that of the contiguity of societies and, resulting from it, the inexorable rise of the open society.[17] That this was an effect of the West's expansion is obvious, and various works show that it was so to their authors. What may be less obvious is a further effect of that relationship: that utopia, in its classical form, would lose its relevance once the world became fully known and give way to other forms of fiction, notably, to the modern realist novel. In other words, a single paradigm can explain both a social and a literary history.

That paradigm is sought here by tracing the relationship between utopia and history through to Enlightenment times. By the latter's end it would culminate in the loss of the last great geographical unknown and in the classical utopia's demise as the world ran out of significant spatial difference. The link between these developments furnishes clues not only to the forms utopia has taken but, more generally, to the way "local truth" gave way to realism and empiricism in the Enlightenment.

CHAPTER TWO

The Discovery of the Austral World

The Ancient World

The concept of an "other half" of the world arose with Greek cosmology in ancient Asia Minor as scientific ways of describing the world supplanted mythical traditions. Among such myths was that of an "earth-disk" rimmed by a river called Ocean, with the sky on one side and the underworld on the other. These older ways were swept up in commercial, social, and intellectual developments that gave rise to geography and were influenced by the Greeks' close relationship with the sea.[1] They had a counterpart in speculation about society itself, a conjunction out of which the literary utopia would be born.

An early geographical concept was that of a spherical world with symmetrical hemispheres and a great southern landmass that counterbalanced the known would (Africa, Europe, and Asia). It is thought that Anaximander of Miletus made a map and envisaged a spherical earth in the sixth century B.C., and in the mid-fifth century Parmenides expressed similar ideas, incorporating an equatorial axis and symmetrical climatic bands or "zones."[2] But a tension between two ways of describing the world—"interested," or mythopoetic, and "disinterested," or empiricist—would continue until quite recent times; in general, the unknown world was defined on the basis of symmetry with the known. The same logic implied that the southern continent might be inhabited, but this idea was rejected—it was thought to be peopled (if at all) by monsters.

This overriding of scientific motives by ideological ones was carried forward by philosophy and theology. In the fourth century B.C. Plato exploited the tension between them by basing his imaginary society, Atlantis, on the notion of an antipodean continent. Aristotle discussed more soberly the questions of a "torrid" or equatorial zone, or whether Africa was circumnavigable, the antipodes inhabited, and so forth. Actual experience was gradually brought to bear on these problems, particularly with the Greek drive eastward to India under Alexander the Great in the late fourth century B.C.

Aegean peoples had made sea voyages in Homeric times, but the Dorians who invaded from the north were indifferent or even hostile to such activities, and by about 1,000 B.C. the Phoenicians controlled the Mediterranean. Arabs, meanwhile, dominated the Indian Ocean[3] where monsoon winds had long been used to reach the east coast of Africa for spices, ivory, metals, or slaves. An Egyptian-Phoenician voyage circa 1490 B.C. may even have rounded Africa from east to west via the legendary Land of Punt (associated with Mozambique or the ancient port of Sofala).[4]

Around 1,000 B.C. the biblical alliance between Solomon and the Phoenician king, Hiram, aimed to exploit the riches of the enigmatic Ophir, which possibly referred to the Punt route. Whatever the case, this tradition later influenced speculation about the Pacific Islands, which were loosely called the "Islands of Solomon" in the period of their discovery.[5] It would be associated as well with the southern continent, an idea nourished by Marco Polo's report of fabulous lands to the south of Indochina. Again, a medieval tradition placed the "Golden Khersonese," a land of vast riches, in a promontory of the southern continent adjacent to Southeast Asia or sometimes of the latter itself.[6]

The Greeks tried (unsuccessfully) to reach the Indian Ocean via Africa, avoiding easier routes blocked by Arab powers. But this was a perilous undertaking: fears of falling off the edge of the earth or of burning up in the "torrid zone" conspired with navigational problems to make the southern regions seem unreachable and terrifying, a perception reinforced by contact with African "barbarians." Some confused Africa with India and the southern continent with both. A Hellenistic cosmologist, Eratosthenes of Alexandria (240–196 B.C.), affirmed that Africa was separate from the southern continent, but in the first century A.D. another Alexandrian, Claudius Ptolemy, still showed (in the first known atlas) an enclosed Indian Ocean analogous to the Mediterranean. The principle of symmetry still held sway, even though Ptolemy claimed to be using "hard" information obtained from a Phoenician hydrographer, Marinus of Tyre.

Ptolemy's geography long dominated ideas about the austral world—not only directly, but because the church fathers later based on it their doctrine of an Old World *oikoumene,* or "community of nations." More scientific notions had, however, been reached by Aristotle, Eratosthenes, and, more recently, by Strabo (ca. 64 B.C.–A.D. 21) and Pliny (A.D. 22–79).[7] Similar forces hindered the growth of knowledge from voyage accounts, which tended to be treated with skepticism, suspicion, or ridicule because of their likely motives. Such accounts might introduce distortions to conceal a useful trade route or exaggerate dangers, real or imaginary. Literary mockery of such "exotic truth" and the prejudice it aroused gave rise to imaginary voyages and utopias[8]—particularly in Hellenistic times when Greeks began voyaging in the Indian Ocean. Alexander sent his captain, Nearchus, down the Ganges to find a sea route home for the Greek army, and although the Greeks were not welcome in the region, they came to know easterly parts of it such as Sri Lanka, the northwest Indian Ocean, and the Red Sea, including Socotra and other islands. The first "tropical island" utopias, the Hellenistic sun states, date from this time.

Roman power fully opened up the Indian Ocean, and the name commonly used for Sri Lanka, Taprobane, may have referred as well to Sumatra. The rutters, or pilot books, for such voyages spread throughout the empire, and one of them, the *Periplus of the Erythraean Sea,* stated that Africa was circumnavigable.[9] Austral speculation, thus, focused by Pliny's time on whether the southern continent could be reached in this way and whether it was inhabited. But no further light was shed on these questions, and in medieval times the Church refused to entertain any such ideas.

Medieval geographers kept alive some of the Ancients' ideas, however, notably those thought to derive from a globe by Crates of Malos (ca. 150 B.C.), featuring two ocean-rivers set at right angles to form four landmasses. It incorporated the five climatic zones: the uninhabitable polar and equatorial zones and two temperate zones containing the continents.[10] In the north were the Old World oikoumene and a land of the Antipodes, or "opposite-footed"; in the south, Africa and a land of the Antoikoi, or Antichtones.[11] This scheme refined older ideas of a single "other continent" and upheld the notion of sphericity (denied by many Romans and by patristic ideology).

Iberian Activity

By the fourteenth century a growing trade in spices and luxuries had generated commercial pressures in Europe and competition with the Arab world for access to such commodities, reopening the quest for a route around the Cape of Good Hope. Ecclesiastical strictures against "worldly" movement were soon swept away and Ptolemaic dogma disproved by increasingly southerly roundings of Africa. Effects of this turmoil appear in literature, particularly with the rebirth of the utopia in the Renaissance; thus, Thomas More in 1516 locates his eponymous island in the Pacific Ocean, discovered a few years previously in the pursuit of a route to the East.

The role of the austral quest in these developments was increasingly distinct from that of the Americas. North America could be reached without crossing the equator and was known to Viking, Irish, and, probably, Portuguese mariners well before 1492.[12] After that time, it soon became part of the Old World orbit. South America, although initially associated with the southern continent (by, for example, Columbus at the Orinoco estuary in 1498), may have been rounded as early as 1507 (see n. 27) and was explored following the Magellan circumnavigation of 1519–1522. Access to the East via Africa, however, was subject to navigational difficulties, Church opposition, fears of monsters or of a torrid zone, and the presence of Arabs in the Indian Ocean or Chinese in the Spice Islands.[13]

But the commercial world was aware from late medieval times of the vast potential of the spice trade and of the profits being lost to powers that controlled the caravan or Red Sea routes to Europe.[14] The Vivaldo brothers of Genoa tried to sail around Africa in 1291, an idea again promoted by the Venetian geographer Marino Sanudo in 1320. This required technical know-how that had to come largely from Semitic sources to which Iberians had more direct access than Italians. It was there, building on an already strong maritime tradition, that the enterprise succeeded.[15] Some Arabian lore, however, entered Italy directly, as did that from the failing Byzantine empire. This included Ptolemy's *Geography*, the textual complement to his maps, which made available from 1409 theoretical and technical advances based on the grid system that, by 1537, had become standard map-making practice.[16]

In 1419 Portugal's Prince Henry the Navigator established a nautical college at Sagres. He was one of the more forceful members of the Aviz dynasty, founded by John I in 1385 and dedicated to building a global empire.[17] Portugal initially sought control of the African gold trade at the Mediterranean port of Ceuta, but from the early fifteenth century aimed to go directly to the source of the gold—the *mina* (mine) in Guinea. Nautical advances enabled voyagers to reach the Gulf of Guinea and the equator by midcentury, by which time the aim extended to rounding Africa and securing the East Indies trade.

Southern-hemisphere navigation called for astronomical tables based on the southerly configuration of the stars and new methods of maintaining a course independent of coasts.[18] A more efficient ship, the caravel, was developed along the lines of the Arab dhow, and a group of Portuguese, Jewish, and German mathematicians called the Junta dos Mathematicos produced tables enabling a position to be calculated by trigonometry (also of Arabian origin). A forerunner of the sextant was developed from the primitive Arab cross-staff, and one degree of latitude was found to equal 60 nautical miles or 17.5 leagues. These advances brought Bartholomew Diaz to the Cape of Good Hope in 1488 and Vasco da Gama across the Indian Ocean to establish a base at Goa in India in 1497. The east coast of Africa was secured, and Malacca was taken from the Arabs in 1511.

Portugal found a closer rival, however, when Spain ejected the Moors in 1492 and turned her attention to the New World. Rivalry between the two powers resulted in a papal division of the world into two vertical hemispheres of influence by the 1494 Treaty of Tordesillas. All that lay to the west of a Line of Demarcation 370 leagues west of the Azores— including most of America and the as yet unknown Pacific—would belong to Spain. Everything to the east, as far as the same meridian on the opposite side of the world (including the Spice Islands), was Portugal's. But this absurd pretention to "trace a line or mark on the ocean" was matched by the problem of accurately defining longitude (one not fully overcome until the invention of a marine chronometer in the eighteenth century). Around this problem of locating the line and distributing rights to lands would crystalize an avatar of the "great austral enigma" of the Ancients, dominated now by official secrecy as well as by the wiles of merchant travelers.

From a modern perspective Spain might seem to have gotten the better of the deal. But the known value of the Spice Islands would have outweighed the merely potential value of regions still unknown, and the Portuguese seem, in addition, to have used their nautical power and geographical knowledge to maximum advantage. They knew the North Atlantic well through links with Vikings settled there and a royal alliance with Denmark[19] and knew the Brazilian coasts well enough to retain the best parts within their hemisphere.[20] They protected this advantage with a policy of secrecy (providing, from 1508, for the death penalty) — details of voyages had to be immediately lodged with the Casa da India in Lisbon and nothing divulged thereafter. Foreigners working for Spain, such as Columbus and Magellan, became known as the discoverers of what others probably knew before them because they were not bound by this Portuguese code.

The eastern Line of Demarcation passed right through the spice-producing region: the Moluccas, Halmahera (Gilolo), Ceram, Amboina, and the Banda Islands. At the time, these were known only as the vague scattering of "Ophirian" islands reported by Marco Polo. Portugal is likely to have explored the area as soon as possible, especially because treaty negotiations continued, leading to the *juntas* (conferences) of Badajoz (1524) and Saragossa (1529). At the latter Portugal bought, for 350,000 gold ducats, the right to a buffer zone extending a further seventeen degrees east of the line through the Spice Islands, excluding Spain from whatever was thought to be of value in that part of the world. Evidence of preparations for this coup has been seen in some scantly known voyages of the time and in the enigmatic Dieppe maps to be discussed.

Early perceptions of the Pacific were influenced by a 1492 globe by Martin Behaim, showing an ocean of fairly appropriate dimensions with a massive continent to the south. A native of Nuremberg, he had migrated to Portugal and probably took part in the Junta dos Mathematicos and, perhaps, in some expeditions. His globe shows an archipelago extending north toward Zipangu (Marco Polo's Japan)[21] and, although still somewhat vague, contrasts starkly with the Ptolemaic image. Ptolemy, indeed, had become an institution, held in quasi-religious awe — atlases were called Ptolemies until the late–sixteenth century. But although vast and richly illustrated, they were slow to absorb the new discoveries (written treatises on the great maritime exploits of the age being almost nonexistent).[22] The Portuguese, no doubt, exploited this conservatism in their policies of secrecy and cartographical distortion.

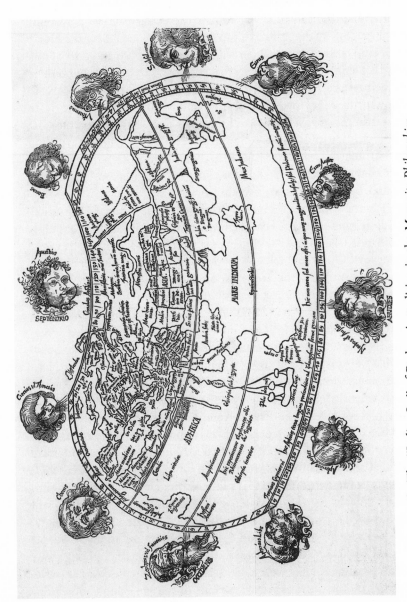

2. The "Indian Sea" of Ptolemaic tradition in the *Margarita Philosophica*
of G. Reisch (1503). Note, however, the caption along its south Coast,
"Here is not land but sea, where there are islands unknown to Ptolemy."
Courtesy of the John M. Wing Foundation, the Newberry Library.

Other traditions, too, tended to ignore the new discoveries: notably the Macrobian, or four-continent, cosmology mentioned above. Formalized around the fourth century,[23] it was carried forward by Isidore of Seville (ca. 570–636) and late-medieval scholastics such as Sacrobosco (John Holywood), Robert Grosseteste, and Roger Bacon. It produced allegorical "T-O" maps in which Asia (including the Holy Land and, far to the east, Paradise) filled the top half of an inverted world while profane Europe and Africa shared the bottom half. Such ideas featured in Ranulf Higden's cosmology of around 1350, *Polychronicon* (a 1527 edition of which still makes no mention of the recent discoveries)[24] or in the 1410 *Imago Mundi* of Pierre d'Ailly. Though outwardly conforming to church doctrine, they, nonetheless, implied that the Antipodes were accessible by sea. Columbus was influenced by them, and it has even been suggested that the name Regio patalis in India (Fringe region in the Indies), appearing in the southern continent on Macrobian maps, referred to Australia.[25]

Another non-Ptolemaic tradition used in the southward drive was the portolan, or sea chart.[26] Other suggestive fragments include a document now lost, the *Newe Zeytung aus Presillgt-Landt* (Recent report from Brazil), in which a Lisbon agent of the Augsburg bankers, Fugger, reported the discovery of a strait south of America. Attributed to the Portuguese mariner John of Lisbon, this voyage is dated before that of Magellan.[27] the Nuremberg geographer, Schöner, mentioned such a strait in 1515, in *Luculentissima quaedam terrae latius descriptio* (A dazzling description of a certain great continent), showing it and the adjacent southern continent on a globe the same year (his earlier Hauslab globe having omitted the continent). Magellan said in 1517 that he had seen the strait on a portolan made by "Martin of Bohemia" (Martin Behaim's son).[28]

Early maps of the Indonesian region feature place names thought to be of local origin (thus, Maletur is Malaya, etc.), and the southern continent is called Beach. These were places on the Chinese trading circuit reported by Marco Polo. The Dieppe maps, however, suggest a more direct knowledge. Produced by a French school of cartographers around 1536–1570,[29] they show the Indonesian archipelago with a continent to the south that appears to be a distorted representation of Australia. The latter's implications, and the question of how such information was obtained, bear not only on the early history of the region but also on the notoriety that characterized it—the mystique that was later translated into a literary theme. Some Portuguese knowledge inevitably escaped their net of secrecy, owing to the participation of foreigners and to internal dissensions and rivalries. Magellan and others defected in protest; Columbus entered the Lisbon scene as a young Genoese merchant; and Germans, Jews, and others were involved. In the East Indies themselves the Portuguese were initially guided by a Bolognese, Vartema, who had been there for more than five years.

An expedition under Antonio Abreu was sent from Malacca in 1512 to explore the Spice Islands.[30] Second in command was Francisco Serrano, a friend (or possibly relative) of Magellan and a man of doubtful loyalties.[31] Local pilots were used and may have been the source for a map featuring Malay place names attributed to the hydrographer Francisco Rodriguez.[32] The fleet sailed east along the archipelago then northeast into the spice region. At Banda a junk was bought to replace Serrano's ship *Sabaia,* lost on the way; it, too, was later lost, and altogether the voyage lasted a year. But questions remain as to where the *Sabaia* was lost, the parts played by Serrano and Rodriguez, whether information gained then was later used by Magellan, and what was done in all that time — given, especially, that the place they chose to "winter" was almost on the line of demarcation. Exploration in the Spanish zone seems a plausible motive that may have been concealed by the official accounts. Serrano emerges as something of an opportunist, and may have passed on such information to Barbosa (see n.31), Magellan, Rodriguez, and — if indirectly — to the Dieppe cartographers. There are other indications, too, of such activity in the region. Colonies established on Timor around 1514–1516 were situated just west of the line and less than three hundred miles from Australia, and an Australian coastal island on the line itself may have been fortified at this time.[33]

Accounts of later Portuguese voyages are even more hazy, owing, perhaps, to tightening security in view of the new treaty negotiations. The latter may, too, have been a factor in Charles V's launching of the Magellan expedition in 1519. A Portuguese armada leaving Goa that year under Mendonza may, in turn, have been a countermeasure and an excuse to enter the Spanish Pacific.[34] Instructed to search for the Islands of Gold, it may have split into several groups of which one coasted the north and east of Australia (possibly as far as the south coast, the site of an unexplained wreck). A route so far south, McIntyre argues, would have generated a distortion in their method of charting by loxodromes (rhumb lines), causing the coast to appear as it does in the Dieppe maps. Here a credible representation of the northern coasts of Australia gives way to a more fanciful southeastward extension, sometimes joined to the traditional southern continent. Others, however, consider this to be an imaginary coastline joining Australia to the northeast coast of New Zealand, whose East Cape would be the promontory named "beautiful cape" (Cabo Hermoso or Fremose, etc.) on various such maps.[35]

Another obscure Portuguese voyage is that of Francisco Gomez de Sequeira northeast from the Moluccas in 1525. Apparently aiming to locate the Line of Demarcation, he reached an island he named San Tomé (St. Thomas). McIntyre identifies this as present-day Faraulep and speculates that the expedition may have had a double aim or even a double itinerary—Sequeira's deputy, Diogo da Rocha, secretly heading southeast to Australasia. Both captains would have sought knowledge useful in the treaty negotiations. So, too, would the Spaniard Saavedra, who on a 1527 voyage from Mexico also reached what McIntyre believes to be Faraulep (which lies on the new line established at Saragossa in 1529).

Accompanying Diogo da Rocha may have been another shadowy figure, the pilot and hydrographer Joao Alfonso. He seems a likely source for the Dieppe school's information about Australasia, whether he acquired it himself, through Rodriguez, or from others such as Serrano. He is thought to have defected with it to France in 1529–1530, having been recruited for or during the 1529 Parmentier expedition to the East Indies.[36] Naturalized by François I, he took the name Alfonse de Saintonge, eluded Portuguese efforts to extradite him, and continued his seafaring career, becoming something of a popular hero. He published a *Cosmographie* in 1545, but it is his semifictional *Voyages avantureux* (1559, although written earlier),[37] that seem to refer to Australia. This information would have been available, along with charts either by Alfonso himself or copied from Portuguese originals, by about 1535–1542 when the first major Dieppe maps were produced.

A likely prototype for the latter is the *Carta Anonyma Portuguesa* (ca. 1533), possibly by Alfonso or plagiarized from the Lisbon cartographer Lopo Homem. In the empiricist or portolan style, it represented only what had actually been seen (thus, the south coasts of Indonesian islands were absent). The Dieppe mapmakers seem to have reverted from this style, combining a traditional southern continent with Portuguese dis-

19

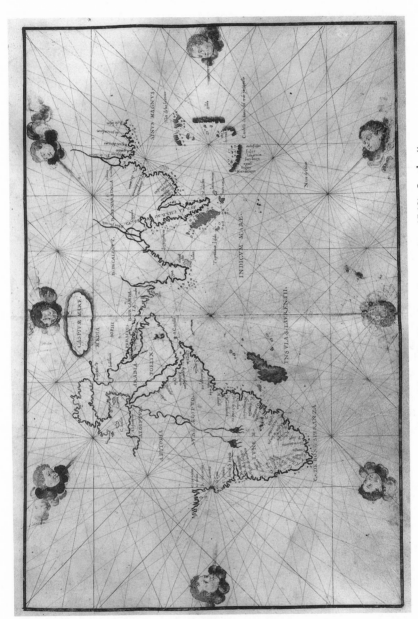

3. Portolan-style world map by Battista Agnese (ca. 1560). In the "empiricist" style typical of this tradition, no uncharted southern lands are shown nor even the south coasts of the Indonesian islands. *Courtesy the Newberry Library.*

coveries in northern Australia. But a Scotsman working at Dieppe, Jean Rotz (John Ross or Rose), perhaps favored the portolan approach and emancipated himself from Ptolemaic dogma. Like Alfonso a man of the sea, he may have been the first to share in the latter's knowledge of Australia; his *Boke of Idrography,* dedicated to England's Henry VIII around 1535–1542, refers, for example, to a "Greate Londe [Land] of Java" south of the Indonesian archipelago.[38]

Spanish activity focused mainly on the central and northern Pacific; it, too, was veiled in secrecy and mingled with Ophir legends. Magellan encountered few islands in the Pacific, and after his death in the Philippines, the fleet was scattered and captured by the Portuguese (except for the *Vittoria,* which completed the circumnavigation). The expeditions of Saavedra and Garcia de Loaysa made no significant discoveries. Loaysa's large fleet was scattered by storms on entering the Pacific; he died during the crossing to the Philippines, and his ship was eventually sunk by the Portuguese. Saavedra reached the Philippines and Moluccas and learned that the remnants of Loaysa's fleet had come to grief there but lost two of his own ships in the process and died during his second attempt to return to Mexico by a southerly route. His crew then joined that of Loaysa in the Moluccas.

Grijalva sailed from newly conquered Peru in 1537, in search of lands thought to be rich in gold. Crossing in the island-strewn latitude of 6°S, he found some in the western Pacific. Villalobos's 1542 expedition ended in disaster but reported Spanish-speaking people in the Caroline Islands (possibly remnants of Saavedra's fleet). Similarly, Loaysa's ship, the *San Lesmes,* may have ended up in the Tuamotu group and given rise to further voyages by the crew or their descendants.[39] A 1564–1566 expedition under Legaspi established Spain in the Philippines; his companion, Urdaneta, and a mutinous pilot independently forged a return route via the north Pacific.[40]

Pedro Sarmiento, a member of the 1567–1569 Mendaña expedition that discovered the Solomon Islands, claimed (on the basis of Inca lore) that a vast continent rose to 15°S, six hundred leagues west of Peru. He and the expedition's pilots, Gallego and Gamboa, contributed to the detailed depiction of a southern continent on late sixteenth-century maps (Mercator in 1569 shows Magellan's mid-Pacific Shark Islands, Los Tiburones, as a promontory of the continent).[41] Published in Herrera's *Historia general* (Madrid, 1601–1615), this first Spanish search for the continent prefigured more spectacular claims by Quirós, to be discussed. Another Spaniard, Juan Fernandez, claimed to have reached around 1576 a land whose description suggests New Zealand — an enigma as yet unresolved, like many others, in this phase of austral history.

From 1571, when Spain's Philippine base was moved to Manila, galleons made the north Pacific passage annually. In the process they became targets for piracy, bringing other nations into the Pacific. Drake's circumnavigation (1577–1580), or the exploits of Hawkins, stimulated English interest in the region and put a damper on Spanish activity, and an English East India Company became active in the Spice Islands in 1601. From 1605 austral speculation was influenced from several quarters: Dutch activity in the East Indies; the propaganda of Quirós; and (in France) the claims of Gonneville.

Pedro Fernandez de Quirós (1560–1614) was a Portuguese pilot working for Spain (which had absorbed Portugal in 1580). He sailed with Mendaña's abortive second expedition to colonize the Solomons in 1595; then, on a voyage of his own in 1606, he discovered the island of Espiritu Santo in Vanuatu (formerly the New Hebrides). He tried to interest the crown in a colonizing expedition there, claiming that it was part of the southern continent. He named the place Austrialia del Espiritu Santo (Austria-land of the Holy Spirit), playing on the word austral (southern) in order to flatter the Spanish-Austrian Habsburgs. These efforts were in vain and ended by destroying Quirós, but they became legendary. Not only did they inspire literary works but the name he invented survived in a modified form and actually appears on early maps of the northern Queensland area. The eighth of his fourteen *Requestes* was published in Latin by De Bry's voyage collection (1613) and then in 1617 in French and English translations.[42]

The Norman mariner Binot Paulmier de Gonneville left Honfleur in 1503 and returned in 1505, claiming to have visited the Southern Land. Having (conveniently?) lost all his papers in a disaster at sea, he made this claim in a sworn statement. He brought with him a native named Essomerik, who was baptized in his name and whose descendant, Jean Paulmier de Courtonne, canon of Lisieux, later canvassed for a mission to his ancestor's land.[43] Although Gonneville's voyage is now associated with Brazil, it was widely believed in the seventeenth century that he had indeed reached the southern continent (which many confused with South America, in any case).

Dutch Discovery

A Dutch takeover of the Far East trade grew out of their involvement with the Iberian world under Spanish-Habsburg rule.[44] The reign of Charles V (1519–1558) grew oppressive as the northern Netherlands gravitated into the Protestant orbit, and this worsened under Philip II (1556–1598). In 1579 the seven northern provinces broke away to form the Union of Utrecht. The following year Philip acquired the throne of Portugal and tried to crush the Dutch by blockading Lisbon, a focus of their (already considerable) international trade. But the plan backfired, and in 1581 the United Provinces formally ceded from Spain. Commercial activity moved north from Antwerp to Amsterdam, and the new state, joined by French and Flemish Protestants, Iberian Jews, and others, developed into a dynamic mercantile society. England was (initially) sympathetic to it, and Dutch trade expanded vigorously around the world.

Spain did not recognize the republic until 1648, during which time the Dutch had access to Iberian maritime lore, including that about the East Indies route. In 1583 Waghenaer published charts and sailing directions in the portolan style, and Linschoten's nautical atlas, or *Itinerario,* of 1596 was researched in Lisbon and Goa. Mercator's famous maps, the *Theatrum Orbis Terrarum* (1570) of Ortelius, and a 1597 map by Wytfliet all reflect Portuguese knowledge.[45] Petrus Plancius, a leading force in the Dutch buildup, also drew on such sources.

Cornelis de Houtman and J. C. van Neck led spice-buying expeditions to the East Indies in 1595–1598, and settlement began in 1596. By 1601 sixty-five ships had sailed, and accounts of such exploits soon began to appear. Domestic and foreign rivalries caused the enterprise to be nationalized, and a strong Vereenigde Oostindische Compagnie (VOC) was formed in 1602 with a government-backed monopoly of trade from the Cape of Good Hope to the Straits of Magellan. It comprised six regional chambers under a board of directors known as the Heren XVII, or Seventeen Lords. Trading stations were established in the Spice Islands, but English competition continued a colonial régime begun in 1619. The ancient port of Jacatra was fortified and renamed Batavia (modern Jakarta).

Explorations proceeded without delay. In 1606 Willem Jansz sailed the *Duyfkin* from Banda down the west coast of New Guinea (past the strait discovered at this time from the other direction by Quirós's companion, Torres) into the Gulf of Carpentaria. Supply problems and violent encounters with locals made him turn back, but his discoveries influenced others, including the VOC cartographer Gerritz. Efforts were made to keep them secret, however, for the VOC "was not very anxious that the up-to-date information thus recorded should be widely known: indeed a request was made to the States General to prohibit the publication of maps, journals and charts without the consent of the Company."[46] But at least one other major cartographer, Hondius, drew on the work of Gerritz.

In 1616 Dirk Hartog visited the west coast of Australia at 25°–28°S, naming it Eendracht's Land after the ship *Eendracht* (Concord). He had confiscated this ship from Jacob Le Maire and Willem Schouten, who were making a circumnavigation (Le Maire's father, Isaac, having left the VOC in 1605 to found an opposition Australian Company in Hoorn).[47] The unfortunate pair were taken back to Holland, and in 1618 Le Maire's company won a court case over the incident. Schouten published his account of it that year and became something of a popular hero at Le Maire's expense, but in 1619 Spilbergen published an account giving Le Maire his due, and an official account, *Spieghel der Australische Navigatie* (1622), also censured Schouten. No further such voyages were made in the seventeenth century.

Hartog had obtained at Ternate Island local knowledge of Australia.[48] Such information had circulated since late in the previous century, when a Portuguese-Macassarese, Manoel Godinho de Eredia, published pamphlets (*Tratado Ophirico* and *Declaraciam de Malaca*) about the region the Portuguese called India Meridional (the South Indies). Eredia planned an expedition to "Nusa Antara" (Australia) for 1601. It is thought not to have eventuated although an earlier one, in 1599 or 1600, apparently did.[49] Here lies a possible source not only for Dutch explorers but also for utopias such as the 1616 *Antangil* (see chap. 4).

In 1619 Houtman named parts of Australia's southwest coast Dinning's Land and Edel's Land and charted the reef known as Houtman's Abrolhos.[50] Further survey of the area was inspired by an English disaster[51] and by some Dutch near misses resulting from the VOC's adoption in 1616 of a southern-ocean route from the Cape of Good Hope to the Spice Islands.[52] This consisted of sailing south to 35° or 40°S, running with the Roaring Forties for 3,860 nautical miles, and then turning north. Because longitudinal distance could not be calculated with any accuracy, overshootings were inevitable, bringing ships up on the Australian coast. The resulting episodes, discussed here and in chapter 7, were to have a great impact on literature.

So was the first known penetration of the Australian interior. In 1623 Carstenz in the *Pera* and Colster in the *Arnhem* coasted the northern areas now known as Van Diemen's Land, Arnhem Land, and Carpentaria. Carstenz saw "a flat and fine countryside with few trees, in which to plant and sow everything, but as far as we could learn and see entirely without water."[53] Colster broke away and explored the western side of the Gulf of Carpentaria while the *Pera* retraced her route and charted the eastern side. This information became publicly available in the maps of Hondius (1630) and Bleau (1635).[54] In the south, Pieter de Nuyts was blown across the Great Australian Bight in 1627 and named the area Van Nuyts Land. In 1628 De Witt was driven onto the northwest coast by monsoon winds and confirmed Carstenz's impressions of an "arid land inhabited by black savages."[55]

Such unpromising indications led to a curtailment of Dutch activity in Australia and, consequently, to the region's fertility as a setting for literary works. It was generally known that the Dutch had been there, but details were sketchy because a new policy of secrecy had set in. In supplanting Iberian power they inherited the old hemispherical rivalries that went back to the Treaty of Tordesillas. Their West and East India Companies, for example, both claimed the right to exploit the Pacific, being "as jealous of each other as they are of the other nations of Europe."[56] They also denied all previous European contact with the areas they explored, thereby adding a further dimension of doubt to what was already, by then, a many-times unknown region.

The *Batavia* Episode

A series of VOC disasters on the west coast of Australia began with the wreck of the *Batavia* in 1629 in the Houtman Abrolhos, a string of offshore reefs and islets at about 28°S latitude. Most of the company got ashore, and the commander of the fleet she had been part of, Francis Pelsaert, headed for the mainland in the ship's boat with the captain and some others. Finding no water there, they sailed on to Batavia. When he returned some months later in the ship *Sardam,* Pelsaert found that the crew had mutinied, murdered most of the male passengers, and organized the rest into a castaway society based on sexism and slavery. This he put down with equal brutality. The story's notoriety greatly contributed to the austral literary theme later in the century.[57] Like later such episodes, it also left unanswered some curious questions about the disappearance of Europeans in the Southland.

Pelsaert had come into conflict with the *Batavia*'s captain Jacobsz, who then plotted mutiny with the deputy supercargo or company agent, Cornelisz. They planned to get away from the other ships, kill Pelsaert and his followers, and go privateering. This plan was partly realized by a storm that scattered the fleet and confined Pelsaert to his cabin. But the ship then struck the Abrolhos, apparently through Jacobsz's negligence (it was a moonlit night, and the reef was by then well known). Pelsaert took command; he could not refloat the ship, but he and Jacobsz got the passengers onto an islet. Cornelisz and some seventy crew remained on board and got into the wine stores as a gale raged. After much discussion, it was decided to leave most of the 180-odd men, women, and children on the islets and go to the mainland, as noted. Pelsaert chose to risk his life by going with Jacobsz rather than stay behind and lose the boat should Jacobsz defect.

The coast proved inhospitable, and some locals they saw fled from them. Pelsaert tried to reach "Jacop Remmesens rivier" to the north[58] before heading in desperation for Java. They reached it after eleven days, and a VOC ship took them to Batavia. Their success was the result of Jacobsz's skill, but he was imprisoned on arrival, and it is not known what became of him.[59] Pelsaert was sent back with the *Sardam,* arriving after several months' delay (presumably because of winter weather).

The seventy crew left on the ship had reached the islets on pieces of wreckage, including, notably, the bowsprit that would feature in the *Isle of Pines* and many other austral works. Cornelisz spent "two days . . . sitting on the bowsprit lacking the courage to jump into the sea; finally he fell into the sea still clinging to the bowsprit as the ship broke up, and in this manner reached land."[60] He then conspired to hijack the rescue ship when it arrived. He ordered that all the other survivors be killed to prevent them from warning the rescuers and also to conserve food. Some were taken to another islet and killed, except for the women and children, who were kept as slaves. On the main islet too, men's throats were cut or they were tied up and thrown into the sea. Cornelisz took as his mistress Lucretia Jansz, a twenty-seven-year-old who had earlier been persecuted for resisting the advances of Jacobsz (events that may have contributed to the shipwreck itself).[61]

A group sent to a third islet was expected to die there but instead found abundant water and food. Led by a soldier named Wiebe Hayes, they repelled the mutineers' assaults on their islet, even managing to take Cornelisz prisoner. When the *Sardam* arrived, Hayes went out on a raft to warn Pelsaert, who landed in force and rounded up the mutineers. The ringleaders were hanged and the rest punished in Batavia except for two, Wouter Loos and Jan Ralgrom de Bye, who were marooned on the mainland with arms and provisions and told to learn all about the country and its people. It was intended to pick them up later, as instructions for later visitors indicate, "but nothing seems subsequently to have been heard of them."[62]

Before leaving the wreck, Pelsaert used divers to recover some of the VOC's bullion. But the location of the site remained a mystery, being variously put between 28° and 28°30'S, 150 miles offshore. In fact the Abrolhos extend from 28°15' to 29°S, fifty miles offshore. The site was finally found, complete with grisly evidence of the violence, in 1963.

CHAPTER THREE

Early Austral Fiction

The Ancient World

Imaginary voyages, geographies, and societies have from early times reflected a tension between two ways of reporting the foreign: the empirical, and that mediated by self-interest or cultural conditioning. The latter is a paradoxical form of truth vitiated by the very foreignness of the observer. But can the former ever fully emancipate itself from it, from history? Early Greek speculation about such problems was more akin to fiction than to scientific ethnography. Pantisocracy (consensus rule), for example, was an ideal associated with primitive society but was difficult to conceptualize within a political framework and often took parodic forms such as sexual communism.[1] A similar tone would characterize Indian Ocean fictions of the Hellenistic Age.

The first known utopia was Phaeacia in Homer's *Odyssey*.[2] Classical Greece produced schemes by a Miletan town planner, Hippodamos; by Phaleas of Chalcedon; by two associates of Socrates, Xenophon and Antisthenes; and by Plato and others influenced by Pythagorean ideas. Sparta was often held as a model of "closed" social integrity; as Greece's only major inland city,[3] it preserved the image of the warrior tribe, by contrast with the Athenian trend toward a commercial "open society." Athens experienced political crisis over this issue at the turn of the fourth century B.C.

Plato was the first to develop the metaphorical possibilities of an antipodean geography and history. His Atlantis was a "federal monarchy" of ten provinces ruled by philosopher kings descended from the sea god Poseidon. With the dilution of their divine blood they had become greedy and set out to conquer Athens and the Greek world. The story is set nine thousand years in the past and is given as historically true, having been learnt from Egyptian sages by Solon, the lawgiver of sixth-century B.C. Athens. The description and (unfinished) story extend over Plato's *Republic, Timeæus, Critias,* and *Laws,* incorporating elements essential to the later antipodes theme: a massive and populous land, existing in isolation.

It was an ambiguous isolation, however, for Atlantis remained paradoxically tied to the world. Although fortified by metal walls and concentric rings of sandbanks (symbolizing its closed society), it was open to the outside via an arm of the sea that reached in to merge with an internal canal system.[4] This simultaneous openness and closure reflected a truth of social history—the inevitable erosion of (inherently conservative) cultural ideals. Implicit here was the rhetorical tension inherent in the representation of other societies, whose most decisive "opening" comes about through representation itself, through being written about. Plato's insight would again come to the fore in Renaissance times when radical global movement renewed the issue of cross-cultural representation, revealing it to be virtually an act of imagination, of subjectivity.[5]

An antipodean continent was again the setting for a mid-fourth century B.C. utopia by Theopompos of Chios, known from fragments in the writings of Elian.[6] It framed Golden-Age myths in an imaginary voyage and stated that "Europe, Asia and Libya [Africa] are islands round which the Ocean flows in circuit, the only 'continent' being that one which men place outside this inhabited earth of ours."[7] Its various nations and cities had morals and laws antipodal to those of the known world. A warlike people, the two million–strong Machimoi contrasted with the peace-loving citizens of Eusebes and had tried (like Plato's Atlanteans) to invade Europe, reaching the Hyperborean lands in the north. Names such as Anostos (a city of "no-return") display a rhetorical negation congenial to Greek and later exploited by More.

Even more explicit was the late-fourth-century *Sacred Inscription* of Euhemerus, a traveler and admirer of Alexander the Great.[8] He recounts a voyage to the eastern confines of the "Indian Sea" (fictionally completing Alexander's Indian Ocean explorations) where he discovered an equatorial island named Panchaya, or the Sacred Isle. Its geometrical perfection was matched by an "ideal" social order, a three-class monarchy. The priesthood was privileged, but the system was without slavery (a regular part of life at the time). But its cosmopolitanism was unrealistic because commerce was suppressed; economic details were apparently rendered superfluous by the island's tropical abundance.

Its stress on formal regularity and on materialist ideas may reflect a knowledge of Asian circular cities,[9] sun cults, and so forth, acquired during Alexander's exploits. By incorporating such elements into the new tropical scene Euhemerus forged a new utopian metaphor linking the material felicity of the tropics to social ideals. The latter were much discussed in the group around Cassander, a successor to Alexander for whom Euhemerus made his voyage.[10] The sun becomes a principle of universality—both religious (in its "panoptical" omniscience) and economic (as a giver of equal opportunity). To imply that "all are equal under the sun" metonymically names the (unutterable) principle of social integration. The equator contributed to this symbolism, which exploited the cosmological traditions mentioned earlier. A satirical charge derived, too, from recent proofs (with Greek voyages in the Indian Ocean) that the torrid zone was, indeed, habitable. Such clashes between dogma and discovery would remain the basic stuff of utopian writing.

A more exaggerated sun state was the *Heliopolis* of Iambulus, a merchant who tells of his adventures with a companion in the Indian Ocean. Captured by Arab pirates, they are rescued by Negroes who take them in but then expel them as scapegoats, setting them adrift to meet a fate that will serve as an omen. If they find a "promised land," the tribe will enjoy six hundred years of peace and prosperity, but if they fail and return, they will be sacrificed as bearers of evil.[11] Fortunately, they find an "island in the sun" after four months. It is circular, five thousand stadia (about six hundred miles) around, and one of an archipelago of seven identical islands—the astral number—lying on the equator.

Perhaps echoing real knowledge of Sri Lanka, the Maldives, or Indonesia, these islands enjoy tropical abundance and an absence of seasons or of any physical principle of difference—qualities matched by the uniformity of the people. These are tall, handsome, beardless, long-lived, and sexually communist (like the hermaphrodites imagined by Foigny in 1676). They are able to hold two conversations at once and practice euthanasia using soporific leaves (another feature of Foigny's work, as is the motif of giant birds, here used to take newborn infants on flights to test their courage). They live in kin groups of about four hundred governed by elders and greatly value education, particularly in astronomy (as, again, in Campanella's 1623 utopia).

Prefigured here, too, is a seventeenth-century concern with language and writing. An alphabet consisting of sixteen characters (four basic signs, each taking four positions) forms a script in Chinese-style vertical columns. (The Panchayans had used hieroglyphics.) Similarly prophetic, particularly of Foigny, are fantastic creatures, one of which has four eyes, four mouths, numerous feet, and blood with magical healing powers as are Oriental astrological and numerological elements and an emphasis on the vegetable kingdom as an ideal environment, dietary resource, and even existential model. Magic fruits bear all year round, including one with white flesh that swells in water to form a kind of bread, and crops grow without cultivation. Such motifs, although clearly a parody of tropical abundance, may again reflect real knowledge.[12]

Again, the island lies in a freshwater ocean with more pronounced tides than the Mediterranean.[13] The sea as a medium of purification and moral redemption was an ancient metaphor (and, again, one later exploited by Foigny); when the dead are committed to it, all of life's differences of class and fortune are dissolved.[14] A related theme is the Heliopolitans' use of their abundant leisure, which they spend aimlessly wandering about together. A parody of primitivism, this seems also to prefigure cults of the "Incomprehensible" prominent in later utopias.

In these figural associations of physical phenomena with social life, a tropical or equatorial scene and the "dislocation" leading to it are key factors. They embodied the tension between a classical nostalgia for the closed society and a new Alexandrian cosmopolitanism in the same way that Atlantis had reflected that between Spartan and Athenian ideals. Imaginary geographies formed, in this way, a basis for systems of allegorical signification, a function that would devolve onto the southern continent with the rise of a fully global perspective.

Its early flowering ended with Iambulus, apart from the *True History* of the Greek writer Lucian (ca. A.D. 125–192). Here the fantastic, parodic bias is pushed to the limit,[15] tilting over into the absurd and providing a model for later inheritors of the style. It becomes self-parody—the culmination of its origin in a burlesque of travel reports and cosmological theories (a similar ritual disembowelment would characterize utopia's later evolution). This period was otherwise devoid of utopias although Roman exotism remained close in other ways to that of the Greeks. Primitivists stressed themes of health, longevity, vegetarianism, or giantism, and social history merged with natural history in the encyclopedias of Strabo or Pliny. But such writers (notably Diodorus Siculus, shortly before the time of Christ) also preserved a record of the earlier Greek utopias.

Lucian ridicules religious or social ideals. The gods and great men of Greece are encountered in farcical settings (which seem, however, to reflect growing knowledge of the Indian Ocean). Tropical imagery and solar metaphor are mocked as is the suspicion surrounding travel reports. Lucian even opens his narrative by proclaiming that he is a liar—adding that, by admitting it, he is being at least as truthful as any philosopher. He tells how he and his crew were caught in a furious storm and driven onto an island in the sky. They were met by cavalry mounted on three-headed vultures and took part in a cosmic battle between their host, Endymion, and the Sun-King Phaeton with his horde of Heliots (Sun People). Endymion won a bloody victory; at the end of the day the skies were stained red.

Phaeton then allied himself with the Selenites (Moon People), whose large flapping ears contrasted with the auditory valves of the Heliots and who were hermaphrodites. Each "married himself" at the age of twenty-five, whereupon a fetus grew in a tumor in the calf of his leg. Another species, the Dendrites or Tree People, made themselves artificial genitals (of ivory for a wealthy man, of wood for the poor). They reproduced by planting a testicle in the ground and growing a large phallic tree whose fruit, an elongated acorn, yielded a baby Dendrite.

Another utopian metaphor, that of symbolic rebirth into a new world, is mocked when an idyllic land is found inside a whale following further misadventure at sea. The whale dies, and the heroes escape to a Milk Island located in a sea of milk. This island, like the legendary Isles of the Blest (here, however, of the Breast), is inhabited by spirits of the dead. Its king is the Cretan Rhadamanthus, the mythical ruler of the underworld; whose rule is absolute—the spirit people are not only without bodies but have no body of laws. Vegetal, climatic, and other themes are also carried to extremes. Numerology is rampant; there are seven city gates, seven rivers of milk, and 365 springs of water and honey. The ground is holy, and its abundance surpasses even Iambulus's fantasies: fruit trees bear thirteen times a year, loaves grow ready-baked, geese fly to the table ready-roasted, and there is a navigable river of wine. The spirits dress in purple spider's webs (Iambulus's Heliopolitans simply used natural fibers) nor does their lack of bodies inhibit the unbridled and public practice of free love.

After seven months, with digressions such as Olympic Games, the protesting visitors are expelled. Rhadamanthus forecasts the rest of their journey, which could be interpreted as leading east from the then-known Indian Ocean through the Indonesian Archipelago to lands beyond. Firstly, five burning islands are to be avoided as an abode of evil;[16] then they will visit a dreamland and, nearby, the Island of Calypso. Beyond these, opposite the known world, lies a great continent that they will reach after many adventures. They set off and negotiate the "purgatory" of burning islands with their suffocating clouds of brimstone, then catch a glimpse of hell while passing through a perilous strait, and, finally, reach the Island of Dreams. It draws away as they approach, but they finally enter its harbor, Hypnos. Later, the narrator walks across a dense jungle, towing his ship behind him; he encounters men with ox heads and man-eating sirens who ensnare victims with their tropical charms. The (unfinished) story ends when the travelers escape from them and are shipwrecked on the antipodean continent.[17]

The Medieval Background

The Romans' lack of utopian literature may be related to their concern with empire rather than with trade or the insular, colonizing mode of society characteristic of the Greeks. This bias carried over into the medieval period with its idea of a purely abstract "elsewhere." Patristic doctrines set in place around the fourth century dominated perceptions of the world for more than one thousand years. Lactantius and Augustine, in particular, scorned ancient speculations about the antipodes, which they declared to be inaccessible or uninhabitable.[18] The former refuted the idea of a spherical earth, the latter upheld the biblical assertion that the only races of men were those founded by Noah's sons Shem, Ham, and Japheth in the Near East, Africa, and Europe. To suggest that the antipodes were inhabited was a heresy for which Virgilius, bishop of Salzburg, was condemned in the eighth century. Later, the scholastics would regard it as an unthinkable departure from the teachings of Aristotle.

Conscious isolationism thus conspired with a more general asceticism to kill off travel, both real and imaginary. But the conditions for its rebirth lay dormant to be reactivated by a later resumption of commercial activity. In the meantime, they gave rise to literary forms akin

33

to utopism, mentioned here because of their later impact on austral literature and because they reflect another aspect of utopism, its profound links with theological imagery. Both the notion of Paradise and of a terrestrial "matrix" (Atlantis or the Hellenistic sun states) derived from archaic Oriental sources such as survived, for example, in traditions of a "Persian garden."[19] Various avatars of the Earth Mother idea have drawn analogies between primal individual experience and that of collective life.

The pivotal concept was that of insularity—as in one's embryonic existence in an amniotic "ocean"; in collective life as part of a (nearly insular) society; or, ultimately, in one's material existence as a node in a cosmic flux. It was from such ideas that utopia derived its idealist aspect. Twin tendencies, theosophical and materialist, combined to inspire "Platonically" closed worlds offering a womblike security.[20] Such symbolic environments had a religious function; into them telescoped the alpha and omega of personal existence. Analogous effects are seen at the global level in notions of the oikoumene (or its antipodean counterpart) as an island surrounded by ocean. The "island continent" (meaning both words in their etymological sense) was the ideal utopian land: a bounded territory, materializing the social matrix that such writing sought to represent.

Paradise and utopia were analogous responses to the same problem: how to articulate an archaic ideal of (en)closure with worldly reality. Theology projected that ideal into a myth that would remain problematical and eventually be fatally demystified by "worldly" developments. Utopia, by contrast, embraced the latter and would play a key role in the advent of realism and empiricism, a role that, however, would eventually entail its demise as well. Insularity in general—whether real or symbolic, individual or collective—is always a lost cause: the memory of a wholeness dissolved in time and space. As with one's splitting from maternal unity to become an individual, a society ideally closed onto itself in cultural homogeneity exists, in fact, in a world that dissolves its traditions and structures.

Even Paradise had a worldly bearing, in that it was thought to lie far beyond the Holy Land. But in utopias a real context of travel and commerce—an imaginary voyage—was either implicit or explicit and lent an air of anxiety or ambivalence. Again, different material images were elicited by the concepts of Paradise and utopia. The former was a peaceful refuge (perhaps, with a token wall of gemstones), whereas the latter's multiple, defensive walls (as in Atlantis or in Asian circular cities) enclosed a refuge from aggression and cultural dissolution. Utopia, unlike Paradise, was situated within worldly dualities of good and bad, interior and exterior, masculine and feminine.[21] Its realism reflected patterns of societal contiguity, essentially, the effects of commercial interaction. The loss of Paradise or of the Golden Age was, thus, implicit in the rise of the fiction that supplanted such myths.

Travel in the early Middle Ages consisted of pilgrimage; commerce (of all kinds) was at a low ebb, and the world was viewed in heavily allegorical terms. Pilgrims remained aloof, notes Campbell, "moralizing the inanimate" and witnessing places as "witnesses" of biblical events. Their transcendentalism overwhelmed what later became "one of the determining tensions of travel accounts: that between the interest of the way there and the interest of the destination."[22] By the seventh century a more empiricist tone appeared, but the basic allegorical bias continued.[23]

With the rise of Islam the East was closed to Europeans and became a place of the monstrous. A fictional natural history arose, partly based on that of Ctesias (ca. 400 B.C.) and fed by the lack of corrective information. The unknown regions were imagined to be the abode of Skiapods (sunshade-footed men), of Blemmyae with heads in their chests, of Dog-heads or two-headed men — traditions later exploited by southernland utopias. It was grotesqueness by default, the obverse of the far-eastern Paradise. The latter, too, appears in allegorical geographies of the time; an eighth-century map shows it on the latitude of Palestine with Adam and Eve leaving for the world, and Cosmas Indicopleustes mapped a rectangular world in the form of the biblical tabernacle.[24] Empiricist representation of such places was forbidden; as late as 1553 the Spaniard Servetus was burned at the stake by Calvin for, among other sins, publishing a map of the Holy Land.

An oblique or marginal reference to the cultural exterior is implicit in all discourse and serves a "framing" function that, if not given, is built. Boundaries, whether territorial or ideological, are both abstractly construed and physically constructed. This is a universal process determined by geospatial patterns and trending toward global inclusion. It is also an essentially passive process; Europe was less an active constructor of a new worldly reality than its site or host, the center of a historical vortex, itself "under construction" in the process. This, too, was implicit in utopian metaphor, the rebirth of which reflected Europe's emergence from medieval isolation.

The latter was decisively breached during the century of Mongol power after the rise of Genghis Khan in 1221. Travelers such as Cadamosto, John of Plano Carpini (1264), Marco Polo (1271–1295), or Friars William of Rubruck (1253) and Odoric of Pordenone (1316–1330) had variously mercantile or missionary aims; but their accounts show a new realism.[25] The breach was further widened by Sir John Mandeville around 1356. His *Travails* (Travel works) were largely plagiarized from the travelers mentioned. Although fictional, they were effectively indistinguishable from real accounts because by his time travel to the East had again nearly ceased. His parody of exotic truth, of tendencies toward the allegorical or the grotesque, was long accepted—even into the seventeenth century[26]—as factual. It was this "rhetorical bottleneck," raising the stakes in a play of fact and fiction, that linked the evolution of discourse and literature to that of geographical knowledge.

Another such influence was the twelfth-century legend of Prester John, a great Christian emperor in the East. As a dream of finding a strong ally against Islam, it incorporated Asian, Indian, and even African elements. Much distorted in transmission (as were all early stories), it was linked to the Crusades and to "Doubting" Thomas's mission to India after Christ's death.[27] The origin of the *Letter* supposedly sent by the prester (presbyter, or priest) himself is in doubt; it may have been composed in Eastern or Western Christendom. Its propagandist nature was later doubled by a nationalist bias in the translations. Details were freely modified: French knights became English and vice versa; a Hebrew version omitted all reference to Thomas or the Christian cause; and fabulous elements (unicorns, griffins, or the exploits of Thomas) were exaggerated. These popularized versions were used in the age of printing and provided flamboyant models for the utopian writing rehabilitated at that time.[28]

Commercial developments from the fourteenth century had an ideological dimension, involving emancipation from Church doctrines. Empirical knowledge of exotic places only gradually overcame dogma. The Prester John story, although probably linked to the travels of Christian merchants, acquired significance for political reasons; Mandeville's tales, too, could have been refuted by merchants. But "low-life" realism did not contribute much to the construction of knowledge in the Middle Ages, which relied on formal, canonical sources. This tension would, as mentioned, underlie the revival of utopism.

In 1215 a Calabrian monk, Joachim, was condemned for ideas that would influence Dante, Columbus, Peter Martyr, More, and others, as well as religious sects such as the Taborites, Anabaptists, or Rosicrucians. They invited speculation about the meaning and location of Paradise and about the possibility of creating an "earthly paradise." This became associated with "worldly" aspirations after the riches of the East and with new ideas of actively improving one's lot within the world, all of which was anathema to patristic doctrines and tended to focus the socioeconomic aspirations of a rising middle class. In both religious and secular terms, the issue of the marginal world took on a revolutionary tinge.[29] Similar motives were implicit in myths of a Land of Cockayne or cornucopia (horn of plenty).[30] Celebrated in popular festivals, these derived from the archaic origins discussed earlier. They, too, combined with commercial factors, the fourteenth-century Church Schism, and an influx of pagan ideas (with the fall of Constantinople to the Turks in 1453) to undermine the unity of the Christian ethos.

The Renaissance of Utopia

Such influences produced a rehabilitation of utopian literature, notably with More's *Utopia* of 1516.[31] It transposed the Platonic metaphor of a worldly matrix into a Pacific setting that was both topical and prophetic of the real "dislocation" of islands there over the following two and one-half centuries.[32] There are various theories about historical sources for the work. Vespucci, on his fourth voyage to South America in 1507, left twenty-four men at Cape Frio. One of them may have returned and met More in Antwerp in 1515 when he was there on a trade mission and began writing *Utopia* (noting that it was a story he had heard there). The narrator, Raphael Hythloday, could, thus, be based on a sailor who told More about the Inca or some other civilization. Other possible sources were Balboa's party, which reached the Pacific at Darien in 1513, or the Spaniards who were living in the Panama area from 1510.[33]

Utopia and its people had been created by Utopus, who persuaded the natives of a peninsula of an unknown continent, Abraxas, to dig a vast canal. The island so cut off formed a crescent folded around a central lagoon, like an atoll, a structure reproducing the bodily (specifically, matricial) form of Atlantis. As with the latter, a tension, an ambiguity, was implied — a simultaneous closure and opening to the world. From their lagoon, for example, the Utopians traded with their neighbors, but its perilous entrance could be negotiated only by their own pilots, and all trade was in their favor.

Geophysical images, thus, give form to the structures of the social world. These aspects of the work are analysed by Marin in an article comparing history and utopia as modes of cultural representation. Myths of origin have used the island as a sign of origin, "a realization of the difference of a world from its unthinkable exterior, enabling it, by that fact, to be conceived . . . in the form of an archaic memory that legitimizes an impure origin, only to itself be forgotten as soon as that function is fulfilled."[34]

This insularity has a bodily dimension; for an island to function as a symbolic origin "it must be offered as a matrix . . . that form of insularity, canonical since Plato's Atlantis, that surrounds the terrestrial fullness with aquatic emptiness only to open up this fullness by a passage. In this structure can be detected the insurmountable problem of origin — the initial contradiction, and an archaic image that space, whether in geography or in fiction, diligently traces out: that of a belly at the same time fecund and fecundated, a womb and a vagina."[35] In this way More expressed tensions arising from the dissolution of medieval society, just as Plato had expressed the destiny of tribal society. Indeed, this open-closed paradigm bears on human history in the widest sense as a structural process articulating (into language and ideology) a collective relationship with a homeland or territory. But with Utopia there is an essential difference in the twin senses of "construction" mentioned. This society is constructed in a literal, concrete sense rather than merely construed as a common origin. Here, "the origins are repressed as such; or, more precisely, the would-be origin is a fiction, a fabrication resulting from a sculpturing of the land: a separation of the land from itself. The island of Utopia no longer functions as a point of origin; a fiction of origin fulfills that image in reverse. Birth is here a movement into the belly. The 'umbilical cord' that Utopus cuts is one attaching the belly to the outside, to the world, to the continent. This is an introjection from the outside to the inside, the birth of another world by introversion: a birth that is a return, not a departure."[36]

This was a metaphor for the origin or identity of modern Britain or of modern statehood generally. "With Utopia as its destination, a history and a politics gives itself its double and its other: it annuls or neutralizes itself by emerging inside of itself, as a poetic destiny of Henry VIII's England."[37] More recast the earth-body metaphor in a global context in line with the new horizons opening up at the time (and, no doubt, with notions "in the air" before the first circumnavigation). The utopia, as an image of society based on the duality of known and unknown worlds, was caught up in an involutional process. Just as global knowledge of the world was imminent, so a new kind of society was being born: a total, abstract state resulting from a coalescence of organic societies and one given a priori as a represented object.[38]

Again, *Utopia* adopts the equatorial setting of the Hellenistic utopias, with all that it signified. Its capital Amaurotum (no-shadows) invokes the solar metaphor of social uniformity and equality—the *homonoia* that was a prominent ideal in Greek thought. Sun symbolism remained as powerful in the Renaissance, a time of incipient social crisis, as it had been for the Ancients. The conflicts to come would call into question the ideal of a unified "Christian republic" and even the very basis of theism itself, giving renewed prestige to materialist and deistic principles. Sun imagery was the germ and symbolic focus of ideological developments that would culminate in the Enlightenment. One source of it had been the failing Byzantine empire, as noted, but more compelling models were soon to reach Europe through contact with exotic cultures where it was a living force.

A major source of these was the Inca, Garcilaso de la Vega, whose *Commentarios reales* appeared from 1609. The son of a conquistador and an Inca princess, he reconstructed his maternal heritage,[39] finding the empire to have originated in the twelfth century when the "Eagle Chief," Manco Capac, was ordered by his father, the sun, to found a two-class society along gender lines. He was to head a superior caste while his sister-wife, Coya, headed an inferior. The city of Cuzco was laid out accordingly, and the dynasty's authority was vested in a deity called Pachacamac (the Unknowable, or Incomprehensible), a "lowest common denominator" deity to which the tribes assimilated into the new empire could bear common allegiance. It could not be discussed and was represented only as something behind a veil. Thus, the structural force of religion was abstracted from any cultural particularity, from time and space. There was no assignable origin, only a force as invisible as the eye of an eagle.

Utopus had similarly subordinated aboriginal cults to a common civic one; they were tolerated but expected to wither away. His syncretism, associated with the ancient Persian solar god Mithra, was assimilated to a political principle, that of "pyramidal" delegation. The basic social unit was a block of thirty families (about twelve hundred people), which elected a syphogrant or "old fool" as its delegate to a local assembly. Tranibores, protophylarchs, and so forth, were elected further up the pyramid, at the top of which the prince, or ademe (tribeless one), was elected from among four candidates. This mechanical process was legitimated by assimilating the prince's role in the human sphere to that of the sun in the material world. Though in theory separate, the two principles fused in practice into an ideology serving as both a political philosophy and a philosophical religion.[40]

The heliocratic theme took a somber, regulationist turn later in the sixteenth century in theocracies of Reformist and Counter-Reformist inspiration. The imprint of the Hellenistic works can again be seen: Kaspar Stüblin's Protestant *Eudemonia* (1553) has an Indian Ocean setting, as have the *Christianopolis* of Johann Valentin Andreae (1619)[41] and Campanella's Catholic utopia, written around 1603 while he was in prison for sedition.

But the original (pagan) sense of the metaphor would, as noted, be renewed from exotic sources: the Tartars, or other Eastern peoples,[42] and the Incas of Peru. It acquired relevance not only from the breakdown of church authority and the rise of materialist and deist currents but also from the rise of political absolutism, notably under the "Sun-King" himself, France's Louis XIV. The heliocratic principle was, indeed, invoked in support of two opposing political models: on the one hand, the republican ideal of uniformity and equality (of rule from below) and, on the other, monarchy as a quasi-solar rule from above. The two agendas would collide in revolutions whose violence reflected the power that was at stake—the scale of the modern state.

Did such models hold, for those who considered them such, the promise of a eutopian or a dystopian future, or did they simply offer a virtue that could be made out of historical necessity? These would be vital questions as a "crisis of consciousness" loomed in the late-seventeenth century, a time when heliocratic imagery reached a high level of development in austral utopias. An issue to be addressed when reading the latter, then, is how such metaphors and themes related to the continued use of an austral setting.

Discourses of Discovery

A paradoxical realism, a "self-destructive tendency,"[43] accompanied the rebirth of utopism. It reflected the commercial realities ever close to such writing and their rhetorical effects in burlesque, parody, irony, or satire — the negative side of cosmopolitanism. It would play a key role in the resolution of exotic writing into genres (direct accounts, histories, encyclopedias, maps and cosmographies, or works of fiction). But a persistent blurring of fact and fiction remained symptomatic of a sixteenth-century resistance to information from the New World. The reaction tended to be one of either parochialism or humanist universalism.

But already, Mandeville's realistic fiction had exposed the fact that truth (particularly about the exotic) has no transcendental basis; it is born of an organic social matrix and is problematized as the latter opens onto a world of difference. In this he carried forward the Menippean style of satire seen in Hellenistic works and (especially) in Lucian.[44] This was an intellectual form of mockery, closely linked to philosophical cynicism and a common source for the utopia and the novel. Satire, notes Frye, combines fantasy and morality. "But as the name of a form (it) is more flexible, and can be either entirely fantastic or entirely moral. The Menippean adventure story may thus be pure fantasy [whereas] the purely moral type is a serious vision of society as a single intellectual pattern, in other words a Utopia."[45] Mandeville's style similarly "suggests neither a scorn for facts nor a mere delight in the picturesque. The material is not our clue to the fictive nature of the *Travels*. . . . The controversy over the 'truth' of Mandeville's document suggests that in it may be found one seed of the crisis over historicity and significance which signaled the birth trauma of the modern novel."[46]

Early discourses of discovery pose problems of genre and reference; they tended to be less concerned with objectivity than with underlying motives and determinants. Irony, moralism, and documentary reporting merged and aroused suspicion (*Utopia,* for example, was long confused with real accounts and remained unpublished in England until 1551).[47] Rabelais in 1532 refers to Pantagruel's mother Badebec as the daughter of the "King of the Amaurotes in Utopia"; his father sends him a letter from Utopia; he himself alludes to a voyage there via the Cape of Good Hope. Such travesties of the documentary function bred, with their learned sophistication, the analytical thinking that gave rise to a modern concern with empirical truth, objectivity, and classification — to a fact-fiction dichotomy that had not greatly bothered earlier ages.

They also had a political dimension: it reflected the rise of a colonial relationship with the New World based on an objectivism that contrasted with older figural or allegorical approaches to the foreign — an "emerging scrupulosity of separation" between accounts of, for example, Utopia and Guiana.[48] The latter, as Sir Walter Raleigh's 1596 El Dorado utopia, contrasted with a colonial project for Guiana published the same year by Lawrence Keymis. Keymis rode a newer wave and sought to "remove all fig-leaves from our unbeliefe."[49]

This sophistication was exemplified by Robert Burton's *Anatomy of Melancholy* (1621).[50] *Anatomy* here meant a dissection or analysis in the intellectual sense — one that, as noted, was related to the novel and eventually merged with it. For Frye, too, the term is "a convenient name to replace the cumbersome and in modern times rather misleading 'Menippean satire'."[51] It elucidates the role of that style in the advent of more self-critical forms of writing and thought. Burton set out to define, analyze, and cure the melancholy that afflicted his age, spanning with his erudition the entire range of human existence from the individual level (where melancholy arises from "humours," "black choler," etc.) to that of "politic bodies." He "offered his reader a survey of the physical and spiritual condition of man, a description of the state of society, and what amounted to a framework for the interpretation of history."[52]

His cure included a rebirth of English society in the New World. It was influenced by images of the austral regions available at the time — those in particular of Quirós and Hall. "I will yet," he proclaims, "make

an Utopia of mine own, a New Atlantis, a poetical commonwealth. . . .
For the site of [which] I am not fully resolved, it may be in *Terra Australis Incognita,* there is room enough (for of my knowledge neither that
hungry Spaniard [Quirós], nor Mercurius Britannicus [Hall], have yet
discovered half of it) or else one of these floating islands in Mare del
Zur (or) perhaps under the Equator, that paradise of the world."[53]

CHAPTER FOUR

Baroque Allegories

Mundus Alter et Idem (1605)

"Another World, and yet the Same; or the Southern Continent, hitherto unknown but recently revealed through the long travels of a wandering academic":[1] this work typifies the style of austral utopism in the early-seventeenth century, exploring satirical possibilities offered by the imaginary continent (which was still a cartographical orthodoxy at the time). It was heavily influenced by Puritan thought and may reflect Hall's own travels in Europe.[2] In the Menippean tradition it mocks discourses of exploration and discovery and is an allegory of man's voyage through life. Mercurius Britannicus (the British Mercury) is a scholarly but innocent Englishman who is talked by his friend Beroaldus into making a voyage of discovery to the unknown continent, only to find himself abandoned there in a world of moral failings.

The austral theme lent itself to this sort of satire.[3] Commercial developments in the region had confounded patristic dogmas about it, yet doubts remained concerning, in particular, the southern continent. Imaginary maps of the latter, based on those of the late-sixteenth century, are included in the original edition of the *Mundus*. The satire also had a basis in political realities: commercial rivalries between English, Dutch, and Iberian interests in the Far East, which reflected religiously based ones within Europe. New World discovery had thrown up new issues of cultural interraction; a primitivist tradition drew on the writings of early explorers (as in Peter Martyr's *Decades of the Newe Worlde*, translated in 1555). The Spanish cleric Las Casas had attacked the actions of the conquistadors, to inspire Montaigne[4] and a Spanish-American "Black Legend."

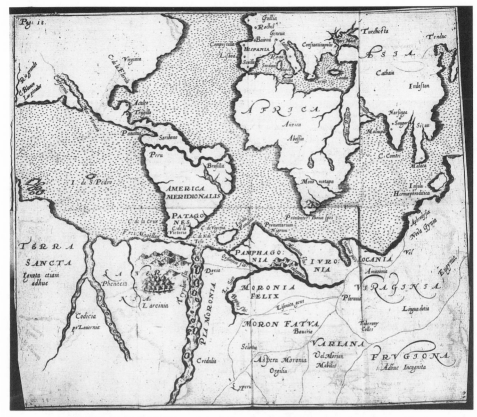

4. Bishop Joseph Hall's satirical Southern Land in *Mundus alter et idem*
(Frankfurt, 1605). *Courtesy the Newberry Library.*

Hall was renowned for his learning, wit, and sincerity and called himself the "first English satirist."[5] His hero visits four allegorical regions of the southern continent. Crapulia (Tenter-belly, in Healey's translation) borders the Indian Ocean and contains the provinces of Pamphagonia (Gluttonia) and Yvronia (Drink-allia). Viraginia (Shee-landt) recalls the Latin *virago* (amazon); Moronia (Fooliana) is a land of folly, especially religious,[6] and Lavernia, or Theevingen, a land of crime (of which Laverna was the Roman patroness).

Before leaving, he debates with Beroaldus and a Dutch friend, Adrian Cornelius Drogius,[7] the virtues of staying in one's homeland. Having posed this question in relation to the Americas, they turn to the "new" New World, the Southern Land. Beroaldus is perplexed that maps still show *Terra Australis, nondum Cognita,* a land that exists but is unknown. In spite of the hero's objections (evoking all the old arguments of a torrid zone, a lack of sunlight, a land inverted or inhabited by monsters), Beroaldus proposes a voyage in emulation of the bold Columbus. Drogius is also sceptical and argues that the continent of myth and legend has already been found—America. But Beroaldus convinces them with a torrent of lore, and they finally set out in the ship *Fantasie.*

Drogius soon gets cold feet, and Beroaldus, too, deserts en route. Mercurius arrives alone in the Southern Land, carried there by "currents unknown to our pilots" after two years in the Fortunate (Canary) Islands and Monomotapa (Africa). His picaresque adventures[8] unfold among provinces, towns, peoples, and topographical features with satirical names. The effect is heightened by the maps mentioned and by realist echoes (thus, Pamphagonia recalls Patagonia, Viraginia is Virginia, etc.).

Pamphagonia, with its Sugar Mountains or Olio River, had dedicated itself to gluttony on freeing itself from Frugiona, a state of frugality. Its capital, Artocreopolis (city of art and creativity) is a circular canal city fortified by walls built of food scraps.[9] The citizens are so fat that they march into battle backward wearing armor on their backs. Their life, education, and government are a constant round of banquets. Leaders are chosen for their gluttony, and ten commandments prescribe consumption at all times. Those who lose their teeth are exiled to a scholastic island called Sorbonia. Punishments are exacted in teeth or, for serious crimes, starvation. Similar customs, based on drinking, prevail in Yvronia.

The hero is captured by the feminists of Viraginia, and at their capital of Gossipingoa is nearly killed as one of their hated neighbors, the Lechiterians. After explaining that he is from England, a feminist paradise, he is left to explore the country. Its provinces include Linguadocia (a land of gossips), Rixatia (of fights), Ploravia (of weeping), Risia Major and Minor (or laughing and grinning), Aphrodisia, Amazonia, and Euginia. The women rule in the interests of peace, reducing men to domestic servitude. But their criteria for leadership are beauty and eloquence, so their parliament is chaotic. Only Euginia (Black-swan-marke) has a workable system—its women live as hermits in the mountains. Still more paradoxical is an "Ile Hermaphrodite" off the coast. These islanders have two sexes (following a logic whereby arms or eyes come in twos) and names like Mary-Philip or Peter-Alice. And because physical attributes are in this world the markers of moral ones,[10] they are morally hermaphroditic as well.

In Moronia, similarly, the climate causes imbalances of physical and intellectual forces that lead to madness. Its provinces are Moronia Mobilis or Variana (Fooliana the Fickle); Moronia Felix (the Fatte), Pia (the Devoute), Aspera (the Craggie), and Fatua (the Fond). The Moronians are generous, garrulous, and always act contrary to logic and custom. They value trivialities such as feathers, despise precious metals (echoing More's Utopians with their golden chamber pots), and measure wisdom by elegance and verbosity. They are ruled by women and greatly respect their Morosophi, or Fool-osophers (monks), who enjoy a life of privileged luxury at their expense. They worship the dead as idols. The capital, Pazzivilla (city of the mad), is anthropomorphic in layout; its head is in the hills, where the upper class lives close to heaven, its lowlier parts are in the valley below.[11] Above them all is the Temple of Lady Fortune, a monastery where monks stage fake miracles.

Moronia Pia, with its districts of Doxia and Credulia, carries the parody of Roman Catholicism to its most vitriolic (it borders on Lavernia). Moronia Variana, inconstant and frivolous, variously calls its capital Farfellia (cf. the French *farfelu,* "up in the clouds") or Papilionia (cf. *papillon,* butterfly). Its laws change constantly, and two academies (the philosophers and the self-taught) noisily debate subjects such as fashion. These qualities are attributed to a perversion of nature and, again, are expressed physiognomically. Moronia Aspera consists of underpopulated Lyperia (Solitaria the Sad) and Orgilia, a land of the proud. Mercurius, daunted by the latter's reputation, does not visit but learns at Pazzivilla that its people are vain, irritable cannibals, and very ugly. Its duke defends himself against his people in a fortress, holding banquets where victims are tortured and eaten.[12]

In Moronia Fatua, Scioccia is inhabited by subhumans who walk on all fours, and Baveria by an ascetic people who scorn even clothing in the pursuit of esoteric knowledge. For the same reason, one of their eyes is torn out soon after birth. This region, also called Asse-sex, is "larger than our three sexes in England."[13] Moronia Felix has further bizarre peoples, one of which, in Lisonia, imitates the styles and manners of others to the point of losing their own personality. This is reflected bodily: they resemble apes in front and dogs behind.

Mercurius stays well clear of Lavernia, a land of unbridled anarchy and criminality. Bands of brigands roam it, speaking their own languages and observing their own cults. There is a plain called Plagianus and a town, Furtofrancheza, that may refer to Frankfurt. (Such details may be linked to an experience during Hall's travels, or to the fact that the work was first published in Germany).

Scholars have tended to study these regions and their implications piecemeal. A fragment about Crapulia, extracted for a 1663 culinary work, represents the whole work in an 1885 anthology of ideal commonwealths edited by Morley. Anderson's edition, a school Latin text, omits the hermaphroditic development. The latter, however, is of central importance; especially in relation to the contemporary work of Thomas Arthus, to be discussed. Such themes join the character Beroaldus in pointing to a moral-satirical style and an interest in the status and role of women that were common to Hall, Arthus, and Béroalde de Verville.[14] Hall traveled to the Low Countries in 1605 with his patron, Sir Edmund Bacon, and could have come into contact with these men or their ideas.[15]

Whatever the case, the theme of gender inversion clearly complements that of antipodean inversion, both literally and symbolically. Precedents for it could be found in "amazon" traditions. Prester John mentioned a region called the Great Feminie where, "when these queens wish to wage war, each of them leads with her one hundred thousand armed women (who) fight bravely like men. No male can stay with them over nine days, during which he can amuse himself and make them conceive. But he should not overstay, for in such a case he will die."[16] Mandeville, too, described a Land of Feminye, and Marco Polo reported incredibly numerous prostitutes in Cathay.[17] The late-medieval *Catalan Atlas* shows the island of Taprobane as a *Regio femnarum* (land of women).

For the southern-land theme, sources were numerous: the voyage-collections of Hakluyt, De Bry, or Purchas; related genres such as geography, cartography, encyclopedias, and cosmologies, and literary tradition itself. Hall was profoundly versed in classical literature and may, for example, have known Elian's Theopompos fragment mentioned earlier. By his time, too, the region was becoming a geopolitical issue and emerging from the legacy of Portuguese secrecy about it. But a tension of fact and fiction persisted, even for the well-informed.

On this point the work has often been misinterpreted. Brown, for example, echoes the views of Drogius in remarking "how little promise those latitudes offered for exploitation. Pure theory had had its day. It had produced the Southern Continent, but could not endow it with wealth. . . . Its singular fitness for Hall's purpose lay, therefore, in that it was not only by tradition remote and uninhabited [but] by demonstration, of no material value, and, therefore, a happy soil for the cultivation of moral and philosophical ideas."[18]

Happy soil it was, but not yet because of any certain knowledge. The question was unresolved and would long remain so. The Dutch had sources of gold, pearls, camphor, sandalwood, and spices in the East Indies[19] and knew that a land existed to the south. Its resources were an open question; indeed, they launched their first expedition to it in 1605 with instructions to look for any such signs. Nor had old associations of the Southland with Solomon's Ophir (see chap. 2) died; Quirós sailed for the New Hebrides in, again, 1605. The *Mundus* was, in its way, a very topical work; interest in *terra australis* was growing.

Hall, in any case, turns the purely economic question into a metaphor — an economics of social relationship. Hence, the hero's progression from the simple pleasures of gluttony to a world of crime. It is doubled by a physiognomical passage from a "normal" bodily physics to one of monstrosity and by a passage from innocence, through contact with the Other, to role reversal and the involution of gender differences. These developments all imply moral structures or configurations of social value, paving the way to a region of crime. To what extent were they theorized in this way by Hall? Were his ideas linked to primitivist sentiments or to a common view of the Southland as a possible new America — whether for the gold it might yield or in terms of souls to be converted?

49

In any case, it was evident that Europe would encompass there its last cultural Other.[20] Austral symbolism impacted in these ways on moral philosophy, Hall's chief area of concern.[21] Mercurius, it will be recalled, argues in the preamble that the incentive to moral behavior is rooted in a commitment to a social culture—to a locale, a homeland. The global explosion of commerce, by contrast, was rapidly dissolving this. Hall compares such effects to those experienced at the personal level in one's voyage through life, by means of a progression from erotic adventure to hermaphrodism or from infantile gluttony to confusion, deception, madness, and crime. Spatial, sexual, and moral inversion overlay each other, implying links between processes at the microsocial and global levels. A voyage to the ends of the earth joins the two levels; the adventures of an individual parallel or "act out" a collective one involving configurations of culture (and, in turn, affecting traditional patterns of behavior).

This link between values on the individual and global planes is figured in the preamble by a reference to the Ophir tradition. Value, it is implied, will be pursued on various levels: firstly, on that of the global gold rush that has led Europeans almost everywhere (except to the southern land) and which Beroaldus finds more congenial than the hero. The quest for value in this mediate form, the "general equivalence" of money, leads, however, only to a regression into infantile somatic immediacy, a world of autistic consumption. The hero discovers not Ophir but Pamphagonia. Similarly, his pursuit of the value traditionally incarnate in woman (as mother, wife, or erotic object) leads, at the far end of Viraginia, to an insular hermaphrodism—an absence of difference. In both cases a normal social economy is reduced or annulled. Analogous effects are encountered in regions of madness—of superfluous or degenerate values. The ultimate such dissolution is that of crime—the direct appropriation of value, short-circuiting its legitimate acquisition through processes of exchange.

Hall's use of the Ophir legend to elaborate this central metaphor is explicitly linked to the traditional symbolic value of woman. As mentioned in chapter 2, Ophir was, at the time, still associated with New Guinea or the "Islands of Solomon" to the east of it. Hall names the region adjacent to the hermaphrodite island Nova Gynia (new womanland: *gyne* is Greek for woman), an anagram of the Latin name for New Guinea, Nova Guinea.[22] The name was, moreover, saturated with economic associations; the original Guinea, on the west coast of Africa, was the "gold mine" that Portugal had coveted at the outset of Europe's drive to the Indies. More recently, Sir Walter Raleigh had portrayed Guiana as El Dorado (the gilded), and this, too, is reflected in a region Hall names (continuing the gyne-Guinea pun) Raleana Guianorum (Raleigh land of Guinea women) situated somewhere southwest of the Moluccas.[23]

To associate the value of woman with that of the land is without doubt the most ancient symbolism in human history.[24] Hall exploits it to the full, making his hero's experience on various planes (geographical, individual, and social) reveal their interrelatedness as aspects of a whole economy of human life. In this way he laid (together with Arthus) the foundations for an austro-hermaphrodite theme that would be carried forward later in the century by Foigny. At the time, however, it aroused little interest — at least in England. But it became something of a classic in continental Europe, with at least four editions by 1664.[25] Plagiarized versions of Healey's English translation appeared in 1669 and 1684, the latter purportedly translated from an original by the Spaniard Francisco Quevedo. In the former the erotic aspect is uppermost; the hero lands in "Psitaccorum regio, or Womandecoia the she-lands (that) bordereth on the domains of the Prince De l'Amour."[26]

Hall inspired contemporary utopists such as Burton and Bacon,[27] English satire of the tradition leading to Swift, and the austral theme flowering toward 1670. But his satirical tone also made him enemies, notably Milton,[28] whose *Apology against Smectymnuus* (1642) cost Hall his bishopric. He was imprisoned in the Tower of London for four months and died in poverty in 1656 despite his services to church and nation (a fate somewhat recalling that of More or many other utopists).

L'Isle des Hermaphrodites (1605)

This "Description of the Isle of Hermaphrodites recently discovered, contained the Manners, Customs & Laws of the Inhabitants" was probably published in the same year as the *Mundus*.[29] It has satirical hermaphrodism as its central theme and, although not itself having any specific geographical reference, was bound with an imaginary voyage that develops the austral theme in a realist direction, anticipating later developments. Taken together, the two works parallel that of Hall and play in the half-light of knowledge about the austral regions at a time of growing public interest in them. Arthus, too, uses that paradox to mock the moral and cultural dissolution of European life.[30]

Critics have assumed, however (following Bayle, the first to seriously examine the hermaphrodite theme), that he intended only an "ingenious satire on the court of Henry III."[31] The title page, it is true, states that the work is "To Serve as a Supplement to the Diary of Henry III" and pictures the hermaphrodite king together with this provocative verse:

> Je ne suis male, ni Femelle
> Et si je suis bien en cervelle
> Lequel des deux je dois choisir
> Mais qu'importe à qui on ressemble
> Il vaut mieux les avoir ensemble
> On en reçoit double plaisir.

> I am neither male nor female
> And well know what it entails
> Which way I make the choice
> But what matter your troth
> Better to have both
> That way you double your joys.

A further "Dionysian" manifesto opens the text: "The world is a buffoon, man a comedy / One wears a dunce's cap; the other is a folly." Pejorative connotations attaching to homosexuality are turned to a critique of the duplicity and hypocrisy of court life. Henri was a weak king at a time of violent religious divisions and a trend toward political absolutism. Siding with right-wing Catholic activists, he sought national unity at the expense of the Huguenots.

But the author's satirical intentions seem to range more widely than Henri and his court. Although the effects he lampoons were manifested there, he seems to project them onto a wider screen in a rather bleak vision of the future. His "anatomy" of them begins with an address to the reader, setting them in the context of a global social history:

The New World has produced so many novelties in this new century that many from the Old, spurning its antiquity, have preferred to seek

52

(at the peril of a thousand lives) some new fortune . . . to overcome their natural inclinations and leave their ancient homelands for fear of becoming victims or spectators to the bloody tragedies played out in that great theater. Among these was one of our Frenchmen, endowed with no less valor than prudence, but in whom a natural goodness had sapped the will or the ability to soak his hands in the blood of his fellows . . . exiling himself and wandering about the world, he saw in the space of a few years all that a curious eye could desire. But at last . . . he felt the urge to see his beloved homeland again. . . . On his arrival all his friends and relatives went to visit him; as much, I gather, to learn some news of the world as to celebrate his return.

Among this crowd was the "secondary narrator" who (as in *Utopia*) relates the traveler's tale. The latter's voyage had been boring him when he was shipwrecked on a floating "hermaphrodite island." He set about exploring its marble statuary and other classical riches and was guided through the royal palace by hermaphrodite courtiers. But he was forbidden to enter a secret chamber to which "none had access but the most familiar . . . for they held their most secret councils there and treated of their most private affairs, calling it roughly what we would term a wardrobe."[32] It was curtained off by a tapestry with cartoon-style scenes in which a figure like a Roman emperor was surrounded by his "companions in arms." In one scene he was stretched out on a table as they used "all sorts of instruments to try to turn him into a woman," without success, because "he remained of the neuter gender." This was Heliogabalus, a Roman emperor renowned for his cruelty.

His fate elucidates that of the French monarch in the power struggles mentioned. Henri III was politically "castrated" by a côterie of courtiers intent on intrigue and duplicity.[33] The French kings sought to replace these parasites with professional statesmen, of whom "the essential selection came in a single century between Henri II and Mazarin. . . . Henri III may have shown the way, but we are not too familiar with that intelligent, cultured king."[34] But Arthus seems, as noted, to associate such developments with a more general trend toward "moral inversion."

Among documents in the secret chamber was the following "Extract from the Laws, Statutes, Customs & Ordinances of the Hermaphrodites":

We, Emperor Varius, the Most Heliogabalic, Hermaphroditic, and Gomorrhic; the Great Eunuch, ever Shameless,

Seek to restore the superb Republic of Hermaphrodites, more or less destroyed during the reigns of Trajan, Antoninus Pius, Marcus Aurelius, Severus, and our other bigoted predecessors. For any self-respecting person must recognize it as the most cultured, most delicious, most corporeal, and most in conformity with the inner and outer senses, and the most agreeable in the world to the human passions.

Accordingly, we have established, decreed, and ordered the following.[35]

What follows is a wholesale inversion of the moral code of the time. The official cult is that of Cupid, Bacchus, and Venus (Roman gods of desire, debauchery, and love), but others are allowed, provided they are not taken seriously as a faith. The Hermaphrodites celebrate their cult with a book "very finely bound, gilded and embossed, half a finger thick and half a foot long; which book will most often treat of love, given that the venereal mysteries are preferable to all others"; their masses are orgies that reach a height of fervor in May, and their priests are "singers, balladeers, comedians, satirists and others of like stuff (who) express most exquisitely and lasciviously the deepest secrets of love."[36] The "most rustic" may feign a sort of reformation, however, and old religions are tolerated as a means of controlling the people.

Emphasized also here is vanity: "We respect good looks and appearances in whatsoever it may be, more than deeds. . . . The will is to be held as reason, and no one shall be permitted to raise himself above the senses on pain of being considered an enemy unto himself. . . . If anyone should wish to stand, we expressly forbid him to remain in one place or in the same pose; the proper thing is to be constantly in motion. . . . We hold prancing and dancing to be the most seemly and agreeable actions."[37]

Their doctrinal canon is based on Ovid, Aristophanes, and other ancient *farceurs* (humorists) on whose authority ecclesiastical abuses, religious wars, and corruption are sanctified. This is set out in eight articles proclaiming their skepticism about religion and explicitly rejecting its allegorical bearing: "we regard as madness any other kind of communion than ours, believing it can only be based on the ancient opinions of the Gnostics."[38]

There are to be "no relations of consanguinity between our subjects except those pertaining to the transmission of goods and possessions"; terms such as *bastard* or *whore* are in no way pejorative, and marriage is retained only because it adds zest to the pursuit of adventures. Those "of a simple, goodly nature, who seek to live without ceremony" are despised — especially by their children, who aspire to a more glorious status. The Hermaphrodites betray and murder their relatives as readily as they would anyone else. Rape, incest, and violence are encouraged, especially if the victim is defenseless. Prostitution is a nationalized industry staffed by *dames d'honneur,* with its own bureaucracy. The juridical system maintains outward appearances of virtue, an ethic of humbug. Of justice there is no question: "We believe that in all things [such as bribery], geometrical proportion should be employed."[39]

The gallant are expected to glorify themselves at the expense of others, for example, by borrowing with no intention to repay. The lands of inferiors may be confiscated without restitution, and taxes are collected by "public surgeons" who bleed the country to fill their own granaries. In war cowardice is rewarded; in peace duels and feats of honor are unknown. Civil servants put their own interests before those of the state. Financiers from the lower classes rapidly grow rich and buy false titles, even though it is obvious that these are bought at the public's expense. Officers appointed to alleviate such abuses are easily corrupted, and the emperor's close confidants are agents of foreign governments. Censors or moralists are "excommunicated and undesirable," and "those who would be traitors to themselves and show kindness to others by their words or their silence should be despised as stupid fools lacking in wit. . . . We absolutely forbid them to be listened to."[40]

Fashion rules: for "clothes maketh the man and not vice versa . . . each may dress as he desires, provided that it be proudly, superbly, and without any distinction of quality or profession. . . . Accoutrements most akin to those of women will be regarded by our subjects as the richest and seemliest, the most suited to the manners, inclinations, and customs of this isle. We desire fashions to change every month, and any who wear a style for longer than that will be seen as mischievous, mean, and uncivilized. But it will be legal to renew old fashions . . . provided that they were current at least seventy or eighty years previously. . . . Everyone may dress as he likes, however bizarre the invention; provided that it expresses what our critics call effrontery."[41] Stars (*nos favorites*) will keep themselves abreast of fashion by passing as much time as possible with their valet (a baroque equivalent of the fashion magazine). Similarly prophetic is a fetishization of commodities. Houses and furniture are owned purely "for appearance's sake" — personal prestige is the only currency or criterion of value.

Again, Varius's decrees concerning food presage a modern artificialism — part of an ethic of representation, a world of deception. The tapestry story included scenes of diners being presented with sumptuous dishes that were only of wax, painted wood, ivory, or stone, and Varius decrees that all food be processed or even refrigerated:

> Let all foodstuffs be disguised, so that none might be recognizable for what it is: in this way our subjects will be nourished in a manner conforming to their personalities. For this reason we hold in high esteem all sorts of pastries and dried and liquid preserves. . . . If they sometimes desire fish, we require that, however near the sea it be eaten, it be marinated. . . . In summer there shall be set aside in suitable places great mounds of ice and snow, in however hot a region, for mixing with drinks; even if this causes extraordinary plagues.[42]

Not only are historical developments targeted but utopian idealism itself. There is a semblance of such provisions but in the context of a society prejudged as evil. The work prefigures an attitude common later in the century and, more distantly, the rise of dystopian futurism. Asylums are provided for "those whom our subjects drive to them by their crimes," and begging is condoned although charity is an "idiocy" because one's purse should at all times be full (except, of course, where a show of charity will bring personal glory). Neither treason nor defamation are crimes and especially not forgery, which is a highly respected branch of the alchemical sciences. Anyone may study these arts and sell their secrets to the rich. "We wish our Masters of the Monies and other officers . . . to be experts on alloys [and] that the most useless professions be those most in vogue, most honored, and offering instant riches."[43]

It becomes clear in these passages, too, that their education involves laissez-faire principles. Children are raised without any discipline but trained to keep up appearances and instructed from the earliest age in the "voluptuous arts." This minimal ideology is imparted with the aid of visual techniques: "Floral and scenic plays are esteemed among our subjects . . . as the easiest and most useful school in which to learn the rudiments of our doctrine."

By the time the narrative moves on to more abstract moral theory, it is clear that Varius is less an imaginary person than the personification of an abstract principle of change, a sort of "anti-Utopus" ushering in a dystopian future. The work is prophetic not only in many of its details but also of the realism of later seventeenth-century utopian satires. Varius actually says so midway through it:

> Moreover we know, with prophetic knowledge, that in centuries to come there will be few Solons, Lycurguses, and Platos traveling the world to gather the best laws or teach theirs to other peoples. On the contrary, the majority of those who travel will generally be the most corrupt and dissolute among their people . . . (but) recognizing that such things are in complete conformity with the humor of this island's inhabitants, who love novelty, we have allowed all sorts of foreigners to live here and after a very short time to occupy all the same positions and enjoy the same honors as the locals . . . , filling them with vice and curiosity, only for them to set sail soon after to wherever they expect to strike as good or better fortune.[44]

This vision of a world of social mobility and its ethical implications goes well beyond satire on Henri III and his court. Other details of its involuted, "poststructural" society—its total abdication from authority—follow. Everyone wears on his forehead (*front*) a medal with *impudence* on one side and *effrontery* on the other to show that he is capable of all sorts of affronts. They shout each other down over the most banal matters, and "when they wish to impose as true something false, they begin with the words, 'The truth is'." Friendships are "strictly for the sake of appearances, or for convenience," and intelligence consists of siding with the strongest. They may seek "enlightenment" so as to be admired in conversation, "for some poor philosopher will gladly, for the few caresses he gets out of it, set down for them on paper what he has spent years of toil learning." But those who profess the "virtuous sciences" are regarded as

> dreamers and pedants, as crazy and irrational; for their theories cannot be founded on human reason, all such things being supernatural. . . . We expressly forbid any instruction to be drawn from them or any change of lifestyle to be made on account of things they say; for we require their interior to be entirely ours and dedicated to our religion. As for their exterior, they may impart it to anyone they wish. . . . The old drug

57

of antiquity is to be held in the greatest disdain, (for) we wish dandies and tricksters to be respected above all others. All kinds of braggarts, clowns, practical jokers, swindlers, seekers of free lunches, kitchen-flies, fair-weather-friends, and other sorts of wits and hail-fellows-well-met will be our favorites."[45]

Later, another view is presented. The voyager's audience is amazed at the rigor of the Hermaphrodite ethos, and one of them stoically responds, "The man of goodwill can be borne upon the great ocean of the world without being carried away by its bitter waters, nor fetching up on its banks and reefs; but, like the sun shining on mud, can see and know the nature of all things without involving himself in them and without drawing his identity from things that should take theirs from him . . . [just as] the geometer measures altitude by having one eye on the heavens and the other on the ground."[46]

He is cut short by the voyager, who goes on to discuss philosophical themes. The Hermaphrodites assimilate "what is called the abstract or separated intelligence, which is none other than divine grace"[47] not to a god or an abstract sociological principle but to the sun. A dualistic (sun-male and earth-female) cosmogony is elaborated at length. The seeming paradox that they had among them people with "such elevated conceptions" is explained by their total indifference to ideology: "They care nothing for what is said about them or their lifestyle; no truth is eloquent enough to persuade them to make the change called conversion . . . although the majority lead the life described, there are also many who prefer virtue to all else. It is true that they are not much in evidence . . . ; they avail themselves only of chance events and circumstances in order to let their light be seen amid such dark shadows."[48]

Their world was, in other words, essentially similar to Arthus's France. This turning-back of the work's ideological trajectory from an encounter with an inverted ethos toward the known one strongly prefigures the later utopia of Foigny and suggests that Arthus may have influenced him. The hermaphrodite theme, too, suggests in both cases a striving for social realism and a critical response to the rise of political absolutism. The latter was, perhaps, seen as intensifying a quasi-erotic relation of mastery and subjection between state and subject. It is toward the state (personified by Varius) that the "passion" of Arthus's hermaphrodites is directed, nor could it, by definition, be directed toward each other. Hence, too, the fact that they are not "their brother's keepers"—a role totally mediated by the state—or, again, the centrality of the feminine role by contrast with its marginalization in the real world. An absolute state reduces the gender roles to near equivalence, so that they can be exchanged or collapse into each other without affecting the social fabric (as might be the case in a kinship-based society).

To what extent was that scenario—or the absolutism it referred to— consciously linked, in these austro-hermaphrodite works, to their geographical theme? With Hall and Foigny, such an association of ideas is suggested by the presence of both themes in a single work. With Arthus, a similar association can be postulated for the reason noted earlier; bound with the 155-page *Isle des Hermaphrodites* is an imaginary voyage of 130 pages, the *Discours de Jacophile à Limne* (Jacophile's letter to Limne). This story, even more stuffed with classical pedantry than the other, is geographically explicit: it is a world cruise that begins in the East Indies.

Jacophile (lover of James) and his friend Opadin sail for Java with a merchant, Socher, from Menlay (Mandalay?). After sheltering from a storm and in the lee of Borneo they continue on to Java and spend twelve to fifteen days at Sunda.[49] Then, heading for Sumatra in a bark with five or six others, they are driven ten leagues from their intended landfall (Ardaqui) to a marshy region behind which is a long escarpment. Its luxuriant gardens, eight fountains, a canal, and bizarre animals and fish make a scene similar to that encountered in Foigny's austral odyssey. "It remained only to see the reasonable animals of the island, and to this end we decided to visit Adrapara, hoping also in this way to find gold mines."[50]

One of them falls ill, and they return to Java. They learn that men there do not involve themselves in public or military affairs after the age of forty-five, even if healthy, and compare this to the norm in Japan. It is, explains a local, because of the rigors of their lives and the burden of children—by that age they are exhausted. Later, the friends join Socher as he takes a cargo of spices to St. Lawrence Island (Madagascar) and the "northern sea." With various digressions they make their way around the Cape of Good Hope to St. Helena and the Canaries where, amid further adventures, Socher sells his cargo of oriental merchandise. More stories and lashings of humanist pedantry color their return to Japan via Europe and Asia.

This very minor imaginary voyage prefigures the realist fiction emerging later in the century and may have been inspired by, or based on, journal accounts. As noted, Foigny probably knew it and the hermaphrodite utopia it accompanies, and *Antangil,* the work discussed next, also builds on the contemporary East Indian scene in ways reminiscent of the Discours de Jacophile.

CHAPTER FIVE

Utopia and Seventeenth-Century Rationalism

The Kingdom of Antangil (1616)

This work[1] displays the geographical realism of Jacophile's travels and other aspects of the literary background, such as the Prester John and St. Thomas legends, and outlines in detail a theocratic state. A strongly polemical interest on the part of its unknown Huguenot author[2] makes it more a treatise than a narrative. Nor is the southern continent visited by the narrator, who merely relates what he learned of it while in the East Indies. That aspect is reduced to a gesture in a preface dedicating the work to the "Most High, Most Mighty and Illustrious Lords of the United Provinces of Holland"—a realist gesture, however, that would become a central feature of later such works. The author had sailed with "Admiral Jacques Corneille Necq,"[3] arriving at Bandung, Java, in 1598. There he learned the Malay (*moclaïque:* 'mock-lay') language and through an Italian named Renuchio met the envoy of "a great Christian king to the south." In Renuchio's presence they exchanged descriptions of each others's countries.

The kingdom is south of Java-la-Grande, extending from 6° north of the Tropic of Capricorn (i.e., about 16°S) down to 50°S on its west coast, the length of which is said to be 330 leagues (one thousand miles). The east coast is somewhat less than 200 leagues long. It is bounded by the Indian Ocean to the north and in the south by a mountain range called Sariché,[4] inhabited by barbarous tribes. On the northern coast is a large estuarine gulf, Pachinquir,[5] about 17 leagues wide and 100 deep, into which flow four great rivers. It recalls the Platonic matrix-metaphor, being "doux & tranquille, comme le nom le porte" (gentle and peaceful, as the name suggests), or, perhaps, Quirós's balmy images

61

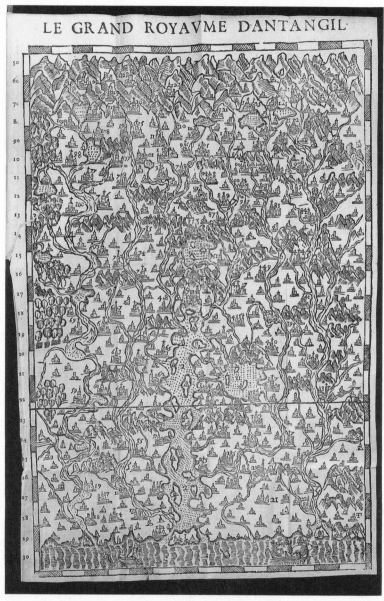

5. Map of the imaginary Kingdom of Antangil (1616), possibly inspired by recent Dutch visits to northern Australia. *Courtesy the Newberry Library.*

Table des lieux principaux tant des villes que rivieres du grand Royaume d'Antangil.

1	L'Isle Corylée.	44	la ville de Bedyl.	87	la ville de Negribaick.
2	goulphe de Pachinquir.	45	la ville de Besan.	88	la ville de Papoda.
3	le fleuve Iarri.	46	la ville de Moulay.	89	la ville de Cabonady
4	le fleuve Bachil.	47	la ville de Sarfi:	90	la ville de Soudacaya.
5	le fleuve Patigi.	48	la ville de Gyla.	91	la ville de Pondarra.
6	le fleuve Alagir.	49	la ville de Pison.	92	la ville de Apy.
7	le fleuve Nochi.	50	la ville de Salyn.	93	la ville de Chinsin.
8	le fleuve Laurys.	51	la ville de Darisé.	94	la ville de Paramoeda.
9	la grande ville de Sangil.	52	la ville de Dingyn.	95	la ville de Nuagia.
10	le lac de Bacico.	53	la ville de Iagava.	96	la ville de Malamata.
11	le lac de Namanga.	54	la ville de Pangan.	97	la ville de Sapy.
12	la ville de Bayacien.	55	la ville de Orip.	98	la ville de Sappy.
13	la ville de Pongacit.	56	la ville de Mado.	99	la ville de Darabengo.
14	la ville de Neffa.	57	la ville de Oracaian.	100	la ville de Capal.
16	la ville de Iambatan.	59	la ville de Tavaconras.	102	la ville de Dylanghy.
17	la ville de Ayam.	60	la ville de Badaga.	103	la ville de Soffo.
18	la ville de Batigay.	61	la ville de Manda.	104	la ville de Gavezala.
19	la ville de Zapare.	62	la ville de Iargary.	105	la ville de Cadda.
20	la ville de Manys.	63	la ville de Balmary	106	la ville de Pandan.
21	la ville de Nigrychamar.	64	la ville de Sagan.	107	la ville de Cambyn.
22	la ville de Tanabirou.	65	la ville de Bainga.	108	la ville de Calmary.
23	la ville de Tyma.	66	la ville de Cayou.	109	la ville de Caesart.
24	la ville de Manco.	67	la ville de Pangali.	110	la ville de Besuidi.
25	la ville de Daramas.	68	la ville de Macono.	111	la ville de Battu.
26	la ville de Tavacassian.	69	la ville de Barnan.	112	la ville de Cryssen.
27	la ville de Curyasava.	70	la ville de Delau.	113	la ville de Baya.
28	la ville de Conda.	71	la ville de Saling.	114	la ville de Salorcha.
29	la ville de Nypis.	72	la ville de Catan.	115	la ville de Negri.
30	la ville de Moncasso.	73	la ville de Icatan.	116	la ville de Pucolitan.
31	la ville de Baycmas.	74	la ville de Ballialayo.	117	la ville de Maixampagi.
32	la ville de Ruma.	75	la ville de Moufo.	118	la ville de Baring.
33	la ville de Baringa.	76	la villa de Daramas.	119	la ville de Macoo.
34	la ville de Berny.	77	la ville de Lande.	120	la ville de Montacan.
35	la ville de Hadina.	78	la ville de Pisou.	121	la ville de Bato.
36	la ville de Negrisaga.	79	la ville de Ican.	122	la ville de Lagasappi.
37	la ville de Cajoumanys.	80	la ville de Domba.	123	la ville de Boanis.
38	la ville de Quicabo.	81	la ville de gymor.	124	la ville de Sebanigri.
39	la ville de Manyta.	82	la ville de Tamapinga.	125	la ville de Gauno.
40	la ville de Tamouta.	83	la ville de Mingan.	126	la ville de Lalau.
41	la ville de Bassongot.	84	la ville de Dalambons.	127	la ville de Darat.
42	la ville de Namanga.	85	la ville de Tombaka.	128	la ville de Gatima.
43	la ville de Sodocan.	86	la ville de Amadate.	129	la ville de Papinga.

Fin de la Table.

6. Legend of towns and rivers of the Kingdom of Antangil (1616). *Courtesy the Newberry Library.*

of "Austrialia." It also suggests the real Gulf of Carpentaria, known to the Dutch by this time through Jansz's 1606 voyage (see chap. 2) and probably earlier to the Portuguese. To the west is a river, the Jarri, that flows into the Indian Ocean (as does curiously, another to the east, the Bachil or Bachir).

This geography may reflect the "Australia" depicted on sixteenth-century maps—not only in form but in the way they incorporated images of camels or elephants roaming in Malay or even Indian landscapes as seen on maps of the Dieppe school or that of Gastaldi (1548). Later in that century, the Venetian Coronelli, too, had provided "vignettes for the unknown interior which include elephants, deer, monkeys and natives in idyllic—almost pastoral—bliss. It is as if "Terra di Concordia" has ceased to have a defining etymology and become a symbol charged with the religious nostalgia that enthused Quirós and the Franciscan missionaries"[6] and, perhaps, the author of *Antangil.*

The imaginary geography (5–6) is detailed and includes a map. The mouth of the Pachinquir is almost blocked by an island called Corylée; the Jarri River is swift and has high banks but is navigable to within thirty leagues of its source. The Bachil is slow, swampy, and navigable right to its source. Other rivers, the Alagir and Patigi, arise in mountains called the Salices, which traverse the country and through which the Jarri and Bachil cut gorges. Thus, the land is well watered and fertile.

The capital, Sangil, is at the head of the main gulf and near a lake called Bacico. A larger lake has mineral springs developed as a spa with "sumptuous edifices." Mineral resources abound and are listed at great length, and pearls are found at the mouth of the Pachinquir. Rich tropical foods are also listed in detail; it seems that the Land of Cockaigne motif is dovetailed into the image of a modern trading state. A navy of galleys supervises travel to and from the kingdom and is kept at Corylée Island, whose volcano serves as a lighthouse.

Sea monsters, tortoises, whales, and "cocodrilles de prodigieuse grandeur" (giant crocodiles) are found in the gulf, and although these latitudes are "a bit southerly for flying-fish, some are seen in summer" (14). All sorts of animals, including camels, are found in the Sariché Mountains where hunting is a favorite sport. A further chapter is devoted to the bird life.

Similarly detailed is the description of the Antangilian state. Book 2

outlines its excellent "Police" (government), with seventeen chapters
on the origin and structure of the bureaucracy. Each of the 120 provinces contains one hundred towns, which, supposing they had on average one thousand persons, would make a total population of twelve
million, a nation of European (or Javanese) dimensions.[7] Each province
has a capital that is also the seat of its judiciary. The political model
is a federal one, a "united provinces" — as might be expected in a work
dedicated to the Dutch authorities. Their communal houses are admin-
istered by headmen in blocks of ten, one hundred, and so forth, on
the familiar pyramidal model. Election to this office depends on being
"the most confident and able" and "knowing down to the last farthing
the value of all material and intangible goods."[8]

Further details of the official cult and the social system fill the remaining books, the tedium of which will be evident.[9] Fourteen chapters are devoted to the military and its system of compulsory service
and eleven to the education system, which corresponds to this society's
division into the "noble and rich" and the commoners. The latter learn
only the basics, whereas upper-class children and any who gain a state
bursary attend an Academy. These, numbering 9,800, lead a regimented
existence for eighteen years in three phases: from six to twelve they study
reading, writing, grammar, poetry, history, music, and the rudiments
of geometry and cosmography. Ten years are spent on mathematics,
physics, metaphysics, medicine, rhetoric, and dialectic, plus some archi-
tecture and science of fortifications. Finally, two years are devoted to
the nation's laws. Theology is kept separate from all this.

The state is a constitutional monarchy; it reflects an interest in Dutch
and English developments of the time and, in France, those following
the assassination of Henri IV in 1610.[10] The effective governing body
is a senate elected by the Council of States composed of one hundred
learned and respected (but not necessarily wealthy) persons aged at least
forty. This senate also elects the king and viceroy. The system is a centralized democracy; power is progressively delegated toward the capital,
Sangil. But it remains largely feudal in inspiration and little concerned
with functional problems at the base of the "pyramid." The executive
function is fulfilled by an elite corps chosen by lot from among upper-
class candidates.

Certain elements of this society are of interest for their prophetic nature as are the indications given about its origins. Its political origins

are dealt with in the section just mentioned; its religious origins in another where it is related how "Idols were Banished and the True Divine Service Established" by a Christian missionary, a disciple of St. Thomas. This "learned Brahmin," Byrachil,[11] was well received at Sangil but martyrized in the provinces.

The legend of Thomas's mission to India influenced (particularly French) literature from the late–Middle Ages.[12] According to the apocryphal *Acts of St. Thomas* (ca. 300 B.C.), he went in the guise of a carpenter and was employed by the Partho-Indian king Gondaphares, or Gundafor, to build a palace. But he gave the money for it to the poor and was only saved from the king's wrath by a vision that came to the latter's brother, Gad, as a result of which both brothers became Christians. On a later visit to the (presumably Persian) realm of a King Mazdai, Thomas's moral rigor led to his death. Gundafor was a real king, but no evidence remains of Thomas's presence in northwest India. Christianity was, however, found to exist on the Malabar coast by Cosmas Indicopleustes in the sixth century, and a Christian tradition was encountered at Mailapur on the Coromandel coast by Marco Polo.

Such coincidences with Antangilian history may suggest a source for the strangely dualistic cult Byrachil established. On the one hand, it is pragmatic or even mercenary: "We do not pray at all for the dead, nor believe in the chimera of purgatory or in any kind of satisfaction in the beyond; for how can a soul pay, who no longer has anything to pay with? And if souls themselves cannot satisfy their Creditor, how will others be able to pay on their behalf?" On the other hand, it resembles a "religion of the Incomprehensible" in its spiritual rigor: "As for veneration and adoration of the cross or of images of the saints, they scarcely mention it; having no images, statues, or representations either within their temples or outside them, except for the cross; and that rather as a symbol or reminder of the death and passion of our Lord Jesus Christ, than to idolize it."[13]

A more immediate source, however, was the sectarianism of the time. One sees, alongside Protestant elements (Calvinist doctrines of predestination to evil or Lutheran justification by faith), Catholic principles of merit through good deeds and proper remuneration.[14] Whatever its intentions, the cult is an ascetic one; fasts and abstinences accompany festivals, and idleness is considered the root of all evil. Even more strict rules apply to the priests, and the cult is highly institutional, perhaps satirically so, reflecting the antipathy many felt toward the churches by this time. Hence, too, its conflation of monetary with spiritual considerations.

By contrast, a conspicuous frivolity is apparent on the "gallant" side of life—that enjoyed by the upper class. Such a combination of moral rigor and privileged debauchery may reflect (as with Arthus or, later, the Marquis de Sade) a nostalgia for the feudal ethos—a vacillation, in response to the modern, between snobbery and viciousness. As Lachèvre observes, the author "has dropped none of his gentlemanly prejudices: he takes little account of the people, he exalts the military vocation, and loves ceremony to a degree that would be difficult to surpass. The description of the pageantry observed on the king's outings takes up no less than six pages: a whole chapter."[15]

As with Sade, too (or with Menippean satire in general), such an attitude tends toward self-parody. A face-value reading is often inappropriate, all the more so when the ideological context was one of oppression and censorship. An ambivalence pervades this scheme, defying easy interpretations of its intentions. Van Wijngaarden concludes that, in political terms, it sought to "construct without demolishing; any direct criticism of the French government is lacking in this first [French] utopia."[16] A similar line was taken by Lanson, Atkinson, and others, and is questionable. Symptomatic of it is the erroneous belief that this is the first French utopia, one that depends on a modern constructivist definition of utopia, ignoring works such as that of Arthus and, in general, the ironical bearing of such writing.

Certain prophetic elements aside, it seems doubtful that *Antangil* was intended as a realizable project. Practical economic aspects are, apart from isolated measures such as freeing the tax system from corruption (a major problem in France at the time) taken care of by the richness of the land and the labor of a working class. The author's concerns were more rarified; it is difficult to see him, for example, as an early communist.[17] His religious thought, too, is neither clearly Protestant nor Catholic, and his political thought is neither decisively republican nor monarchist. The ordinary citizen, no less than the "Most High Lords" of Holland, would have found the work difficult to take seriously as a positive project.

There may be reasons why it was at least ambivalent, if not frankly dystopian. The life of Joachim du Moulin, for example, was very difficult after the death of Henri IV; he was forced to wander the country, hiding his children under haystacks, for fear of detection by the Catholics.[18] Such an experience would seem more likely to have disposed him toward cynicism and satire than toward positive idealism. Even if he were not the author, the same would have been essentially true of other Huguenot ideologues at the time. *Antangil* may simply reflect a collapse of the author's cultural and ethical world, a dystopian vision of the way Europe seemed to be going.

This view would bring it into line with the trend of ideas at the time, one of growing ambivalence and skepticism about old ideals of all sorts. The trend was correlated, in imaginary voyages and utopias, with a new realism, both geographical and social. This, for example, is one of the first works to make the vastness of the southern continent symbolize a rising political absolutism with all its social, economic, administrative, and military ramifications. The centralized modern state, as an accumulation of "social capital," was a reality that would be brought into even sharper focus by later utopias based on the southern-continent theme, notably those of Foigny and Vairasse, who may well have drawn on this earlier work.

The Antipodes (1640): A Dramatic "Tour de Farce"

The austral theme was not only exploited by writers of prose. It was put to theatrical use by the English playwright Richard Brome in a five-act play performed in 1638 and published in 1640. This was the period just before the outbreak of the English Civil War, one of events and problems that profoundly affected the English theater and are crucial to an understanding of the work. Brome turns the analogy between antipodean travel and moral inversion to the purposes of dramatic psychotherapy on various levels ranging from the individual to the collective. He also builds on Burton's development of the "anatomy" or "skeleton" as a metaphor for formal analysis[19] and was inspired, no doubt, by Hall's *Mundus* and other Menippean prose satires.

When he wrote the work in 1636–1637, London was in the grip of a plague that, together with political troubles, severely affected public morale. Theaters were closed despite their therapeutic value in such crises. Brome (like his mentor, Ben Jonson) was acutely aware of this function of comedy and sought to give it a political extension. But the

Caroline theater, appreciated by Charles I and Henrietta Maria,[20] was in opposition to a rising tide of Puritanism and would again be closed in 1642—this time, by a "political plague." Brome foresaw this "*Epidemicall* ruine of the *Scene*"[21] and wrote *The Antipodes* under its shadow. In it he explores the cathartic function of drama at the level of the body politic,[22] an effect achieved by addressing the latter not directly, but obliquely—by way of a reference to its absolute exterior, the antipodes.

The patient is ostensibly Peregrine, a sort of eponymous hero who personifies the uprootedness felt by his age, not only that resulting from the immediate factors mentioned but, more broadly, as the effect of a century and a half of peregrinations to exotic places. An influx of cultural novelty had shaken the medieval stability of the European's self-image, his sense of belonging to a centered tradition. Peregrine is obsessed with the literature of travel and its doubtful truth and, especially, with Mandeville's *Travails* and their images of antipodean monsters; he believes himself to actually live in such a world.

His cure follows a formula found in Burton's *Anatomy of Melancholy*, that of an "invention" (in the old sense, of a discovery or revelation).[23] The patient is led to invent or discover (to himself) his condition of alienation. But what Burton had associated with English melancholy in general, Brome links more explicitly to the Puritan spirit. Such reflexive engagement had also been Jonson's aim in *Every Man out of his Humor*,[24] in which the audience was asked to imagine a mirror "as large as is the stage whereupon we act, / Where they shall see the time's deformity / Anatomized in every nerve, and sinew."[25] The public therapeutics aimed at by Jonson, Hall, Burton, Brome, and others involved an almost structuralist analytics; one accruing from an abstractive overview, an "exorbitance."

This is the nub both of Peregrine's condition and of its cure. A confrontation with the world of his imaginings, calling the bluff of his obsession and recentering him in his immediate world, is to be induced by staging an imaginary voyage to the antipodes.[26] It takes the form of a byplay orchestrated by a "Doctor of Physick," Hughball, and acted out by the household of the "fantastick lord,"[27] Letoy. The latter is an aristocrat who, having escaped ruin under the Puritans, keeps this troupe of players both for his own entertainment and for the benefit of others. The lead roles are taken by his servants, Byplay and Blaze.

Peregrine is brought to Letoy's London mansion by Joyless and Diana, his jealous old father and young stepmother. They outline his condition: his childhood obsession with travel literature[28] and the early marriage that had unhinged him. No less distressing than his own obsession, indeed, is that of his wife Martha, with becoming a mother; "for though they have been three years wed, / They are yet ignorant of the marriage bed."[29] A vital clue is that Peregrine

> talks much of the kingdom of Cathaya, Of one
> great Khan and Goodman Prester John
> (Whate'er they be), and says that Khan's a clown
> Unto the John he speaks of; and that John
> Dwells up almost at Paradise. But sure his mind
> Is in a wilderness.[30]

Hughball's diagnosis focuses on the prominence of Mandeville in Peregrine's fantasies. A 1625 edition of this "popular old collection of cock-and-bull stories"[31] shows its enduring fascination at the time. Peregrine, clutching a copy of it, assures Hughball that Mandeville went everywhere — even to the Antipodes. The doctor replies that he himself knows the customs and morals of the Antipodeans well and offers to take him there. Peregrine eagerly assents and is put into a drug-induced sleep to wake up amid the antipodean byplay after what, he is told, was a voyage of eight months. The latter is referred to as a "country sleep" (the name given to sojourns there of unmarried ladies from time to time).[32] Peregrine's cure is compared to a gestation; one which, moreover, will cause his wife to become actually pregnant.

The inner play is introduced by Letoy's curate, Quailpipe, who explains its essential point (and, as will become apparent, that of the work as a whole): "Our far fetch'd title over lands and seas / Offers unto your view th'Antipodes." A reflexive vision is to be procured through confrontation with a world so foreign as to drive the patient back to the familiar — an extreme form of the "exotic truth" found in travel reports.

Accordingly, an inverted morality unfolds: sergeants run away from a gentleman debtor, who seeks to be arrested; a wife abuses her husband; old men go to school; poets and statesmen trade places; lawyers and merchants refuse payment; a young aristocrat begs for a meal. Peregrine, invested as King of the Antipodes, is forced to question the wisdom of these antipodean ways and, through a concern for his imaginary kingdom (which is his own state of mind), begins to "discover" a cure. When he finally takes matters into his own hands, Byplay reports that

> He has got into our tiring house amongst us,
> And ta'en a strict survey of all our properties:
> Our statues and our images of gods, our planets and our constellations,
> Our giants, monsters, furies, beasts, and bugbears,
> Our helmets, shields, and vizors, hairs, and beards,
> Our pasteboard marchpanes, and our wooden pies.(69)

In other words, he has grasped the theatrical nature of social role-playing and is returning to normality. On the erotic plane too, a dénouement is brewing: Barbara is offstage educating Martha, assuring her that "You shall get a child by't." More scenes of gender, moral, or occupational inversion are played out, and Hughball detects a further germ of lucidity when Peregrine refers to contemporary hopes of a moral reformation in the colonies: "What if I crav'd a counsel from New England? / The old will spare me none."[33] "Is this man mad?" he asks, in an aside, adding confidently, "My cure goes fairly one." He presses the point home by spelling out the follies of Peregrine's kingdom and, when the latter demands in a rage, "Will you make me mad?" he observes that "We are sail'd, I hope, / Beyond the line of madness."

This "line" signifying psychic and moral equilibrium is, of course, the equator. What follows shows how fully Brome exploited old metaphors of a "worldly body" and the sexual symbolism of the two hemispheres. Peregrine's rage is transmuted into lucidity by a timely reunion with Martha who, dressed up as an Antipodean princess, is presented to him as a bride. He protests that he is already married and even invokes "Mandevillean" associations of the female with the monstrous to avoid this fate. "For the safety of your kingdom, you must do it," insists Byplay (102), and he submits.

Brome's insight into the theoretical possibilities such devices afforded goes beyond the popular nature of the imagery he starts out from, the "familiar comic territory the work moves over."[34] The development of a subplot focusing on Joyless and Diana brings out its full implications, doubling Peregrine's rediscovery of the real world and raising the main theme onto the plane Brome intended, that of a "public therapeutics."

71

A manipulation of the mechanics of dramatic representation turns passive voyeurs into active self-analysts, the effect he sought to realize for the theater at large.

With the cure at a turning point, an abrupt return to normality is called for. The inner play is abandoned; Peregrine and Martha retire to their chamber, and Letoy calls to Joyless and Diana, "Your parts are next" (104). In one sense, no doubt, this implies their private parts, on which their own neuroses are focused. Peregrine's problem was from the start recognized as a family one; Blaze observed on their arrival that "they all ail something" (14). The parents were among the audience of the inner play, Diana, as victim of the jealous Joyless, finding especially interesting the idea of antipodean gender inversion. She flirted with Hughball and then with Byplay, provoking the jealousy of Joyless — edging him toward the role of "patient," whereby he, too, might be cured of an imbalance that leaves him "as far short of a competent reason as [Peregrine] was of late beyond it."

During the inner play, furthermore, Letoy directs Joyless and Diana to a window in his chamber overlooking the stage from which they are to observe the rest of the action. Haaker notes (80n) that "a person in one of these balconies could see the inner stage and would be clearly visible to the spectators in the theater," doubling, in other words, their speculary relation to the play in the mirror-effect mentioned earlier. The joyless couple, no less than Peregrine and Martha, are made objects of scrutiny — by Hughball and the rest of the audience and, ultimately, by the audience of the outer play. Their position enables them to see both the inner and the outer workings of the play and its effect of inspiring introspection so that by understanding its therapeutic action they can begin to discover their own problems — to become, in effect, an audience to themselves.

Then Joyless and Diana, too, are instructed to retire to their chamber. But Joyless finds himself locked in a labyrinth of dark rooms and suspects Letoy of cuckolding him. As he bemoans his predicament, he begins to realize that he, like his son, is undergoing a therapeutic passage through a moral "antipodes" — that Letoy's blatant affront is a means of freeing him from his puritanical anxieties:

> This is sure the lordlier way, and makes
> The act more glorious in my sufferings. Oh!

> May my hot curses on their melting pleasures
> Cement them so together in their lust
> That they may never part, but grow one monster.[35]

As his despair becomes suicidal, Barbara and Blaze join him and discuss their infidelities during the past night—she with Hughball while spying on Peregrine and Martha and he with the butler. (It is no longer clear whether they are play-acting or not; the inner and outer plays have telescoped into one.) Brome counsels an acceptance of moral "peregrination" although not to an extent that would lead to monstrous, "antipodean" inversion. The need to find the line between the latter and its polar opposite, puritanical rigor, is nicely expressed by Blaze:

> "Nay, facks, I am not jealous.
> Thou knowest I was cur'd long since, and how.
> I jealous! I an ass. A man sha'nt ask
> His wife. . . . But she must *think* him jealous." (110)

Similarly, Diana proves her virtue by resisting Letoy's advances, even when offered money. The dénouement resolves all such tensions, and Joyless is reunited with Diana. Letoy had intended only to test her virtue for it transpires that she is his daughter. This is revealed with the appearance of Truelock, Letoy's old friend and (it had been thought) Diana's father. Thirty years previously, the two men had conspired to substitute Letoy's newborn daughter for that of Truelock (who had died), a secret kept even from their wives and inspired by Letoy's belief that Truelock had fathered both babies. He had later been disabused of his fantasy by his wife on her deathbed and, as a result of this crisis, had taken up his mission of dramatic psychotherapy.

With Peregrine cured, it remains only to inform him that, because his stepmother is Letoy's daughter, he is the great lord's heir. Hughball warns that this may ruin his cure, but Letoy presses ahead. The revelation is followed by a grand final scene that completes the telescoping into each other of the inner and outer plays. Allegorical figures of Discord and Harmony and their followers (Folly, Jealousy, Melancholy, and Madness on one side; Mercury, Cupid, Bacchus and Apollo on the other) mingle in a dance and Harmony triumphs over Discord, who with her followers is banished from the scene.

This facile ending underlines the essential point of the play—its allegorization of the stage itself. The world here transcends its function of providing a backdrop for dramatic action; it becomes a part of that action. So, too, does the audience in a progressive enlargement of therapeutic scope. Brome's manipulation of the speculary mechanics of the play enabled him to "merge two worlds of illusion into a third world of reality [and] to demonstrate concentrically the relative ratio between social consciousness and harmony: the greater the bounds of social consciousness, the greater the harmony and happiness. . . . Both worlds, finally, are set within the still greater play, the sphere of reality, in which the audience recognizes its own part in its drama of human follies. Structurally a tour de force, the play presents a three-level message which takes the unsuspecting patients, the joyless ones, unawares. It is by means of instructive entertainment, however, that each, within his own sphere, is brought to his proper center. Thus has comedy assumed its role as doctor of the age."[36]

Critics agree that it was his most ambitious and controversial play. "Unlike the plays using place-realism, [it] has a hypothetical rather than an actual setting," notes Shaw[37] in tracing Brome's progress toward a "turning of the generic form upon itself." This reflexive, involutional use of scenery (as found in the utopian tradition)[38] would underwrite important developments in prose realism later in the century in, as noted, prose versions of the antipodean "byplay." The latter was a dramatic equivalent of the utopian novel's central feature—that it was a "history of a history."

Again, the antipodes theme was for Brome a means of encoding his satire, of carrying it forward under conditions of censorship and refining (in spite of, or even because of, those pressures) his understanding of his craft. An obsession with exotic novelty, he says between the lines, is the hallmark of an insecure society and its literature. Far from succumbing to it, he works through it to an analysis of cultural processes. So, too, would the writers of the prose avatars mentioned—often Huguenots, whose situation was analogous to that of a Caroline playwright under the Puritans. *Antangil* had paved the way for such a response, but Brome's play clearly prefigures the literary revolution occurring later in the century. By being turned back on itself, driven into itself by censuring forces, such writing led to a deeper examination, a *mise en abyme*, of its rhetorical status and capabilities, one that inaugurated the abstractive thought of the Enlightenment.

The Century to 1668

A quest for certitude about the exotic, both geographical and literary, became apparent by the late sixteenth century. With it came a departure from older styles characterized by irony and a relative indifference to empirical fact—from, in other words, a "closed society" mentality. Commercial forces led to more accurate mapping of the New World and a more objective appraisal of its peoples. In English utopism, the tone evident in More's *Utopia* began to be overridden by directly political motives, both republican and colonial. A similar trend underlay developments in all areas of life—religion, politics, scientific method, linguistic theory, and literature.

Around the time of Burton's "utopia of mine owne," Francis Bacon embodied the idea that science and technology might redeem man's fallen state in a *New Atlantis*. This was a Pacific island 5,600 miles in diameter, whose Spanish-speaking people traced their ancestry over three thousand years to a time when "the navigation of the world (specially for remote voyages) was greater than at this day. . . . The Phoenicians, Tyrians, Carthaginians, Egypt and Palestina, China, and the great Atlantis (that you call America), which now have but junks and canoes, abounded then in tall ships."[39] Its city of Bensalem had a House of Salomon, or College of the Six Days' Works, devoted to scientific research. Its spies roamed the world in search of "light" (knowledge), and officers called depredators, miners, compilers, benefactors, or lamps conducted experiments.

Bacon's role in the turn to scientific empiricism is well known. Influential in another way was Campanella, whose *City of the Sun* (1623) emphasized science and education but subordinated them to a more classical theocratic state. He and his German associate, Andreae, influenced the theological aspect of utopism (see chap. 3, n. 41), which often embodied millennial notions but, increasingly, sought to achieve an earthly paradise through political action.[40] In the 1620s a political theorist, Samuel Hartlib, projected the ideal state of Antilia.[41] Projected for Virginia or elsewhere under various names, it finally became the *Macaria* of Gabriel Plattes,[42] a fifteen-page scheme "whereby Utopia may be had really, without any fiction." *Nova Solyma* (New Jerusalem) was a 1648 Christian republic attributed to Milton but actually by a friend of Hartlib, Samuel Gott.[43] It echoed Quirós's projected colony of that name on Espiritu Santo Island (see chap. 2).

An austral setting featured in Benjamin Worsley's *Profits Humbly Presented to His Kingdom,* a republican and capitalist scheme. Harrington's *Oceana* (1656)[44] was a South Sea island utopia based on ideas from the English Revolution (many of which were later put into practice), notably, that of pyramidal representation. Restoration utopias reflect the fall of republican ideology. Usually anonymous and tending to revert to baroque or even medieval themes, they still often used an austral setting. A "new" *New Atlantis* appeared in 1660, and the *State of Noland* (1696) was an England set in the southern continent, arguing the Whig case against James II's policies.

But scientific themes tended to supplant politics, just as, earlier, politics had taken over from religious concerns.[45] The Royal Society was founded in 1660 by a group carrying on the legacy of Bacon, and a French Academy followed in 1666. Space flight became a literary theme in 1638 (the time of Galileo's defense of Copernicus) with Francis Godwin's *Man in the Moone* and was exploited by Cyrano de Bergerac in his *Histoire comique des Etats et Empires de la Lune* (1657) and *Etats et Empires du Soleil* (1662). It went further than austral travel in spatial displacement but, in so doing, lost the crucial element of realism. The same might be said of voyages to the center of the earth, such as Margaret Cavendish's *Blazing World* (1666), a vast thermodynamic metaphor embodying political ideas. Still further removed from traditional spatial allegory was the voyage in time. The futurist utopia was anticipated in France (which otherwise had produced no utopias since *Antangil*)[46] by the anonymous *Epigone, histoire du siècle futur* (1659). Attributed to Jacques Guttin, it described France in the reign of Clodévée (Louis) XVIII in the late eighteenth century.[47]

Such themes were generally symptomatic of a rhetorical tension that was becoming acute, a desire both to embrace the new empiricism and to retain older certitudes of an allegorical order—the "Peregrine" syndrome. The trend reflected, no less than in earlier times, Europe's evolving relationship with its exterior, and its literary expression focused ever more explicitly on the austral unknown and its exploration (in 1660 an influential cosmography by Peter Heylin gave a list, headed by Hall's *Mundus,* of literary references to the antipodes).

This relationship becomes evident in the fortunes of the theme from 1668, which was also a watershed year in the changing landscape of European thought more generally.

On one level, it was expressed as a "physical anxiety" — a writer's identity was transcended by his experience, engulfed by the multifariousness of the world. Cyrano, for example, countered this threat with "a Dionysian fusion with nature. But between the one solution and the other, his hero does not pretend to choose: he wishes simultaneously to be and to know."[48] At another level it bore on theories of language — its origin, and the idea of creating a universal or "natural" language. Nor are the two levels unrelated. For in this millennium of full meaning, the word would be made flesh; it would be at once absolutely spiritual and absolutely physical, transcending the historical tension between the two.

The age was fascinated by concepts of the ideogram or pictogram; of a "cratylist," or one-to-one, relation between sign and thing. Inspired by Jesuit missionary reports from China or by Egyptian hieroglyphs, such schemes proliferated from the middle of the century. They began with Bacon and Godwin; the former had coined the term *real character* and believed that an original, nonconventional language was still used in China and written with pictograms. He envisaged in *The Advancement of Learning* (1605) a natural grammatics "such as should diligently examine the analogy or relation betwixt words and things." Godwin then invented such a scheme, which was later either ridiculed or used as a basis for more realistic efforts.[49]

Those influenced by it included John Wilkins (*The Discovery of a New World . . . in the Moon,* 1640; *Mercury: Or the Secret and Swift Messenger,* 1641); the German sinologist Müller; and Cyrano, whose "Grandees," the elite of his moon society, have a hieratic language and can speak in music. The Moravian Comenius, invited to England in 1641 by Hartlib, advanced such ideas and dedicated his *Via Lucis* (1668) to the "Torch Bearers of an Enlightened Age, Members of the Royal Society of London now bringing real philosophy to a happy birth."[50] He proposed *pansophia* (universal knowledge) and a universal language as the way to return to the unity of a world before Babel. In France the Cartesian Géraud de Cordemoy advanced similar ideas in his *Discours physique sur la parole* (1668).

Speculation on the origin of language obliquely called into question the chronology (and, with it, the truth) of the biblical creation, and it grew with the progress of global knowledge. Isaac La Peyrère thought many accounts of lengthy chronologies might be found "in the South-

ern Parts, if they were but known to us."[51] Around 1650–1670 many
believed the antediluvian world had been well populated and culturally
advanced, and some tried to prove that the primal language was Chinese. Athanasius Kircher asserted in 1663 that it had evolved after the
Flood from Egyptian influences.

Language schemes appeared from 1657 to 1687 by Beck, Becher, Schott,
and Dalgarno (who influenced Leibniz in this direction). The most ex-
tensive and influential of all was John Wilkins's *Essay towards a Real
Character and Philosophical Language* (1668). The idea was, of course,
a utopian paradox, and its Chinese basis was an avatar of medieval perceptions of the East — an effect of isolation. As the East became better
known, the illusion was dispelled. By 1668 a disillusioned Wilkins realized that "a more scientific set of artificial characters would have to be
constructed. . . . Nevertheless, he was unhappy that they could not be
natural."[52] Such, too, was the mood generating at this time a new
literature of imaginary displacement, one that pointed the way beyond
the century's rationalist fantasies.

CHAPTER SIX

Real and Imaginary Voyages

The Voyage of Bontekoe

A further element of the nonfictional background in this period influenced writers of fiction. It mingled the real with the unreal, the plausible with the implausible, and involved ordinary people in extraordinary events at sea. It elucidated how these impacted on thought and behavior and the role of a leader in interpreting or inflecting them to edifying ends—the way such events had, in an age suffused with religious ideas, an allegorical bearing. Such adventures were described in the memoirs of a VOC captain who served in the East Indies from 1618 to 1625. Published in Hoorn in 1646 (the year before the *Batavia* story), this became one of the most popular books of the Dutch seventeenth century. Its sincerity and topicality raised it into an epic; a "voyage of Bontekoe" became synonymous with a saga of accident and adventure.[1] He was a fatherly figure, who sought consensus and maintained morale in perilous situations.

His story complements fictional voyages and utopias by showing how a ship's company was a microcosmic society, or colony, equipped not only for material survival but with systems of hierarchy, role structures, and cultural traditions—in short, with a portable ethos.[2] Religion and the mystique of leadership are constant themes as might be expected in a life of fear, deprivation, and unexpected rewards; Bontekoe emerges as a Moses- or Noah-like figure. His account involves themes germane to the later imaginary voyage (storm, shipwreck, and contact with strange peoples) and, in particular, certain motifs peculiar to the austral cycle, such as riding on spars.

Bontekoe grew up in Hoorn during the VOC's expansion in the East

Indies. In 1622 he took part in its attempt to open trade with China, a hegemonist policy that became genocidal and was discontinued. He seems to have had little taste for such activities although he was not engaged in any political way. His voyage out took him past the Cape of Good Hope to the Bay of Santa Lucia in Madagascar (where he would call on his return voyage, a symmetry prominent, like Madagascar itself, in later fictional works). Unable to land, he rested the crew at the uninhabited Mascarenes (Réunion Island), a sort of Eden, or Land of Cocaigne, where dodos and other creatures could be caught by hand. Then at an island off Madagascar, "before the great Bay of Antongil,"[3] they noted the simplicity and gaiety of the islanders when one of the sailors played the fiddle but "found in them no sign of any knowledge of God or any religion."[4]

In mid-Indian Ocean disaster struck when coal in the bilge caught fire. Water thrown on it made choking sulphurous fumes, and the fire reached some barrels of oil. It finally ignited the gunpowder, and in the explosion Bontekoe was blown into the air. On coming to in the water, he had the mainmast on one side and the foremast on the other. "I climbed into the mainmast and laid myself down thereon (and) a young man did bubble up beside me. . . . I saw near him a spar or yard floating, and because the mainmast (on which I lay) rolled continually from side to side so that I could not well remain on it, I said to him: 'Push that spar towards me, I will lie on it, then pull me to you and we can sit together'" (41–43).

Seventy-two survivors set out in two small boats for Batavia with almost no food or water. Bontekoe made a sail from their shirts and with the carpenter (who had his compass and dividers) improvised a sextant. "I also cut a sea-chart on the board aft and laid the island of Sumatra therein, with the island of Java and the Strait of Sunda that runs in between."[5] Guessing the strait to lie due east, he cut each day's estimated run into the board. But things grew desperate despite his assurances that land was near and some providential meals of seagulls and flying fish. Reduced to drinking seawater and urine, the men began to discuss eating each other.

He managed to stave off this catastrophe until, after thirteen days, an island was sighted.[6] It was uninhabited and offered only coconuts on which they made themselves sick. Farther along the Sumatran coast the locals proved hostile, and they narrowly escaped massacre, losing sixteen men. After further such episodes, the Sunda strait was reached, and a Dutch fleet took them to Batavia.

Bontekoe's adventures around the archipelago and in China left him with a strong urge to return to Holland for they "would be but poor entertainment were we not supported by the hope of once upon a time relating (them) at home; for in that very hope do we call our journeyings 'travels', otherwise such hopeless wanderings would be no better to a man than exile" (128). Returning through the Indian Ocean, he again struck disaster in the form of a hurricane. The ship, its bilge pumps blocked with loose pepper, nearly sank, and the mainmast had to be cut away. Afterward Bontekoe gave some spars to another surviving ship (despite the objections of a less-charitable crew) and reached the Bay of Santa Lucia to refit his ship. He then carried on (again with a reluctant crew captivated by the local women) around the Cape of Good Hope and finally reached Zeeland via St. Helena and Ireland. The other ship, he learnt, had reached the Bay of Antongil (where Willem Schouten, a passenger in her, had died and been buried).

Bontekoe's story illustrates a point crucial to imaginary voyage literature of the ensuing period: if a narrative so seemingly allegorical could have been pure documentary fact, it is not surprising that fictional versions of the theme were often confused with fact. Such confusion, indeed, bore allegorical implications for the new age of empiricism.

The Isle of Pines (1668)

This nine-page pamphlet (Neville 1668a) appeared anonymously in London as, it seemed, an insignificant erotic fantasy in the Restoration manner. But it became an overnight sensation because of its erotic aspect and its imaginary geography and, above all, its claim to be a true story. It was written by a republican politician and political theorist, Henry Neville, and, as was common with such works, the title page outlined the main elements of the story.

It begins with a trading voyage to the South Seas in 1569. The young hero, George Pine, sailed in the *India Merchant* as the captain's secretary and servant. They followed the normal route via the Cape of Good Hope but off Madagascar were carried away by a violent storm and wrecked on an unknown coast. The only survivors were Pine, the cap-

The ISLE of
PINES,
O R,

A late Difcovery of a fourth ISLAND in

Terra Auftralis, Incognita.

BEING

A True Relation of certain *Englifh* perfons, Who in the dayes of Queen *Elizabeth*, making a Voyage to the *Eaft India*, were caſt away, and wracked upon the Ifland near to the Coaſt of *Terra Auſtralis, Incognita*, and all drowned, except one Man and four Women, whereof one was a *Negro*. And now lately *Anno Dom.* 1667. a *Dutch* Ship driven by foul weather there, by chance have found their Poſterity (ſpeaking good *Englifh*) to amount to ten or twelve thouſand perfons, as they ſuppofe. The whole Relation follows, written, and left by the Man himfelf a little before his death, and declared to the *Dutch* by his Grandchild.

Licenfed *June* 27. 1668.

LONDON,
Printed by *S. G.* for *Allen Banks* and *Charles Harper* at the *Flower-Deluice* near *Cripplegate* Church, 1668.

7. Title page of The Isle of Pines (1668) by Henry Neville. *Courtesy the Newberry Library.*

tain's fourteen-year-old daughter, two young maidservants, and a Negro slave girl. They crowded onto the bowsprit as the ship broke up and, riding on it, were washed into a creek. They set up camp in this idyllic spot, and after four months Pine found that "Idleness and Fulness of every thing begot in me a desire of enjoying the women . . . ; the truth is, they were all handsome." The handsomest bore him a son, the captain's daughter and the other maidservant (who was "something fat") had daughters, and finally the Negress (with the consent of the others) "brought me a fine white Girl." They laid their bevy of babies on moss "and took no further care of them, for we knew, when they were gone more would come, the Women never failing once a year at least. . . . There being nothing to hurt us, we many times lay abroad on Mossey Banks, under the shelter of some Trees."

The women bore seven to thirteen children each before the second generation took over. Pine became a patriarch, ruling with his "favourite consort," the captain's daughter. After twenty-two years, the Negress died, followed by his other wives, and when he was sixty he called a gathering of his descendants, 565 in all. They formed four tribes descended from Pine's wives, distributed territorially (for "we would not pester one another"). Exogamy became the rule, "not letting any to marry their sisters, as we formerly did out of necessity." Completing this parody of the biblical creation, Pine ordered that the Bible he had salvaged from the wreck be read once a month at a general assembly.

He buried his wives in a grave "where I purposed to be buried myself," placing them (as in life) in order of proximity to himself, according to what he saw as a natural hierarchy. At eighty, having "now nothing to mind, but the place whether I was to go," he bequeathed his "Cabin and Furniture" to his eldest son who, with the eldest daughter, had founded a royal dynasty. At eighty-nine and almost blind, he called another gathering of his people, who now numbered 1,789. He placed a written account of their history in the care of his son and bestowed on them the name of "the ENGLISH PINES, George Pine being my name, and my Masters Daughters name Sarah English (etc.) I informed them of the manners of Europe, and charged them to remember the Christian Religion, after the manner of them that spake the same Language, and to admit no other; if hereafter any should come and find them out." This injunction had been forgotten by the time a Dutch ship arrived in 1667.

The work purports to be an authentic document: Pine's narrative, later acquired by the Dutch visitors. Reports of visits to exotic places were common in those days, and this one might have seemed merely an erotic embroidery of the style. But the effect of its claim to offer news from *Terra Australis* was electric. As one critic notes, "so startling a popularity, so widely shown, was a tribute to the opportunity rather than to the contents of the piece."[7] The commercial world was avid for information about that possible "new America," and by the end of the year the work had been published in Holland,[8] France,[9] Germany,[10] Italy,[11] and New England.[12]

Exactly one month after the original (of June 27), Neville published a "New and further Discovery" of the island, "In A Letter from Cornelius Van Sloetton a Dutch-man (who first dis-covered the same)" (Neville 1668b), an extension of the story purporting to be by the previously unnamed Dutch captain. The original piece was inserted into it, and the resulting thirty-one-page quarto edition was given a definitive title (Neville 1668c). Further details included the present population of the island and its exact location (76° longitude 20°S latitude).[13] The Dutchman (whose name is now spelt Sloetten) is given a first name, Henry—that of George Pine's first son, and of Neville himself. In addition, two prefatory letters from an Amsterdam merchant, Abraham Keek, mention a French sighting of an Isle of Pines in the Atlantic Ocean.

Neville thus elaborated on his invention, citing an independent witness to boost its credibility (a few years later, Vairasse would further exploit this art of fictional documentation). But "the ruse did not contribute to such a purpose, as the combined parts did not enjoy as wide a circulation as the first part."[14] Again, his deliberately rough text ("desiring you to bear with my blunt Phrases, as being more a Seaman than a Scholler") may reflect, beyond the new vogue for such a style, a real source in a sailor's journal or tavern tale. Such a theory is further suggested by internal analysis and, in particular, by comparing the circumstances of the work's appearance with real events in Australia.

Sloetten describes his voyage from Amsterdam (in a ship of that name), following the East Indies route until, off Madagascar, "we were incountred with a violent storm, and the winds holding contrary, for the space of a fortnight, brought us back almost as far as the isle *Del Principe*."[15] On landing at the latter they asked the inhabitants, "WAT EYLANT

IS DIT? to which they returned this Answer in English, *That they knew not what we said.*"[16] The Dutchmen, amazed to find "so many that could speak *English,* and yet to go naked," were hospitably received. They experienced the usual novelties of such encounters: exotic fruits, naked but demure women, a visit to the chief, and so on.

They questioned William Pines (George's grandson) about how his people came to be there, speaking English yet with no apparent knowledge of navigation. William replied by telling the story of his grandfather's arrival and producing his manuscript (the original nine-page text is inserted here). He went on to relate the island's history during the intervening decades of rapid population growth, territorial expansion, and disorder: "amongst them mischiefs began to rise . . . they fell to whoredoms, incests, and adulteries; so that what my Grandfather was forced to do for necessity, they did for wantonness."[17]

The intervening Pine, Henry, had mobilized the community against the "wickedness of those their brethren," the Phill tribe (descended from Philippa, the Negress—a racism normal at the time). Their leader, John Phill, was thrown off a cliff and the rest were pardoned. A moral reformation followed, with laws proscribing rape, adultery, assault, fraud, sedition, and irreligion. Henry appointed a leader from each of the four tribes to an executive council that reorted to him annually. He then lived peacefully until the age of ninety-four.

The Dutchmen assured William of their good intentions and witnessed one of their monthly religious gatherings. This, preceeded by several marriages, consisted of hours of prayer, sermons, and abstinence. A hunting party found the hinterland well populated by natives living simply (and terrified by guns) and described it in arcadian terms.[18] They reached the other side of the island, which was about two hundred miles by one hundred, with mostly rocky and inaccessible coasts. Burial customs were also observed (flowers were placed on the body, then each mourner heaped a stone on it) and an English christening ceremony that George Pines had instituted.

Before leaving, they built William a wooden palace and he (although apprehensive of the imminent revelation of his island to Europe) hosted a magnificent feast. But then further civil disorder broke out, again caused by the Phills—their new chief (another Henry) having ravished the wife of another chief. With Dutch assistance, he was brought to justice and thrown off a cliff. After loading up with produce and specimens (the fauna was so tame that it could be "picked" as at Bontekoe's island) the visitors left.

Their return, via parts of Asia "under the great Cham of *Tartary*," is punctuated by further erotic curiosities. At Madagascar they experience an earthquake and report the inhabitants to be "very Unhospitable and Treacherous, hardly to be drawn to Traffique with any people" (a detail Foigny may have drawn on). Sloetten finally reiterates that his account is true and adds in a "Post-Script" a detail he had forgotten (the islanders' reactions on hearing an Irish crewman play the bagpipes)[19] and a call to "civilize" (colonize) the place.

Neville (1620–1694) was a member of Parliament and part of the Puritan group around James Harrington. Although a zealous republican, he was suspicious of Cromwell's autocratic tendencies and suffered accordingly, being banished from London in 1654. He resumed his parliamentary career from 1658 until the Restoration but then, suspected of involvement in a 1663 republican uprising, retired from active politics. He devoted himself to theory, translating Machiavelli and writing *Discourses Concerning Government* (1681) that Hobbes admired.[20] Such details may suggest (as with the author of *Antangil* or other Huguenots) a propensity to realism or even cynicism.

His *Isle of Pines* has been disregarded as literature and seen at best as a forerunner of the Robinsonade, a view colored, no doubt, by moralistic considerations.[21] Yet it occupies an important place in the exotist tradition. Its eroticism would inspire Foigny, Vairasse, and others, and its sexual cornucopia and quasi-Adamic populating of a land by one man epitomized new philosophical and political concerns.[22] Neville had written a *Parliament of Ladies* in 1647, which resembled Hall's early works and other satirical "governments by women."[23] Such satire pointed up gender issues that in *Robinson Crusoe,* for example, are conspicuous by their absence. Indeed Neville, as German critics early noted, is an "anti-Defoe"; his fantasy is the obverse of Defoe's ascetic, womanless one.[24] They are diametrical approaches to the same problem: the one moral but sterile, the other vulgar but pregnant with meaning.

This is graphically illustrated by an engraving from an early edition of the *Pines* captioned "How they were cast away." It shows how Neville exploited the bowsprit theme inherited from the *Batavia* and Bontekoe accounts. The wrecked ship, a royal coat of arms emblazoned on its stern, represents the ship of state (no doubt, that of Restoration

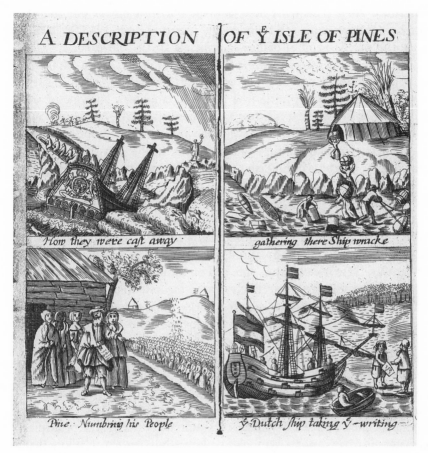

8. Illustrations in an early edition of *The Isle of Pines. Courtesy of the Huntington Library.*

England). As it strikes the new land the bowsprit breaks off, and on it escape the five who will found a new society—appropriating, in this way, the phallic symbol or power-principle of the old order.

The human element in this splitting off, moreover, is an explicitly popular one: it consists of three representatives of the working classes, one of the petty bourgeoisie (the captain's daughter), and one of the totally dispossessed (the Negress). The new state will be one of, and for, the common people; it is they who inherit the bowsprit and set off to be fruitful and multiply in a new land. In this way Neville's fantasy reflects his roots in English republicanism and, more generally, the proximity of utopias of the time to colonialism and all its sociological implications.

It shows, furthermore, that a splinter from an older state (whether republic or colony) is, in the first place, a material or corporeal one—a group of people. As the great migrations of Europe's dispossessed got under way, these five castaways appeared on the literary scene as archetypal figures, signifying by their lowly status the essential nature of that diaspora. It was mainly the powerless ones—those reduced to a struggle for physical survival by oppressive ideologies—who left to form new societies in the New World.

Again, the ship of state was an ideological vessel that contained the desires of the masses in the interests of the powerful, an effect achieved through moral codes based on religious asceticism in an alliance with the Church. But that basis of its power is here subverted by "low" individuals. The new society has, as its unifying or religious principle, a materialist basis, not a symbolic bowsprit but a literal phallus, that of Pine himself, from which every member is descended. Pine personifies the new physicalism taking form by that time: he is an archetypal modern citizen, emancipated from the old social order and its metaphysical underpinnings. The work, thus, had more profound connotations than its erotic aspect suggests.

Similar motives are reflected in Neville's treatment of gender configurations and their traditional association with a social hierarchy. Beneath the appearances of arrant sexism lies a subversion of that hierarchy. One finds here no fully masculine figure in such terms. Pine is a male but has no status in the eyes of the (Old) World; he is of feminine, or inferior, class. The person with superior social status, the captain's daughter, is female, and apart from them there are only female servants. How (the respectable reader might have asked) could a credible state be founded by such flotsam and jetsam of social life?

As the story indicates, their society was, indeed, flawed. It could scarcely be said that Neville was setting up a eutopian ideal except, perhaps, in a flippantly sexist and racist way or in terms of Land of Cockayne traditions. As a polemical work, however (and Neville was a political man), it can be seen rather as expressing a trend of social history, as an abstract vision of political and colonial aspirations. Perhaps, Neville saw in the latter a trend toward the physicalism we now know, a "world of body" valorizing material goals, and sensed how it related to changing geopolitical configurations as the New World was settled. In any case, his intentions were clearly not of a projective order. Although a republican, he imagines not an ideal republic, nor any kind of republic, but a monarchy.

His goal was realism—both the social realism just outlined and a more immediate one that underlines it at the narrative level. As Ford puts it, to assume that the work was a eutopia in disguise "is to introduce an element unnecessary to explain the vogue of the relation. It passed simply as a story of adventure, and as such it fell upon a time when a wide public was receptive to the point of being easily duped. . . . There are few contemporary references to the relation of either Pine or Van Sloetten, and those few are of little moment. If the seamen, who were in a position to point out discrepancies of fact in the story, made any comment or criticism, I have failed to discover them."[25] More recent evidence on this question is discussed in chapter 7.

As a narrative, the work—especially the later addition—is prosaic and dull. Sloetten's closing apology seems, ironically, to anticipate that of Ford.[26] The work may have appealed at the time for the allegorical reasons mentioned (as had those of Hall, Burton, Brome, and others).[27] But the explanation of its sudden and short-lived popularity does not lie in that direction. Neville exploited a specific interest on the part of the public, one soon withdrawn when not satisfied by what he offered. The immediate impact the *Pines* had and the question of its inspiration seem to relate to a sensation created by real events in Australia: the VOC shipwrecks and maroonings discussed in chapters 2 and 7. The world was avid for news about the Southland and, specifically, about those events; but the VOC had a policy of suppressing its diffusion. It is also, presumably, because they were successful in this that no hard evidence of a link between the events and the literary works in question has survived (although the connection is later made by Vairasse and Smeeks). The theme has, accordingly, been put down to mere coincidence or literary resourcefulness.

This transmission from real events to novels is clarified when the set of works from the *Pines* to *Robinson Crusoe* is examined in the light of real cases of shipwreck and marooning in the Southland. These contained a naturally utopian element: the large numbers of people who disappeared there would have given rise to speculation about possible contact with local inhabitants or, at least, about castaway societies. One such incident, the loss of the *Batavia,* was well known. It featured maritime adventures like those experienced by Bontekoe, the use of a bowsprit to reach the shore, a scandalous lapse of morality among the survivors, and a documented marooning, and is certain to have inspired Neville.

But rumors about other events in the region may have been catalyzed around 1667–1668 by the return of a person or persons involved in them or of their story (whose publication the VOC was able to block, at least in Holland). Such a story would have created by its notoriety the conditions in which literary versions of it could flourish. The story may be lost, but the set of works beginning with the *Pines* points to its existence, and that work's popularity attests to its notoriety. It is difficult to explain its reception in any other way.

Such is the present line of inquiry into the "novel" uses of the Southern Land theme from 1668. Earlier ones, including those in English political utopias, had been more directly allegorical. But the *Isle of Pines* shifts the theme onto a new, more esoteric plane, that of narrative realism. The old problem of the traveler's tale had reared its head in the context of new events in the Southland and, more generally, of the growing knowledge of the region. Its potential commercial value aside, New Holland became an object of "pure" empiricist inquiry in the new fashion. Neville's play on the epistemological issues it represented was symptomatic of a new worldview, one for which it is the empirical world alone that is in view (rather than, through it, the "viewing community"). His austral encounter represents a departure from that of Hall or Brome, for example.

The Hairy Giants (1671?)

An undated apocryphal voyage account similar to the *Isle of Pines* soon appeared,[28] claiming to be the translation of a report by a Dutch captain, Henry Schooten (who introduces it in a letter echoing that of Neville's Abraham Keek). His name and that of his mate, Cornelius Groot, recall those of Neville and his characters with their scabrous overtones (notably, Henry Cornelius Van Sloetten). It suggests, too, various real names figuring in the austral story: Willem Schouten, the navigator, and Wouter Schouten, a VOC ship's surgeon who published his memoirs in 1676 (see chap. 7). This again reflects a high level of English interest in Dutch maritime activities, such as caused the Dutch discovery of Australia to first become a literary theme in England.

A notice "To the Reader" surveys the history of voyaging and the famous or infamous episodes it gave rise to. Schooten tells how he had boldly (notwithstanding problems of austral voyaging, such as scurvy) undertaken the explorations still to be made:

> Several Discoveries was made . . . , and yet there remains above a fourth part undiscovered; this gave me encouragement to take upon me this Adventure, though not without great trouble and care . . . (and) in four days after I came out of *Fretum le Mair*,[29] I discovered the Land, which in the following Treatise I give you a relation of.
>
> I do not doubt but this Discovery will be beneficial to *Europe* many ways; first as it may encourage several others to proceed in the like Adventures which may happily find out other Lands, and likewise these particular Islands may be beneficial, they being very fruitful, not over peopled; abounding with many rich Mines [etc.]. The Inhabitants are a people very humane, witty, and intelligent, ready to receive any Instructions, and may be easily brought to Traffick.

A "Description of the Islands of Benganga and Coma" follows. In January 1669 Schooten left Amsterdam in the *Flying-Faulcon*[30] to explore the South Seas. Skirting the "Streights of Magalan" and "Terra del Fuega," he passed into the "Main-Ocean called Mare del Zur." At 275° longitude 50°13'S. latitude (between Patagonia and the islands to the south of New Zealand) he discovered a land with good harbors. It consisted of two islands about three hundred leagues (one thousand miles) around, joined by a strait he named "Fretum del Schooten."

91

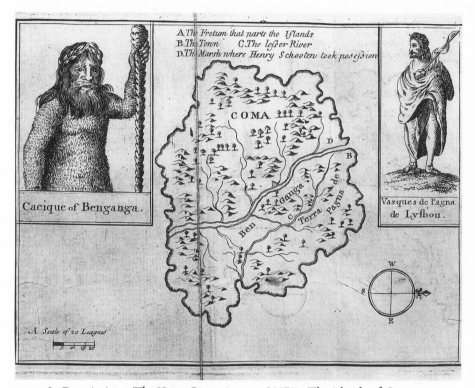

A. The Fretum that parts the Islands
B. The Town   C. The lesser River
D. The Marsh where Henry Schooten took posession

COMA

Cacique of Benganga.

Vasques de Pagna de Lysbon.

Ben Ganga Terra de Pagna

A Scale of 20 Leagues

9. Frontispiece, *The Hairy Giants* (anon., ?1671). The islands of Coma
and Benganga (possibly inspired by Drake's alleged discovery of "Elizabeth Island" west of Cape Horn) are divided by a sinuous strait, a common feature of early representations of the Southern Land. *Courtesy the
Newberry Library.*

There, "we could discover on the Banks, People of an extraordinary size, and hairy."[31]

A "canoo" came out from a cluster of grass-covered mounds with a European in it—a Portuguese who had been wrecked there and become naturalized. He came aboard and invited the ship's company ashore, being "Governour of this Town, and *Cacique,* or King of that part of the Country." The scene was decidedly Swiftian; the natives "were all hairy, having no other Cloathing than what Nature had furnished them withall; and the least of them by computation above Eleven foot high; by these Gygantick men, we were safely conducted to the Town, which consisted of about a thousand Houses, built of Timber, and covered over the top with Boughs of Trees wreathed together; and over them were placed very curiously Greensads, which make their Houses look like so many Hills covered with Grass."[32]

Section 2 relates "The Adventures of *Vasques de Pagna* from the year 1646 to November 1670 as it was related by himself to *Henry Schooten.*" De Pagna, also a compulsive explorer, had run aground between the two islands. With two other survivors he had salvaged supplies from the wreck and set up camp. Within a few months the companions died and he was left in a desperate condition with his supplies running out. Placing himself in the hands of Providence, he left a message for any other European visitors and set out in search of salvation. On encountering the hairy people he was afraid but found them to be "more fearful of me, admiring at my Clothes and Complexion (and) making offers to adore me, supposing I was a god; but I did what I could to hinder them."

They decided that he was "of Cœlestial Extract, and fit for no Company but the Gods and Kings. At this Palace I fared very well . . . by ingratiating my self with the *Cacique's* Daughter, whom I found very ready to receive any kindness from me; her Father likewise casting a pleasant aspect on both, did give me encouragement to make some offers of Amours, which was kindly received, and we in a short time married according to the Custom of the Countrey." He was given two hundred slaves and invited to found a town on the island.

De Pagna (an anagram of *pagan*?) entertains his guests lavishly and shows them his town, the hollow tree he slept in as a castaway, the church he had built, and so forth. His "Lady" and twenty-year-old son were about twelve feet high, a sixteen-year old son more than ten feet, and two daughters nine and seven feet. The second son and elder daughter were, unlike the others, smooth-skinned. As cacique (priest-king), he had converted the locals and founded a priesthood. He then outlines "the Government, Religion, and Customs of the Inhabitants: With the nature of the Soil, and several Commodities of the Island Benganga." It had been governed for one thousand years by the Gangois family— that of his father-in-law, who

> is called by the name of Conumbro Bengangois: his chief seat is Cubugnello, the Town where I was Entertained and Married. He is the Absolute Monarch of the Island, and hath Fourty petty Kings that live about him, that do Homage. . . . They worship in all parts of this Island, except mine, the Devil, who appears to them very often in a misty cloud, uttering or mumbling out some words concerning his will. . . . They believe that they that live well here, and do no man any injury, and obey the Laws of the *Cacique,* they shall enjoy much happiness after death, in pleasant fields, behind the Hills. At three times of the year they offer Sacrifices to their *Dieu* (as they call him) who appears in a Cloud upon a high Mountain all the time of their Sacrificing; and these Sacrifices are sometimes Goats, and sometime Children.

Marriages are arranged by parents and, if approved by the couple, sealed with a dowry and with sacrifices offered by the "Fritazeer" or priest. They are monogamous and bound by a severe morality. "Both Men and Women here are very chast and temperate in meat and drink: their Women are not so fruitful as in *Europe.* . . . Theft and Murder are here severely punished with cruel Tortures unto death." With such a régime they live for up to one hundred and fifty years, and "the like reason might be given for their extraordinary stature." The women are "very comely, and well featured; their faces indifferently smooth, but the Men are so rough and hairy in the face, that they look like so many Island-shocks."[33]

Their "Commodities" include sandalwood ("Saunders"), palm products, "Konock a sort of paint, Cassanack a kind of Pults [pulse] of which they make their bread,"[34] goats, deer, fowl, fish, otters, and beavers. There are gold and silver mines, but they prefer to adorn themselves with the pearls and amber that abound there. They drink palm wine, which "is very pleasant and spiritous, intoxicating the brain, as soon as the most generous Wine in *Europe*" and have "a certain Tree which they call *Cocotonuch,* of the Bark of which they weave a Cloth which serves them for Hammocks and Mantles which they use in the Winter time."

De Pagna describes the government of "Terra de Pagna," the area within ten leagues of his capital, including four towns ruled by deputies. Its laws are "of two sorts, after the manner of the *Europeans,* viz. Ecclesiastical and Civil: My eldest Son I have made Judg in all Civil matters; and my second Son in Ecclesiastical: The Ten Commandments is the rule of our Government; the Lords Prayer and Creed the rule and foundation of our Devotion." During a banquet, "his Lady who had learnt to speak *Portuguese,* made several Enquiries of us concerning *Portugal* and *Europe;* asking us if *Europe* was as big as this World she lived in?"

Finally, the visitors left and a sad de Pagna "made us promise that (if God would permit) we would return again, or at least acquaint the *European* World with this place, and more especially his own Country; desiring them to send over some Religious men to assist him in planting the Gospel amongst these miserably deluded people." On a coast where few giants were seen, they stopped off and "struck down our Ancient in token of possession, giving it the name of *Coma,* by reason of the Hairy Inhabitants." Ten months later they returned to Amsterdam "sufficiently satisfied with our Discovery." Schooten and Groot sign off, swearing as master and mate that "this is a true Relation of our Voyage and Discovery."

An appendix sets out "The Qualifications of Such as undertake a Voyage for Discovery: With several Precepts to be observed by them." They should be of middle age, fit, vigorous, courageous, and schooled in the appropriate disciplines. They need a good ship, well armed, provisioned, equipped with "Instruments for prospection and observation," and crewed by "healthy, stout, resolute Blades." The whole company should be alert and accurate in their calculations. Logs, charts, and journals must be kept faithfully, as well as records of wind and weather patterns, courses and distances sailed, soundings, and any hazards or compass variations.

In remote places they should "use their utmost endeavour to understand the Religion, Customs, Manners, and Commodities, with the Inclinations of the Inhabitants, and commit it to writing." They should seek "a convenient River . . . whose banks are distant from Woods or other Ambushcado's" and, once ashore, "go well armed, that they may awe the Natives; who . . . will be ready to offer divine adoration to them; but let them be very prudent in this case: neither absolutely hindering it, yet modestly denying such adoration . . . for by absolutely hindring their Adoration, they thinking you to be men, will make other attempts upon you, as the *Indians* did upon the *Spaniards* at their first coming thither, by holding them so long under water till they were confirmed they were mortal." Fair treatment in trade and other dealings is enjoined.

On this note, the pamphlet ends. It is typical of post-1668 austral fiction in a number of respects: its Dutch basis; its story-within-a-story structure (a utopia within a voyage); a chronology (1646–1670) approximating that of other such stories; and satirical and narrative elements that anticipate the works of Foigny, Defoe, Swift, and others, and carry on ancient such traditions. Finally, its appendix embodies the progression from literary speculation to colonial "projection."

It bears notable similarities to a later work, the *Travels of Hildebrand Bowman* (1778), based on Cook's second voyage to the South Pacific a few years previously. There, too, the words *endeavour, resolution, adventure,* and *discovery* — the names of Cook's ships — feature prominently (cf. also n. 31: Banks was the celebrated naturalist on Cook's first expedition in 1769–1772). Such coincidences suggest, at the least, that the pseudonymous Bowman had read *The Hairy Giants,* probably in its 1766 edition. But it might be further inferred that the date of 1671 for the original edition, known only from this later one (see n. 28), was a misprint, either accidental or deliberate, the true date being 1771 and the author someone interested (or even involved) in Cook's first voyage.

There may, too, be a historical basis for the work in Sir Francis Drake's adventures at Cape Horn in 1578 on his way to the Pacific. Having lost his companion vessels, Drake in the *Pelican* (renamed *Golden Hinde* following this episode) passed through the Magellan Strait but was storm driven around the area west of the cape. He encountered, at 57°S, a land he named Elizabeth Island, where he found a good anchorage in twenty fathoms and stayed for several days. The island, unlike the desolate landscapes of Cape Horn, was said to have "herbes of great virtue," and so forth, but it does not exist.

A sandbank rising to about sixty fathoms in the area, however, known since 1885, may be the sunken remains of the island Drake (not a man given to idle fabrications) visited. The area is geologically unstable and such a subsidence may have occurred in the intervening centuries.[35] Such an island would have had strategic interest as a base adjacent to the southern continent so that the question of its existence could have inspired a work like *The Hairy Giants* in 1671 (or even, with the revival of such concerns, in 1771). The work's dating remains, however, an unresolved enigma.

CHAPTER SEVEN

Shipwreck and Marooning
in the Southland

The *Vergulde Draeck* Episode

The VOC's second major disaster in Australia was the loss in 1656 of the *Vergulde Draeck,* a large *jacht,* or fast ship, built during the Anglo-Dutch war of 1652–1654 and involved during her brief life in the VOC's contribution to it.[1] In October 1655 she sailed for the East Indies but on April 28, 1656, was wrecked on the Southland as was learned on June 7 when seven sailors arrived at Batavia in her pinnace after an epic "voyage of Bontekoe." Of the 190 reported to be aboard when she called at the Cape of Good Hope, 75 (including the captain, Pieter Albertsz) survived as the ship sank quickly, losing a cargo valued at 185,000 guilders (including 78,600 in cash). The Batavia Council met that day, reporting, however, a complement of 193 and giving the wreck's position as 30°40′S, about six miles from the coast (the actual position, discovered in 1963, is about three miles offshore and 33 miles farther south, at 31°13′S).[2] Such discrepancies are part of the ensuing saga of intrigue and scandal, which would be a major source of inspiration for novels from 1668.

The *Witte Valck* (White Falcon) left the following day for a substantial recovery operation. She was to join the *Goede Hoop* (Good Hope) in the Sunda Strait and search the coast from 32° or 33°S latitude, find the survivors, retrieve as much cargo as possible, and chart the area. She followed these instructions but was unable to land a boat party in the heavy midwinter conditions. The *Goede Hoop* did manage to, after the two ships had become separated, but three of the party disappeared,

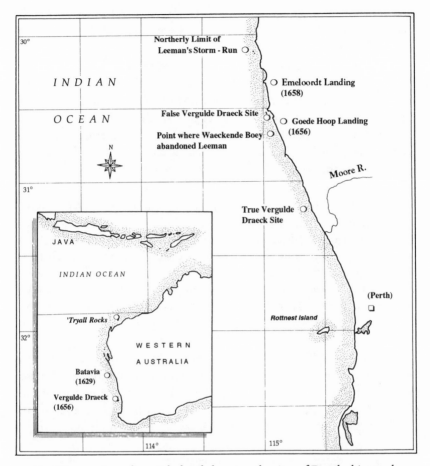

10. Western Australia, with detail showing the sites of Dutch shipwrecks that inspired austral fictions in the late seventeenth century. *Courtesy the Newberry Library.*

and another eight sent to search for them were also lost together with their boat. The *Witte Valck* returned in September and the *Goede Hoop* a month later.

The governor-general then asked his counterpart at the Cape of Good Hope, Van Riebeeck, to instruct Batavia-bound ships to search the coast en route. A memo to this effect outlined the events so far: Albertsz had stayed behind to prevent a repetition of the *Batavia* scandal; little in the way of provisions or water had been salvaged from the wreck; and as the pinnace left, the others had been about to trek inland to search for food. As for the *Goede Hoop* searchers,

> they did not fail to do their utmost to sail to the ordered spot [30°40'S] . . . , and they have been several *mijlen* [ten or twelve miles] inland. They had sailed a long way along the coast but have seen neither wreck nor people. Instead they have lost eleven of their own men. Firstly, three, who seem to have lost their way in the bush, and after that another eight, who, having been sent ashore with the boat to look for them, have never appeared again. The boat was found smashed to pieces on the beach with which the crew is probably lost, too.[3]

Nothing was done (oddly) that summer, but in April 1657 van Riebeeck ordered a search and gave the captains charts, directions, official reports, and some survivors' letters brought to Batavia by the *Vergulde Draeck*'s second officer in the pinnace.[4] The *Vincq* made a landfall at about 29°S—well north of the wreck's reported position and even further north of its true position—and proceeded north briefly before abandoning the search because of bad weather.

It was then decided to mount another expedition the following summer (January 1658). A medium-sized ship with the enigmatic name *Waeckende Boey* (Watching Buoy) and the smaller *Emeloordt* were prepared, with instructions to proceed south and then east for a landfall at 32°–33°S and to work up the coast searching and surveying. They were to spare no pains to

> find the wreck if it still be there, and . . . to see whether on that spot or thereabouts a road or footpath leading inland can be found, in which case you shall . . . examine it in case some of the people could be found.[5]

100

They were to signal constantly with fires on the beach and cannon shots. Salvage was to be attempted if possible, for which purpose, "in order to make the crew more zealous, we have approved that out of what shall be acquired and salvaged by them a proper share be apportioned to be distributed among them."[6]

Disparities between the two vessels and the temperaments of their skippers seem to have contributed to another unsatisfactory outcome. The *Waeckende Boey* was a *fluyt* (flûte), a maneuverable ship with pear-shaped sections, square-rigged on three masts, and with a crew of forty. The *Emeloordt* was a galliot (a type of North Sea whaler averaging about seventy feet, gaff rigged and steered by a tiller over the transom) with a crew of twenty-five.[7] She was at a disadvantage in view of their orders to stay together and suffered damage in the heavy conditions encountered. Her slow progress under skipper Aucke Pieters Jonck seems to have frustrated the *Waeckende Boey*'s captain, Samuel Volkersen, who had to backtrack on occasion.[8]

On approaching the coast they parted company, reporting the circumstances differently, and did not meet again until a brief encounter near the supposed wreck site two weeks later. Volkersen's landfall was at Rottnest Island, as ordered, that of Jonck[9] near Cape Leeuwin to the south. Both made their way north, and by February 28 Jonck had reached the vicinity of the Moore River (near where the *Vergulde Draeck* lay although he saw no such signs). The *Waeckende Boey* was sighted and rejoined, but as they headed out to sea in deteriorating weather they again became separated, perhaps deliberately.

There are also discrepancies in their reports of the ensuing weather conditions. Jonck "did not record which way the *Emeloordt* sailed but said that by nightfall the wind had abated somewhat. . . . [He] was making for land again on 7 March when a morning shower swept in from astern and the sea began to flatten—a good sign for making the land and shallows." The next day, he sent a party ashore.[10] Smoke had been seen and interpreted as signals, and they had replied with cannon and a flag:

whereupon they lit more [and] we decided to send our boat there, with nine stout men and the first navigator-officer. . . . But the moment they touched shore, the smoke or fire was extinguished. Seeing this, our sail-

101

ors turned around, since it was also getting very late. . . . I suspect that
this fire is no honest work, for it was lit at least two *mijlen* [about eight
miles] from the other one and was extinguished at once. We resolved
to send the boat again tomorrow to try our luck again.[11]

Further signals were not answered, and a landing could not be made
until the next afternoon when a large fire was seen in the same place.
That night a party of nine stayed ashore. On returning, they described
the coast and related an encounter with local inhabitants.

We had been near three houses, and five persons of distinction and of
very tall build were there who beckoned us . . . and sympathetically put
their hands under their heads as a signal of sleep.

But we, not being simple enough to put ourselves in the hands of
such savage people as we have had good example [of], returned to our
boat (whereupon) they came up on to the beach. We signalled with our
lantern and flag that they should come to us, but they were very timid
and we couldn't get them near our boat. They departed from us at dusk
and we rested all night in our boat.

On land we found much low scrub and in some places also seeding
land which they burn off in some places, arable or seeding land, but
we saw no fruit but some herbs that had a fragrant scent. We saw nothing more of fresh water or trees going inland, but many sand dunes
as we walked along the beach and inland three *mijlen* [twelve miles],
but saw at night many fires being lit.[12]

A further sweep southward revealed nothing and Jonck left for Batavia, reaching (with difficulty) the Sunda Strait and meeting up with
the returning Volkersen. The pair conferred there before sailing on to
Batavia.

Volkersen's searches began earlier, lasted longer, and were equally
bizarre. He initially moved north to the vicinity of the Moore River—
about twelve miles[13] south of the true wreck site—and sent First Officer Abraham Leeman ashore with a landing party. They were greeted
by many large fires and could be seen by telescope marching north with
their pikes, cutlasses, and muskets. They did not return the next day
but new fires were seen. When he returned the following day, Leeman
reported seeing many signs of the *Vergulde Draeck,*

but no footprints nor any place where people had lived, although they had gone far and wide, both inland and along the beach.

The signs of the ship on the coast which they had observed are as follows: a heavy beam, a piece of oak planking, a small keg, buckets, thwarts of the boat, pieces of chests, staves and other similar rubbish.

It was noteworthy that a number of pieces of planking had been put up in a circle with their ends pointing upwards.[14]

Volkersen saw little significance in these finds and carried on north (the supposed wreck site being well to the north although he must have suspected that this was the true site). As he was leaving, a double misfortune occurred: an anchor was lost, and a swell capsized and sank the pinnace being towed astern, leaving only a smaller boat carried on deck. Next day the latter was put ashore in the Moore River area, but nothing was reported, and the following morning (February 28) Volkersen made for 30°40', the supposed wreck site. Passing the true site (31°13'), he reached a point he gave as 30°40' (but which Henderson reckons was 30°50'). Here the boat was sent ashore, and as it left fires were seen—signals, it was hoped, from the survivors. It returned in heavy weather and broke its mast and would not have reached the ship if the latter had not fortuitously drifted downwind to it when her anchor cable parted, Volkersen having had no intention of helping the hapless crew.

The *Emeloordt* was encountered, as mentioned, following which Volkersen stood well out to sea and turned south as "with only brief respite, the wild seas and high winds continued."[15] Finally (as the *Emeloordt* was leaving the Southland), he returned to the Moore River in moderating conditions, but bad weather again developed, and he put in to Rottnest Island to careen the ship.[16] On another run up the coast, Leeman landed north of the Swan River and trekked north. Further wreckage was found around 31°30', and by March 22 the true wreck site was (unwittingly) reached.

Here began the dramatic events in which the expedition culminated. Volkersen was impatient for progress; perhaps, he sought the glory of bringing back survivors or treasure or hoped for gain of a more nefarious kind, or simply feared lingering on such a perilous coast. Whatever the case, he sent Leeman ashore despite signs of deteriorating weather.

The wind veered south-southwest and threw a heavy swell onto the coast. Leeman became trapped inside the reefs that skirt it, unable either to land or get back to sea. He tried anchoring, but the storm became so violent that he had to run north before it, careering among the reefs all night and the following day. Eventually, he made for an islet where they were "thrown over the rocks about as far as a pistol-shot" by the waves[17] and staggered ashore. They had some water, bread, and bacon, and the island had seals and birds. But there appeared to be little prospect of rejoining the ship.

Volkersen, himself caught on a lee shore, waited until morning and then gave them up as lost and headed for the open sea. When conditions eased, he ran up the coast to the same spot but saw no signs of life. Then, as he was leaving for Batavia, "we saw a fire (and) hoped it was lit by Christian people, either the *Draeck*'s or the [*Goede Hoop*'s], since we had never observed such a fire."[18] With the wind rising, no boat, and only coral to anchor in, Volkersen hove-to until the following day. But by then the ship had drifted at least twenty-five miles to the north.

The fires were signals from Leeman and his men, who had retraced their storm-driven tracks.[19] With little water, but fortified by seal meat, birds, and Leeman's prayers, they had sailed south looking for the ship. At the point where they had parted no sign was seen and, reduced to drinking urine, they returned north to an island where they rested, fed on seals, and set up rostered watches. It was here that the ship was sighted and fires frantically lit.

In despair the fourteen men set out in pursuit of the ship, but she had gone. Leeman put in to the island they had previously reached and prepared to sail to Batavia. He raised the freeboard of the boat (an open vessel of about twenty-eight feet) using seal skins, made running rigging out of the gunwale fender, carved the course to be covered on a board at the stern, improvised a pair of dividers, and had a sail sewn out of blankets.[20] But the boat leaked, and the venture appeared (although he pretended otherwise) hopeless.

They sailed through Houtman's Abrolhos and past the Zuytdorp cliffs, d'Edel's Land, Eendracht's Land, and Dirk Hartog Island before leaving the coast for Java. After only three hundred of the thirteen hundred miles they were drinking urine and seawater. They had sea parsley and dried seal meat but were too dehydrated to eat. Constant bailing was necessary, and Leeman had to maintain strict discipline. His compass was wrecked four hundred miles from Java, and he had to navigate by the stars. Three men died; but on the twenty-eighth day, just as the last of their fresh water was running out, Java was sighted.

Aware of hazards both nautical and human, Leeman put in and sent five men through the surf. They found water and coconuts but then refused to return to the boat. A youth[21] and another man were sent to recall them, but they, too, simply ate, drank, and slept. Later the line that had been run ashore parted, and Leeman and the three remaining men (who could not swim) moved to a safer spot for the night. The next morning they beached the boat and also found water and coconuts but were cut off from the others by dense jungle. Then the boat broached in the surf and was wrecked. The four set off westward on foot (they were even further east than Leeman's estimated position, east of present-day Patjitan) and after many hardships and an attempt to steal some prahus (double-outrigger canoes) were taken in by hospitable Javanese. They were later taken to the city of Mataram, where they remained for two weeks as hostages of the local sultan, Tommagon Pati. The VOC negotiated for their release, and they finally reached Batavia via the VOC station at Japara on the north coast.

Leeman gave the Company his account of the episode. Volkersen, meanwhile, had been killed in an obscure incident some weeks previously. A VOC report noted that he had "left behind a boat with fourteen men under the first officer, writing off the same too thoughtlessly," and that the two captains "did not take sufficient care to remain together [so] we have ordered the Lord Fiscal of India to examine them before the Council of Justice."[22]

This was accompanied by the captains' logs as well as that of another ship nearly lost on the same coast in 1658, the *Elberg.*[23] Another search was made in 1659 by the *Immemhorn,* and in 1660 the VOC concluded, "Now that all missions have been fruitless, we will have to give up, to our distress, the people of the *Vergulde Draeck,* who have found refuge on the Southland."[24]

Wouter Schouten's Version of the Story

The scandalous overtones to the *Vergulde Draeck* disaster were compounded by the fact that eight cases of bullion lay on the Australian coast. Such factors contributed, no doubt, to the episode's translation into a literary theme. When tracing the latter it is worth comparing the various accounts, which vary among each other at critical points, and at others fall silent altogether. The archival pages that might tell us what became of Volkersen and Jonck, for example, are missing, nor is it known what role the second officer of the *Vergulde Draeck* played in the searches after his voyage to Batavia, what happened to the letters he carried, or his later career. Such material was not, in any case, available to the public, which probably learned of these events through oral sources: either from officials with access to VOC records or from the protagonists themselves. Unknown also is the fate of those who became separated from Leeman in Java.

There was, however, a published account of that saga in the "Voyage to the East Indies" of Wouter Schouten (no relation to the navigator Willem Schouten), his memoirs of a tour of duty as a VOC doctor from 1658 to 1665. But reasons both textual and chronological argue against this as the main source for the austral novels. For one thing, the novels seem to refer to details other than those of Leeman's voyage. For another, Schouten's version differs from that of Leeman himself in ways that suggest a confusion of several rescue missions or even with other models—the *Batavia* story or that of Bontekoe. It appears, indeed, to report the story in an almost novelistic vein. The following is a summary of it.[25]

As soon as the news reached Batavia that the ship *Dragon,* en route from Holland to the Indies, had been wrecked on the coast of an unknown Southern Land, the flûte *Watching Buoy* was sent to rescue those of the crew who had got ashore, and whatever was left of the cargo.

The flûte, being directed by those who had escaped from the shipwreck in the ship's boat and brought the news to Batavia, reached the place where the *Dragon* had gone down, and anchored in the spot best suited to her mission. The boat was immediately prepared to search the shore for the survivors. *It first went to the wreck,* over which waves were breaking; then made for the *spot where tents had been erected* when the ship's boat left, for those who had to remain behind and await rescue.

When the crew got ashore *they found the tents smashed to pieces,* and not a single person was found anywhere in the area. Their surprise was considerable. They searched everywhere for clues that might indicate that some small vessel had been built; but could find neither auger nor hatchet nor knife, nail, etc. Nor was there any inscription *or other indication* by which the fate of those people might have been conjectured.

When the boat returned to the ship with this news, it was decided to search further inland and along the coast. To this end several groups were formed; but with no more success than before. However much they shouted, called or fired musket shots, all was in vain, and as far as I know it was never found out what had become of those people.

So they went back *to the wreck,* from which nothing could be salvaged: the waves having carried away the planking and hatches and smashed the whole vessel to pieces, such is the power of the sea on that coast. It was decided therefore that the best plan would be to return, since nothing more could be done and the risk of losing the flûte in this region of sudden storms was evident. With this in mind the boat was sent ashore for water. But those sent to a small river that had been sighted, instead of hurrying back, wandered about and disappeared.[26]

Meanwhile a violent storm was rising and the ship had to get out to sea, where it waited for a while. But when the boat did not return, it was assumed that it had been lost; so that the return to Batavia proceeded, and a report was made there of all that had taken place. . . .

Those marooned there numbered *thirteen men,*[27] who were soon exhausted, weak and thin. Hunger and the cold, wet conditions began to overcome them, and they thought themselves condemned to die there. There was nothing to be had from the wreck: the waves had scattered everything about. Finally in their search for something to eat they noticed among the rocks some large *sea-slugs,* and a smaller variety, which came out of the sea; and these tasted good enough to seem excellent to starving men.[28] . . .

Eventually . . . they quit this place where they had found only arid deserts and mirages, and where there lived *neither man nor beast.*[29] The sterile land was soon lost to view astern, the *second officer*[30] of the flûte finding himself in sad company, and guiding its course by the sun, moon and stars.

Of Leeman's landing on the south coast of Java, Schouten notes that "among their number of *thirteen, nine* could swim.[31] These, despite the

107

opposition of the other four, plunged into the sea and, notwithstanding their weakened state, reached the shore." Again, the four remaining in the boat discovered the following morning that "the *current had carried them* to a quite different part of the coast, where there were no more valley, river or coconuts to be seen." But according to Leeman, they had moved on deliberately the previous evening, and at the new place did find coconuts, and so forth.

Later, the four are said to be taken in by "an old Indian *hermit* who lived alone in that deserted place," living with him until found by "a band of *Javanese rogues.*" The hermit interceded on their behalf, and the vagrants then "offered to help the Dutchmen as charitably as if they had been civilized folk, capable of tenderness towards their fellows. They even offered to take them to Japara." But according to Leeman, their hosts were a group, and they became hostages of the sultan. Again, they "arrived at the city of *the Mataram,* the *Emperor of Java,*[32] and finally reached the Dutch base at Japara, where they gave some reward to their faithful guides. . . . But as for their *nine* companions, I have not been able to find out whether anything more was heard of them."

Further Discoveries

Nineteenth-century Australia learned of various wrecks on its west coast. The circle of timbers at the *Vergulde Draeck* site, for example, was reported in Major 1859, and speculation arose that the lost bullion was buried there. A circle of stones found in 1875 at about 30°40′S was excavated (without result) in 1931 and 1939, and in 1931 about forty old silver coins and the remains of a chest were found at the mouth of the Moore River.[33] A human skeleton was also found in the area but not expertly dated. Another coin was later found on the banks of the Moore River about forty miles inland, but it is not known how it got there or what became of it.[34] In 1964 Henderson and Fred Edwards (who, as a boy, had made the 1931 discovery) located the site of Edwards's find—a cave shelter with "neatly stacked small rocks at the entrance" in some cliffs known as the Eagle's Nest. This was approximately the location of the "houses" mentioned in note 12.

At this time too—the year after the *Vergulde Draeck* wreck was found by Henderson—excavation began at a site believed by the prospector (on the basis of a parchment map bequeathed to him years before by a Dutchman whom he knew only as "Harry") to be where the treasure was buried. Harry claimed descent from one of the *Vergulde Draeck*'s crew and that the map had been handed down to him.[35] A cave was found fifty feet down, but the hole filled up with water and, despite further efforts at great cost, nothing was found.

The wreck itself[36] yielded (along with an illicit cargo of elephant tusks) about half of the estimated forty thousand lost coins. Ninety-two percent of them were two-, four-, or eight-real pieces from the Mexico mint (the most common coins circulating in 1656), and a few from the Potosi and Seville mints. Most were dated between 1590 and 1654; but one was dated 1655, raising the question of how it could have reached the Netherlands in time for the ship's departure in October 1655. It may suggest a later presence at the wreck site.[37]

Such details further underscore the notoriety of the *Vergulde Draeck* story and its literary potential. That the disaster had occurred was public knowledge as van Riebeeck noted in his instructions to the *Vincq*: "It is well known in and outside the Council how this ship has unexpectedly run into the Southland at *about* 30°40′."[38] But details were not publicly available, and even had they been, the picture would still have been a confused one (as Schouten's account suggests). Apart from the presence of treasure and the secrecy and suspicion that goes with it, there are anomalies about the numbers involved in the disaster and its sequels (although crew numbers were often falsified to the captain's advantage; this and the carrying of illicit cargoes were regarded as inevitable).[39]

Nowhere in the accounts is the name of the *Vergulde Draeck*'s second officer mentioned although he was clearly a central figure in the drama.[40] His sailing of a boat to Batavia was at least as heroic an exploit as that of Bontekoe or Leeman, and he was the only person able to locate the wreck. This may have something to do with the discrepancy between its stated location and the actual one (to which, nonetheless, the *Waeckende Boey* gravitated). It suggests a blurring of latitude on the part of the VOC or that officer, deflecting any other searchers to the north. It might explain, too, the lack of coordination on the 1658 expedition (Volkersen concentrating on the real area and shaking off Jonck to this end) or the loss of the *Waeckende Boey*'s pinnace and anchor at the true wreck site (two items essential for an unofficial attempt to recover the treasure) or, again, the fact that no serious consequences resulted from Volkersen's conduct.

Similarly ambiguous were the Company's views about the reception the castaways might have had in the Southland; indeed, they parallel much utopian thinking of the time. They were expressed as late as 1696 when Willem de Vlamingh, en route to Batavia with three ships, was instructed to make yet another search in Australia.[41] The question of their grounds for such optimism begs that of what they knew about the Australian world, both human and physical. On the one hand, a high VOC official, Nicolaas Witsen, warned (in the instructions to de Vlamingh) of the violence and barbarity of the Southlanders—a perception probably conditioned by earlier encounters in the north (see chap. 1). Accounts of the west coast landings suggest, however, that the aborigines may not have been so violent. But the idea of Europeans becoming integrated with them was inconceivable—a "utopian fantasy."

Officials, publishers, and critics were no less prone than novelists to confusion on this point. The only surviving account of the visit of de Vlamingh's ship *Nijptangh* was published in 1701 and bound with Dutch translations of the utopias of Vairasse and Foigny (see chaps. 8, 9), which led many to believe that the latter were also documentary accounts of Australian societies.[42]

Another discovery on Australia's northwestern coast is worth mentioning here. In 1838 the explorer (and later governor) George Grey was in the Glenelg River valley, which runs into Collier Bay adjacent to Brunswick Bay—the conjectured destination of the Portuguese Nusa Antara expedition mentioned in chapter 2. He found some extraordinary cave paintings, including a tall, brightly colored figure that he took to be a priest, likening the scene to Ezekiel's "Men pourtrayed on the wall, the images of the Chaldeans pourtrayed with vermilion." There was also a large sandstone carving of a human head, well worked and apparently beyond the technical means of the Aborigines. As proof of antiquity, "the edges of the cutting were rounded and perfectly smooth."[43]

This may suggest an earlier Portuguese visit or even contacts of greater antiquity from the Near or Middle East. An earlier presence, say of Persians or Nestorians, might explain the "almost Byzantine" style of the artwork Grey saw or, again, the recurring mention of white men in early reports about the region.[44] There are reasons—political, technological, and oceanographic — to suppose that such contact could have taken place in a manner similar to those of the seventeenth century.

The *Batavia* episode had catalyzed exploration of the Southland under Van Diemen (governor from 1636 to 1645) as had the experience of de Nuyts on the south coast two years earlier. The Dutch were interested in extending the southern ocean route to rich markets opening up in Chile and, of course, in the unresolved question of New Holland's own economic value. G. Pool set out in 1636 to explore the north and west coasts, at least to the Abrolhos, looking for signs of a north-south passage that divided the continent and investigating the inhabitants — their race, religion, society, and economic resources.[45] He was to look for the *Batavia* convicts and, if possible, circumnavigate the continent. But he was killed in New Guinea, and the voyage largely failed in its objectives.

These were achieved in 1642 by Abel Tasman.[46] He established that New Holland was separate from the southern continent although the extent of "Staaten Landt" (New Zealand, encountered to the east) remained in question. In 1643 Brouwer, accidentally driven into high latitudes, confirmed Tasman's findings. But the VOC was not satisfied and sent Tasman out again in 1644 with instructions to sail around the continent and explore its northern and eastern regions. This voyage, by contrast with the earlier one, is poorly known and was followed only by brief west coast visits (by Jan van der Wall in 1678 and Willem de Vlamingh).

The only other significant visit for many decades was that of the English adventurer-explorer William Dampier in 1699, which stimulated British interest in the area. Information had earlier reached Britain as a result of Tasman's activities; thus, an anonymous letter found with a chart in the India Office archives in 1891 is thought to have been sent in 1644 by the English Resident at Bantam. It points out that

The Dutch have lately made a new discovery of the South Land in latitude of 44 degrees and their longitude 169, the draught whereof is herewith sent. They relate of a gyant-like kinde of people there, very treacherouse, that tore in peeces lymbemeale their merchant, and would have done them further mischiefe, had they not betaken them to their shipps. They make mention alsoe of another sort of people about our stature, very white, and comely, and ruddy, a people gentle and familiar,

with whome, by their owne rellations, they have had some private confer-
ence. We are tould that the Dutch Generall intends to send thither againe
and fortifie, having mett with something worth the looking after.[47]

Interest in the austral world from the late 1660s was in the main
stimulated by published accounts of Tasman's first voyage, "the real motive
of (which) was the speculative hope of finding wealthy lands in the south
and east—a hope clearly expressed in the [VOC's] resolution."[48] The
account of Arnold Montanus in 1671, based on the journal of the expedition's surgeon, Hendrik Haelbos, contains details not found elsewhere and has been seen as an ethnographic supplement to Tasman's
report.[49] Van Nierop's 1674 account of the voyage (based on Tasman's
journal) was highly influential; it was translated by Robert Hooke in
1682 and appeared in travel collections by Narborough and Harris around
the turn of the eighteenth century.

In addition to such accounts the public had access to maps showing
the new discoveries with just enough information to arouse its curiosity. They appeared in voyage collections such as that of Thévenot (1663)
and showed an almost complete outline of Australia's west coast (except
for the region of the VOC disasters), north coast (shown as continuous
with New Guinea), and south coast, with Van Diemen's Land (Tasmania) and New Zealand's west coast suspended in an empty ocean.
Speculative completions of this tantalizing picture naturally resorted to
Quirós's description of the "Austrialia" he thought he had reached in
1606 as, notably, in Foigny's *Southern Land, Known*. Empiricist advances
were made in geography: for example, Pieter Goos was an Amsterdam
bookseller who popularized the charts of Hendrick Doncker. His influential *Nieuwe Werelt Kaert* (New world map) of 1666 shows Tasman's
Australia freestanding, with no southern continent. But it remained un-
changed until 1675, and "the geographical representation of Australia
offered on this map was to be retained for the next hundred years, except for the hypotheses of the French School of cartographers."[50] The
latter, indeed, were not far removed from the literary form the Southland took from Goos's time.

CHAPTER EIGHT

The *History of the Sevarites* (1675–1679)

A Series of Doubles

Probably the best-known utopia of the 1668–1708 phase is the *History of the Sevarites* by Denis Vairasse, or Veiras. The work of a Huguenot living in England, it shows the influence of seventeenth-century English utopism and was first published in English.[1] When Vairasse returned to France, he published it in French with Louis XIV's approval in 1677.[2] A Seconde Partie, Tome II (second part, vol. 2) was added the same year, followed (oddly) in 1678 by volume 1 and in 1679 by volume 3. These additions again had royal privilege even though they are increasingly critical of the political and religious establishment in France.

A condensed version of the Seconde Partie was translated and added to the original English text as "A further Account . . . more wonderful and delightful than the First," and this, too, was published in 1679. In the view of Lanson (see n. 2) the addition was a "mere novel," sacrificing the philosophical interest of the book. He considered that Vairasse had had control over the first English edition but not over the later one either because the publisher feared the rigor of his ideas or because there were "more lucrative speculations to pursue." Such hypotheses are examined here by reference to evidence both internal and external and, in particular, to indications that a true story from the Southland had found its way into Europe's literary consciousness by about 1668. In France, too, the charmed life of this critical work in a time of strict censorship needs to be explained. An undue focus on its ideological aspects may have obscured (as with the *Isle of Pines* and other such works) the even greater significance of its relationship with historical events.

The identity of the "editor," le Sieur D.V.D.E.L. (Denis Veiras d'Alais

113

THE
HISTORY
OF THE
Sevarites or *Sevarambi:*
A
Nation inhabiting part of the third
CONTINENT,
Commonly called,
Terræ Auſtrales Incognitæ.
WITH
An Account of their admirable
GOVERNMENT, RELIGION,
CUSTOMS, and LANGUAGE.

Written
By one Captain *Siden,*
A Worthy Perſon,
Who, together with many others, was
caſt upon thoſe Coaſts, and lived
many Years in that Country.

LONDON,
Printed for *Henry Brome,* at the *Gun* at the Weſt
End of St. *Pauls* Church-Yard. 1675

11. Title page of *The History of the Sevarites* (1675) by Denis Vairasse. *Courtesy the Newberry Library.*

en Languedoc), remained uncertain until the nineteenth century, and the story was variously thought to be by the Captain Siden who narrates it or by some literary figure such as Bayle or Leibniz.[3] Vairasse, like other authors of austral novels, is an enigmatic figure, variously an adventurer, scholar, and diplomat.[4] Well born and educated, he studied law and was probably influenced by Cartesian and skeptical philosophies. After the death of his parents, he left the legal profession, sold his inheritance except for a small farm, and traveled in Europe. He served in Louis XIV's armies and is thought to have settled in London sometime before 1665. There, he associated with figures such as Locke, Shaftesbury, and Pepys and pursued a diplomatic career, but this came to an end when his patron, Arlington, fell from power in 1674. He moved to Paris around 1676 and exploited his knowledge of geography, languages, grammar, and exotic cultures by giving lectures, which were attended by intellectuals from all quarters. He was friendly with the geographer Sanson and (although nominally a Protestant) with the Jansenists.[5]

This sort of readership, too, was impressed by the bold propositions in the *Sévarambes*. The work enjoyed a reputation throughout the century before the French Revolution,[6] largely for ideological reasons, as a vehicle for "Enlightened" ideas. At least initially, however, its claim to be a true story was also significant. As mentioned in chapter 7, a Dutch translation of it was bound with an account of de Vlamingh's visit to Australia and widely taken to form part of it. Vairasse went to great lengths to exploit such confusions so that his work merged into the prevailing aporia of fact and fiction concerning the Southern Land and its discovery.

The Sevarite land is encountered at 40°–42°S; which, along with details such as a mountain range seen to the south, evokes Tasman's descriptions of Tasmania and New Zealand or the tantalizingly incomplete maps of the region at the time. It retrenches the old myth in the light of new information, making a utopian setting out of what still remained unknown. An elaborate preamble sets up this effect in the manner familiar since More's *Utopia*.

Siden—an anagram of Denis—is a Dutch sea captain who died while returning from the Southland and entrusted a manuscript recounting his adventures there to the ship's doctor. This account had been passed to D.V.D.E.L. for translation and publication, being in Latin, French,

Italian, and Provençal (languages Vairasse knew). It begins with a bio-graphical sketch that corresponds to what is known of Vairasse's own life—an early career in law, a "violent" desire to travel. But Siden parts company with the author when he sails for Batavia on April 12, 1655, aboard the VOC ship *Golden Dragon*.[7] In August she was wrecked on an unknown Southland shore[8] and the castaways discovered a utopian civilization. The latter is outlined in a number of works[9] and is only briefly discussed here where the primary issue is the story's relationship with the real events it refers to.

The coast was uninhabited, and Siden organized the survivors into a colony. His first task was to distribute 74 women among 307 men, a problem he solved by resorting to rank. The officers received one wife each, and the sailors shared the remainder on a roster system. The theme, probably inspired in part by Neville's *Isle of Pines* and other erotica of the time was no doubt based largely on the *Batavia* mutiny.

In the interior is found a marvelous city, Sporounde, but its gracious citizens say they are only the "rejects" of a much more glorious me-tropolis further inland, Sevarinde, capital of the Sevarite empire. There, only the most perfect are tolerated. The castaways move to Sporounde, and a venerable guide named Sermodas explains the elements of Sevarite philosophy. Each guest is given a female slave; for here a strict sexual economy prevails, proscribing both abstinence and excess and regulat-ing the minutest details of conjugal practice—even a couple's nights of "association."

Traveling on to Sevarinde, they undergo medical tests and don Sevarite dress (which distinguishes the various classes of this society). They are again provided with females and observe a mass marriage in which the two sexes form lines and parade before each other and each man chooses a wife. Leftover women are taken into the households of state officials, who are allowed polygamy as a reward for civic duty. Adultery, how-ever, is severely punished. This system, doubling Siden's polyandrous one for his castaways,[10] had been instituted by their "founding legis-lator," Sevarias.

The latter's name, again, is an anagram of Vairasse. It is evident too that the prefix *sev-* in these names implies a severing or sundering (in French, too, *sévrer* means to wean, separate, or deprive)—again, in the manner of More's Utopus as creator of the Utopian island. Thus, Se-varias doubles the author and Sevarinde the Indies; it is a part of the world so remote as to be split off from reality. It also implies severity—a satire on excessive moral rigor (as will be seen, such a tone becomes manifest on several levels).

Another aspect of its "enlightened" system is its natural theology. The Sevarites worship the sun and have in their temples a crystal globe radiating light, a many-breasted female idol symbolizing the motherland, and an image of Khodimbas, an Unknowable deity hidden by a black veil. These were ideas in vogue at the time (see chap. 3). They are also great engineers, building architectonic prodigies (like those of Utopus or of Foigny's hermaphrodites). Examples are a tunnel through a mountain range, by which Sevarinde is reached (in the symbolic rebirth typical of utopian novels), or the alternative route over the mountains by funicular railway. Other wonders include systems of fishing and hunting using trained animals.

The journey there is an initiation into this civilization; the aim (as in Brome's play) is to initiate the reader into a new way of viewing the world. It is also a penetration to the center of a perfect, geometrical structure. The nation's capital lies at its center, at the center of an island in the center of a lake,[11] and is symmetrical. The buildings are square (number four, central to alchemy and numerology, features prominently). A communal dwelling, or "osmasy," is set aside for the visitors, with Siden (who is received at the palace of the Viceroy of the Sun)[12] as its "osmasiont," or chief. The newcomers are integrated into local life with reduced working hours so they can learn the new ways. They study technologies that Sevarias had introduced (such as an alchemical means of transforming sand into rich soil)[13] and the collectivist economy.

The imaginary history is further amplified from book 3 (the part Vairasse added after returning to France) and narrated now in the third person. Sevarias was a Persian prince and high priest of the Parsee sect, steeped also in Byzantine and Western culture. As a refugee (like many Huguenots) from Muslim persecution, he had traveled the world with his teacher, a Venetian named Giovanni, finally deciding to create an ideal society in the Southland. The ensuing history of colonization displays, with its geographic and ethnographic details, Vairasse's erudition; for example, a military system complete with amazons reflects the Tartar or Scythian models available at the time from travel accounts.

Sevaris (as he then called himself) arrived in 1427 with an army of six hundred Parsees, who were later joined by a further thousand. The natives were persuaded by the magic of firearms of his right to rule as well as by his claim to be an envoy sent by the sun to renew their corrupted sun cult (echoes of the Spanish conquest of America, of More's Mazdaism, or of the Christ story might be detected here). The native "Sephirambi" were divided (like Europe's Christians) into two warring factions: the Prestarambi in the north and the Stroukarambi in the south. The latter were under the sway of impostors such as Omigas, a pontifical figure who (like the Inca Manco Capac) claimed to be descended from the sun and imposed priestly power by staging false miracles. This was a powerful critique of ecclesiastical abuses of the time. The Stroukarambi persecuted the Prestarambi (Protestants) but were defeated when Sevaris allied himself with the latter.

Sevarias, as he became known (reflecting the author's name-change when he went to England), did not claim to be literally a "son of the sun," only its representative or viceroy. He also gave a popular bearing to his rule by marrying (like Alexander the Great) a daughter of each vanquished leader. But it becomes clear that the rationalist system he instituted was no less prone to elitism and abuse than that of the old impostors as is underlined by the long story of a later imposter, Stroukaras, in the final book. Such complications call into question easy "eutopian" interpretations of the work.

Successive viceroys are recalled, with their exploits. They are elected despots, morally responsible for the well-being of their subjects (unlike the real monarchs obliquely referred to, specifically, Louis XIV). Although ultimate sovereignty and property rights are vested in them, their election is the culmination of a process of pyramidal representation, and their authority is similarly delegated down through a pyramid structure. In general, the system echoes that of More. But on this point, too, the question of Vairasse's true intentions is a complex one.

Later parts become progressively distant from Siden's first-person narrative and its double, the story of Sevarias. The "Manners and Customs" of the Sevarites are described in a familiar utopian manner, dealing with class structures, health, marriage, laws, education, religion, and political institutions. Digressions proliferate on their ceremonies and doctrines and on their language, which is an example of the universalist schemes then in vogue. Despite their collectivist economy (with communal storehouses, and so forth), a class-system persists — marked, as noted, by the use of dress. Education is provided by the state from the age of seven when children are taken from their parents. It is the same for boys and girls despite their very different adult roles. Marriage is compulsory at eighteen for women and twenty-one for men.

When the focus shifts to the Dutchmen's life there, Siden suddenly declares his desire to return to his family in Holland. The viceroy reluctantly consents, and he makes his way via Persia to Smyrna (Izmir) in Turkey where he boards a Dutch ship bound for Holland. But he is mortally wounded in a hostile encounter with the British Navy (a real one, which occurred on March 15, 1672, and precipitated war between the two countries). Before dying he commits the account of his adventures to the ship's doctor, as mentioned, so that it becomes, in every sense, a "testament."

Interpreting a History

How, and why, did Vairasse's utopia depart from earlier seventeenth-century styles? Two apsects of it might provide a useful approach: first, its interest as a political utopia, a blueprint for the Enlightenment. Central problems here are the meaning it gives to concepts of representation, equality, and cultural identity. Second, a more historiographic approach can link these provisions with real exotic models and the narrative itself with real events of the time.[14] In the end it is necessary to articulate these two approaches to fully appreciate the bearing of either and the complexity of Vairasse's thought.

A series of societal models is presented. That of Siden takes a militaristic line (echoing, perhaps, Cromwell) but is short-lived and overshadowed by the erotic aspect. Giovanni had proposed a seven-class system (again, the astral number) for the new society, and the two indigenous societies provide further models. But all of these are incidental to the Sevarite one. Here, the osmasies (each with about one thousand residents) are represented by osmasionts or coenobiarchs in a local assembly, which in turn elects brosmasionts (each representing eight osmasies) to an Ordinary Council. Through seniority, these become members of an upper house, the Great Council or Senate, consisting of twenty-four members with the title of sevarobast. Four of them are elected as candidates for the post of viceroy when it falls vacant and draw lots to reveal the sun's choice of a successor.

In theory, power is delegated toward the center of the society, a paradigm doubling the centripetal spatial and narrative configurations mentioned. At the heart of the imaginary society, of the Southland, and of the story is found an absolute social ideal — pure democracy. But that long and tortuous convergence, that voyage of discovery, reveals the contrary — power radiates in practice from the center, or apex, and is disseminated outward and downward by the delegation of an authority attributed to the sun. The system's religious basis, in other words, is at cross-purposes with its ostensible political structures. Contradictions appear as well in its egalitarian economic system. Its hierarchy of sexual privileges (the lowest officials are allowed two wives, osmasionts three, and so on up to the viceroy, who takes twelve) is, like the use of uniforms as markers, merely another way of delineating a class system (than, e.g., the money-based system that Giovanni had proposed).

At the ideal center, then, is found only paradox. The society proves to be caught in an all-too-real tension between divine and profane forces, public and private ends. Its attempt to rid politics of greed and ambition by substituting other forms of incentive for monetary ones (sexual privilege or social respect) fails to account for the fact that these are equally susceptible of becoming personal ends, displacing civic duty. Vairasse's society, although undoubtedly a vehicle for radical Enlightenment ideas, was not such in any simple, projective way. Indeed, its attitude begins to appear — as "Enlightened" positivism recedes into the history of ideas — at least ambivalent if not frankly dystopian. It suggests that projective attempts[15] to harness religious forces to political ends, whether passively or by actively collapsing politics and religion into a single process, ignores the essential function of both.

Primitive pantisocracy might be such a marriage of basic principles, but it is to be found in man's past, not in any conceivable (let alone constructible) future. The historical pluralization and massification of society brings a conflict of organic cultures, a need for political processes of delegation and integration and, with them (as Rousseau would point out), inevitable inequalities. Again, to posit deism or materialism as the basis of a universal humanity is profoundly contradictory. Religion is in essence a process of internal integration, structuring a community by excluding an ideological exterior — a process of differentiation. Organic religions reflected the givenness of physical boundaries, hence, inversely, the need for a universalist avatar to take the form of a utopia "severed" from the real world. Religious toleration would come about not through any intentional project but through a general defusing of religion as a structural force with the cultural interchange resulting from commerce and travel.

These were realities that *terra australis incognita* was uniquely suited to illustrate (Foigny, writing at this time, uses the device even more cogently than Vairasse). In the story Siden's (Denis's) decision to leave implies a disillusionment with the utopia's inner contradictions. These are reflected on another level, too, in the insinuation into the story of recent developments in Australia. They are variously accurate: Siden sails with the *Vergulde Draeck* but on the wrong date, and his 380-odd castaways recall not the 75 from that ship but the 250 or so from the *Batavia* (or the crew of the *Trial*). The *Batavia's* influence in the erotic area, too, was noted although it is only partly valid to associate Siden with Cornelisz, the leader of that mutiny[16] because in many ways he is closer to a Pelsaert or a Bontekoe.

Vairasse pretended to solve a great enigma of the time: How could so many people[17] simply disappear in the Southland? Had they died or been massacred or, perhaps, joined a local society? Siden tells all: they had gone inland and joined the Sevarite civilization, and he had stayed for about sixteen years. His account of the episode had reached the world by way of a ship's doctor and a sympathetic editor. Given the confused nature of reports from distant parts at the time, this would have seemed plausible enough—no less so than stories of miraculous voyages in open boats, Patagonian giants, men with tails (orangutans),[18] or the claims of Gonneville and Quirós to have visited the Southland (both of which had come to the public's attention in 1663, see chap. 1).

Again, it might be thought that Siden's story was based on that of a real ship's doctor, Wouter Schouten (see chap. 7). But this appeared in 1676, one year after the *History of the Sevarites*. Vairasse was, however, in Holland on a mission with Buckingham in 1672 and probably learned of the story then, further seasoning it by involving Siden in the naval incident of that year. He also mentions in his "Notice to the Reader" a real VOC lawyer, Pieter Van Dam,[19] who attests to the authenticity of Siden's account, and Maetsuycker, governor at Batavia from 1653 to 1678 and organizer of the *Vergulde Draeck* searches.

The "editor" claims to have been shown a letter by a Frenchman, who had recieved it from a Fleming named Thomas Skinner in reply to his inquiry about Skinner's involvement in a shipwreck in New Holland. The Frenchman made the request on behalf of a Savoyard gentleman who had heard of this episode. Skinner's reply, however, related not his own experiences but those of a Flemish sailor named Prince, who had sailed in the *Golden Dragon*. Skinner may have been a real person[20] or a character based on Abraham Leeman, first officer of the *Waeckende Boey* (see chap. 7), as, too, may Prince. It is even possible that this was a veiled reference to the unknown second officer of the *Vergulde Draeck* or to a companion of his in the small boat he sailed back to Batavia or on the rescue mission he accompanied. There may, too, have been others who experienced shipwreck on the Australian coast and returned to tell the tale but who for some reason referred to Leeman's story rather than their own.

When introducing volume 1 of the French Seconde Partie in 1678, Vairasse calls a further real witness, Du Quesne-Guiton (1653–1724), a Catholic nephew of Abraham Duquesne, the Huguenot admiral of Louis XIV's navy (whose family Vairasse knew). He, says Vairasse, could verify the story, having spent several years in jail at Batavia (which he had, from 1670 to 1673). Certain other details in the story, such as a bizarre creature called the Bandélis, may also have derived from this source (another Duquesne, Henri, later led an Indian Ocean colonial project). Another real witness called here is Gerard Janzsoon Putsman, burgomaster of Delft and a VOC director.[21]

Some editions of the French Second Part are prefaced with a letter summarizing the First Part and purporting to be by Dr. Van der Haert, the ship's surgeon who relayed Siden's manuscript. He says that as the son of a Frenchwoman he had lived in France from the age of fifteen to twenty-three before traveling in Turkey and the Holy Land. Curiously, he addresses D.V.D.E.L. as if the latter were not also the editor of the 1675 English version, a person he refers to as "our friend." Such details may hold clues to the identity of that person as well as to Vairasse's sources and the extent of the work's factual basis generally.[22]

Cited later is Skinner's letter. It gives the dates 1656 or 1657 for the shipwreck and a latitude of 23°S, whereas the text asserts that Siden and his companions came to grief at 40°S in 1655. On the obvious question of a factual basis for this letter, Von der Mühll in 1938 admitted defeat but was prepared to believe that it was authentic. Australia does have a reef-bound coast at 23°S, but no wreck is known to have occurred there by this time; the nearest was that of the *Trial* in 1622 at 20°21'S.[23] As noted earlier, the locations of both the *Batavia* and *Vergulde Draeck* wrecks remained uncertain until 1963, which, whether accidental or deliberate, had a great bearing on subsequent events. Skinner's letter refers to the latter disaster but gives a position nearer to the former (and even nearer to the earlier English one); it seems to reflect or invoke this confusion in the same way that Siden's narrative conflates elements of the two major disasters along with possible others.[24]

Whether or not Skinner, Prince, or Van der Haert were based on real people, there were certainly good reasons for inventing or distorting such sources: notably, Dutch official secrecy and Vairasse's need (as a diplomat) to be discrete about information he became privy to. Was it a coincidence, moreover, that Maetsuycker's term as governor-general ended in the same year that Vairasse's Seconde Partie was published? In addition to such factors was the rhetorical motive mentioned, the need to preserve the utopian secrecy of the land visited. Vairasse dovetailed that need to the knowledge emerging from Dutch activities in the area, and perhaps introduced distortions of time and place to forestall accusations of fraud or abuse of confidence. In any case, readers had no means of verifying his story, a problem that was especially acute in France.[25]

The work was a garbled assemblage of actual (if not always totally factual) information — the first novel specifically based on the shipwrecks in Western Australia. Playing on the unverifiability of those events, it built on Neville's initiative a few years earlier and gave new impetus to utopian satire. It also put literature in the vanguard of intellectual developments of the day — a search for pure knowledge, unbound by "local" interests (such as had produced, for example, the allegorical Antipodes of earlier ages).[26]

Again, the convolutions of the tale of Skinner and Prince suggest a need to displace authorial responsibility, to erase traces, one analogous to that which, under conditions of censorship, motivated authors to camouflage their political commentaries within novels of this type. The catalyst for that device was, it seems, a real situation of censorship and official secrecy, one of a commercial rather than political order and played out in the antipodes but strikingly anagolous to the French political context. VOC secrecy can explain, too, the mystery surrounding the source of the story in question.

Another comparable literary hoax was the François Leguat story touched on previously in which Leguat and seven others try to found a Huguenot colony on uninhabited Rodriguez Island in the Indian Ocean but are forced from their paradise by the lack of women.[27] It resembles those of Vairasse, Neville, and others both in its sexual theme and in confusing fact with fiction. Long considered fictional,[28] it is now known to relate an attempt to colonize Bourbon island (modern Réunion) in 1690 by the Henri Duquesne mentioned. He wrote a 1689 memoir ("Recueil de quelques mémoires servant d'instruction pour l'île d'Eden") outlining the project.

Such writing also manifested the rising empiricism of the age by giving a heightened profile to the physical side of life. As the *Isle of Pines* shows, this trend not only generated erotic themes but bore on deeper problems of political representation or, generally, of the social distribution of power. The new prestige of the physical shows in Vairasse's reliance on the testimonies of doctors, his dedication of the work to Riquet, or his Baconian concern with scientific knowledge (which his utopians, like the New Atlanteans, gather in the real world).

It is further manifested in his invention of a natural, or cratylist, language. A sort of verbal hieroglyphics, it relies heavily on onomatopoeia and methodically builds complex forms out of simple, concrete ones in such a way as to structure meaning rigidly. Its numerous basic elements (ten vowels, thirty consonants, and even more diphthongs and triphthongs) are further distinguished by tonal variants, cases, declensions, and other syntactical structures. Like other such schemes, it sought to transcend the local variability of language by engineering an absolute conformity of sound with thing.[29] To this end it adapts phonological, lexical, and conceptual elements from living or dead languages (mainly Greek, Latin, and Persian, however, rather than the usual Chinese).

But such monosemy is possible only to the extent of a society's closure from space and time. Language communities have neighbors and evolve. The oblique function of language (beyond particular speech acts) is — like that of religion or other manifestations of culture — to connote a collective difference, to structure a group. Language reflects a syntax of interracting individuals rather than an abstract process of nomination.[30] Vairasse sought to make language (his own, as well as that of his utopians) double the world and its history. His work is characterized by a dependence on the Old World; its use of historical sources extends far beyond previous borrowings of a novelistic décor.[31] This was an enterprise fully in line with the spirit of his age and with its undercurrent of cultural imperialism.

The Utopian Theater and Its Double: A Divided World

In this doubling of worlds and words, credibility becomes a central theme. Vairasse separates himself, on this point, from the "ingenious imaginations" of Plato, More, Bacon, and other utopian forbears; his story, he asserts, is true. Although this gesture was as old as the genre itself, it took on new meaning in this dawning age of empiricism, especially because the story seems to have indeed been based on a true one.[32] The common thread in these crossovers between fact and fiction or nature and culture is the epistemological *mise en abyme*,[33] a telescoping of things, ordering their significance, that would become paradigmatic for Enlightenment thought. Vairasse seems to already raise it as a conscious principle.

Similarly, he joins Neville in introducing to utopism an evolutionary element: a progression from primitive or castaway societies to the absolute statehood of modern Europe. Implicit here is an ideology of progress that, with the Industrial Revolution, would assume explicitly technological and political forms. Here, in an embryonic form, is the political avatar of the epistemological process mentioned: a stasis or statism raising society to a new level of abstraction. As Leibacher-Ouvrard observes, "In this chaining together of the various stages is seen a methodical progression toward a higher degree of coherence, conferring on the story the dogmatism of univocity. . . . Past and present are structurally and thematically linked on the basis of a partial retelling of the primary story of colonization. This *mise en abyme* . . . offers to the reader a multipled image of the Same. . . . In more than one sense, utopia is here a state."[34]

This paradigm extends to all aspects of the work.[35] Along with a doubling of histories goes that of places, characters, and institutions — especially religious sects. The fate of sects in a globalized and secularized world epitomized, as noted, that of local pretentions to universality in general. Already breached by culture contact, they would be further relativized by the advent of an Enlightened search for truth

125

through a rationalist *mise en abyme*. A resurgent colonialism, too, was bound up with this shift from older ways of apprehending the world (those of the closed society) to a global, empiricist one. It brought new ways of relating to cultural otherness based on the principle of doubling or assimilating the Other (in the manner of Sevarias).

Here, as in religion, the determining factor was not the content of particular ideologies but the context in which they encounter each other. Imperialism is an intermediate phase in a (theoretical) global history; not yet affecting closed societies, it may again disappear in a world where the reality of cultural difference is fully interiorized and transcended. Between these poles lies the world as we know it, that of a "classical" cultural metabolism in its twin forms of imperialism and fashion.

Locke, whom Vairasse knew and who moved in similar circles, was also interested in colonial developments and was well informed about world events. Vairasse's vision of a founding legislator who rationalizes cultural differences may be associated with the thought, or even the person, of Locke.[36] The individualist bias of his sensationalist philosophy (or of the Protestant ethic it reflects) is evident in Vairasse's *History*. There, personality is problematized not within the imaginary society itself but by a heightened tension between it and historical reality. Indeed, the Sevarites' appearance, language, sexual mores, and economics reduce them to the status of cogs in a social machine.

These were familiar positions of the classical utopia, but they no longer retain, here, their tone of exemplarity. A merger with history renders the whole scheme problematical. By drawing attention to the story's rhetorical and scenic framework Vairasse introduces an ambivalence—a collapse of the comfortable here-there, Same-Other dichotomies that had cradled utopian literature. It reflected changes that the genre's narrative basis, the voyage of discovery, was undergoing, changes affecting its utopian cargo and heralding later developments in which the latter would be jettisoned. The utopian genre itself, one might say, was falling victim to shipwreck on the southern continent.

Even the author himself was caught in this destabilizing machine. He merges into Siden, then into the more legendary Sevaris-Sevarias through transmutations of his name, a cycle that is reversed when Siden reappears, returns to the real world, and eventually metamorphoses (by dying) back into the author. The narratorial voice is displaced, indeed, several times; from Vairasse to Van der Haert, then on to Siden, after whose account another of the castaways, Maurice, introduces the utopian society, a function then taken over by Sermodas.

This telescoping of narrative elements into each other and of the whole into contemporary history also marks the point at which utopia emancipates itself from English political developments. Hence, too, the incongruity of casting Vairasse as an idealist in the latter sense—for no sooner is his utopia "discovered" than it is rejected by Siden (Denis).[37] In this way he helped build a paradigm that would dominate the genre until the late–eighteenth century.

Nor was this a purely literary phenomenon; as noted, there are grounds for believing that a real castaway story, or its notoriety, underlay such developments and the thematic unity of the austral novels. Dramatic events were known by the 1660s to have occurred in New Holland, but details were not available until Vairasse and others pretended to supply them. Thus, he introduces his French Seconde Partie by defending the original work against sceptical critics. He notes that since it was published he had met the du Quesne-Guitton mentioned and that

> various people have told me of difficulties they had with it; but because they only read the beginning, they had nothing substantial to say on the matter. Among those who discussed it with something constructive to offer was one of the most learned men of our time, whose works are admired by all of the enlightened both for the force of his reasoning and the sublime nature of his thought and his purity of style. One day he told me he doubted very much that the *History of the Sevarites* could be true because he did not believe there were such good people in the world. Indeed, if one considers carefully the manners, religion, government, and culture of this people, one finds it difficult to believe that there could exist on earth such an honest and virtuous nation. We offer the public the body of this false or true history and beg the reader to excuse our omissions and printing errors.[38]

That person may have been Locke, and it is notable that, after mentioning his interest in the work, Vairasse slips from "I" to "we" as if to suggest some collaboration. The last two sentences here speak volumes. On one level the admission that the history is *either* false *or* true could refer to the friend's doubts about the possibility of such an honest and virtuous nation. In this sense it would suggest a parody of Noble Savage primitivism (and elucidate its close relationship with utopian writing). If the friend were Locke, again, it could be seen as a clue to the background of his sociological thought.

On another level this apology may refer to the secrecy surrounding the *Vergulde Draeck* saga. In fact it probably referred to both sources of inspiration — given the breadth of Vairasse's learning and his interest in current affairs. Again, it may be significant that the title of the First Part says it contains an "Account" of the Sevarites' government, but this, although correctly translated "un compte exact" in the first French edition (Barbin 1677), was changed in subsequent editions to "un *conte* exact" (a precise *story*).

Did Vairasse turn an ambiguous story into an ideological effect, or was it the other way around? Was the idea his own or another's? Or did it simply reflect historical circumstance? Various evidence suggests that he (perhaps in collaboration with Locke or another) embroidered a contemporary Dutch anecdote. A possible means by which he could have obtained information about VOC activities in Australia is found in the biographical information mentioned at the outset. It includes a story about his dealings with an English adventurer, Colonel Scott, whom he had known in London around 1670 and met in Holland in 1672. A bon vivant, Scott regularly visited him in Paris and lent him money. Around 1678 Scott was imprisoned by the Admiralty, under Pepys, for spying; and in retaliation he accused Pepys of involvement in the Papist Plot and of selling secrets to France. Pepys fell from power in 1679 and sought to clear his name by discrediting Scott. Vairasse appears to have served his purpose by betraying Scott and to have been well rewarded.[39] In 1680 he wrote a long letter in English detailing Scott's espionage in Holland and on behalf of France. Although this evidence does not itself refer to VOC classified material, it may suggest a means by which Vairasse could have obtained it.

There is also the question of earlier Australian contacts, touched on at the end of chapter 7, which may have a bearing on the explicitly Persian basis of the *History*. A possible source here was Francis Pelsaert's *Remonstrantie* about the Mogul's India (where he was the VOC representative before his voyage in the *Batavia*). Again, winds and currents in the southern Indian Ocean are such that vessels would be carried toward the coast of Australia if driven south from the main trading routes. The latter were regularly sailed at least as early as the tenth century, a time when the area was dominated by Persian mariners.[40] The ships of that time appear to have been seaworthy, well stocked, and able to survive such an ordeal.[41]

Muslim expansion from the eighth century particularly affected Persia's Zoroastrians, who refused assimilation in the manner that Vairasse attributes to Sevaris. Their main refuge was India, where they founded the Parsee sect, but it is possible that some migrated elsewhere and, either accidentally or on purpose, ended up in Australia. Vairasse notes that Sevarias, following his successful implantation, was periodically visited by Parsees who, "seeing reborn in him, as it were, the splendor and ancient glory of their nation, almost effaced in their own land, eagerly came to offer their services to this restorer of the Persian name."[42] Again, the imminent fall of the Byzantine empire in the thirteenth century created similar conditions; perhaps, the "Byzantine" or priestly figures found in cave art in northwest Australia, mentioned in chapter 7, might be viewed in this light. Did the learned Vairasse know of any such lore and use it in concocting his *History?*

CHAPTER NINE

Splendid Isolation

The Southern Land, Known

The "classical" voyage-utopia culminates in another work by a Hugue-not refugee, this time to Switzerland: Gabriel de Foigny's *La Terre Australe connue* of 1676. A short but highly structured and complex work, it again plays on the enigma of *terra australis incognita*. Foigny was, until his thirties, a Franciscan monk, but his licentious behavior obliged him to quit the order, and he fled to Geneva as a Protestant. There he fell afoul of a strict Calvinist morality and eventually returned to die in his native country and religion. But he left a brilliant literary testament reflecting this double, symmetrical rejection. The austral voyage here becomes a metaphor expressing his life experience and, projected onto a global screen, acquires the stature of a philosophical treatise.[1]

It is the first-person narrative of Nicolas Sadeur, a Frenchman "con-ceived in America and born on the ocean; a too-telling presage of what I would one day become." His father, an engineer, was returning in 1603 from a job in America when the ship was wrecked near Cape Finisterre. The newborn Nicolas (named after the patron saint of sea-farers) lost both parents, who died in their efforts to save him. He then became the object of a tug-of-war between would-be adoptive parents, and learned that he was a hermaphrodite (although, as later develop-ments show, this was only a symbolic hermaphrodism).

With the help of Portuguese Jesuits he entered the Villa Franca house-hold, a noble family opposed to Spanish rule in Portugal at the time. He grew up with the young count, a boy his own age, and received a good education.

But when the time came to travel to the university at Coimbra, the feelings of guilt resulting from his earlier experiences flooded back as an irrational conviction that his presence aboard a ship would inevitably lead it to disaster. A succession of (mis)adventures followed that were linked to the political situation mentioned and involved three further shipwrecks in the course of which Sadeur became adept at surviving such disasters. He gained mastery over the watery element he had feared from the beginning.

The sea becomes in the work a metaphorical double of that other medium of communication, language. For it is his intellectual qualities that enable him to experience incredible adventures and convey them to the reader. The sea that bears him on his voyage of discovery is a medium of communication between lands and nations, and its analogical relationship with language turns out to be a central theme of the work. It complements the other main theme, hermaphrodism.

It bears him, eventually, to the Great Southern Land. On the way he falls in with pirates, is rescued by a captain hoping to ransom him for a rich reward, endures ferocious storms, and so forth. He embarks for the East Indies, stops over at the Zaire River, and with some companions makes an expedition into the heart of Africa. There he finds a chaos of natural wealth combined with human apathy or degeneracy (which he sees as directly resulting from it). This episode forms a thematic relay or springboard relative to the fully imaginary scenario to be encountered in the southern continent. There, such qualities will be fully antipodal to European norms; an artificial perfection of the environment will be complemented by human perfection (or what is initially postulated as such).

Sadeur's ship is carried away by a ferocious storm off Madagascar and wrecked on "Trinity Island" in the southern ocean.[2] Having learned to survive such disasters by floating on a plank (a parody of Christ's crucifixion), he floats away on the door of the captain's cabin and, after a series of hardships, arrives at the southern continent. These include a brush with death when he finds himself on an island that proves to be a whale and a mortal fight with some giant birds (a familiar theme in austral literature). His victory over these is watched by some "Australians" (sic), who rescue him and, because the birds are their worst enemies, hail him as a hero.

Thus, too, he arrives naked and exhausted—a stark illustration of the traditional symbolic rebirth into a utopian world (and of its real

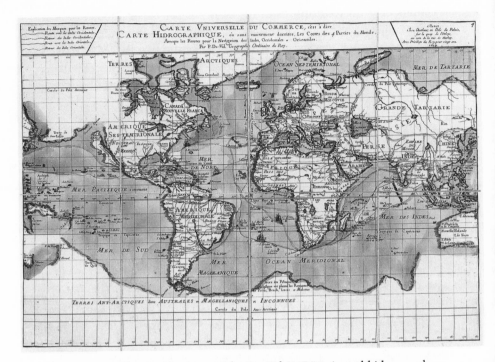

12. A typically post-Tasman map by Du Val (1674) mixes old ideas, such as his "Terre des Perroquets" (Land of parrots) or "Terre de Quir" (Land of Quirós), with new information. His vague connection of a traditional southern continent to the real Australia recalls the earlier "Dieppe" school of French cartography, and the gap on Australia's west coast reflects Dutch attempts to ignore or censor information about their disasters there. This map sums up common conceptions of the region at the time when the most vivid austral fictions were written. *Courtesy the Newberry Library.*

basis in the destitution resulting from shipwreck). This is also providential, in that the Australians do not know the use of clothing[3] and are able to see, furthermore, that Sadeur is a hermaphrodite like them. In this way he gains access to a society that normally kills any castaway "half-men" (monosexuals, who cover their "shame" with clothes).[4] Further developed here is the metaphorical sense of hermaphrodism; for it is Sadeur's ability to embrace ambiguity or duality in the conceptual and cultural senses that enables him to be accepted into their culture.

His continued survival also depends on the patronage of an old hermaphrodite, Suains, with whom he enters into a series of philosophical dialogues. They compare European and Australian society—their respective customs and ideas—in terms familiar to readers of voyage or missionary accounts of the time. As reports of an encounter with an "Indian sage,"[5] for example, a central issue is the seeming contradiction between monotheist principles of unity and the sectarian or nationalist violence endemic to European society. For Australian society has transcended all such inconsistencies; it represents the postulate of a fully rational monoculture. They are perfectly homogeneous, without cultural, racial, national, ideological, or any differences (even sexual) among them. Politically, they are (or claim to be) totally "neutral."[6]

Sadeur learns about their way of life and their world. They strongly recall the Heliopolitans of Iambulus (see chap. 3). They are eight feet tall, beardless, handsome, of reddish complexion, immensely strong, and identical. They live in geometrically precise apartment blocks called *Hiebs,* four to a cell (like monks). These are arranged in quarters that, in turn, form *sezains* or sixteens, the basic unit of society. Each sezain has a *Hab* (temple) and a *Heb* or House of Instruction.

The hermaphrodite way of procreating, however, remains a mystery to Sadeur because the Australians never discuss it. All he can gather is that their "fruit" gestates somewhat in the manner of Lucian's Selenites (see chap. 3) then simply drops onto a bed of leaves of the magic *Balf* tree and is rubbed with them. The parent's milk is so nourishing that for two years the child needs nothing else and produces almost no excrement. Adults, too, eat little (and then only in secret), and their raw fruits are so rich that they scarcely defecate once a week. All physical functions are regarded as shameful and irrational.

Their education is long and comprehensive, and they emerge at the age of thirty identical in knowledge and abilities. The entire population of 144 million (the number of the saved in the biblical Apocalypse) is totally homogenized, and each sezain is permanently ready to receive visitors; so that travel throughout the southern continent is free and easy. In case of a military alert, they crowd to the spot from around about, forming themselves spontaneously into military units, deploying themselves to best advantage, and fighting valiantly to the death; all without any need of leaders or training. In effect, they have the rationality associated (already in Foigny's time) with social insects or beavers.

That rationality is even imposed on the land, which has been leveled into a regular escarpment descending from polar mountains to the coast (varying in latitude between 30°S and 50°S). In this way every part lies toward the sun and has the same climate. The continent's topography (perhaps reflecting what was known of the Australian interior by this time) mirrors the ideology of its people—it is a monological, featureless platitude resulting from an absence of structuring binarities.

Their time is similarly organized. The day is divided into three parts, which subgroups of each sezain spend in various activities on a roster system. One part is spent in the Hab in silent worship of the *Haab*, or Incomprehensible;[7] another at school in the Heb; and the third in their gardens, where Balf and other miraculous fruits grow. They also have recreation periods in which they perform "exercises" (alchemical experiments with Balf juice, seawater, or vitriol that produce ludicrous prodigies) and play games involving feats of dexterity with their medieval weapons, mainly the halberd, a spear with an ax head. Their nights are spent in Balf-induced sleep.

Their language, too, is totally rational and artificial—another universal scheme in the manner of the time. But that of Foigny, whose professional interests included grammar and languages, is distinctive and complex. Its vowels and consonants each name an object or quality and are arranged into clusters that denote the entire range of concepts or referents encountered by an Australian. In this way any confusion of meaning (and the arbitrary nature of language in general) is eliminated; one becomes a philosopher as soon as one learns the first elements of speech. A large part of their communication is, indeed, purely silent—a sharing of identical thoughts.[8]

At the age of thirty-five they become "lieutenants" or candidates for full adulthood. Much later in their long lives, after serving as teachers, they seek permission in the assembly to return to their natural home (death). If it is granted, they consume a large quantity of Balf and pass through intoxication (a state otherwise foreign to them—another parody of religious asceticism) into an eternal sleep. Their names and places in society are taken over by their chosen lieutenants so that the population remains constant. Earlier generations, though, had been so afflicted by life's irrationality—by the paradox of mortality—that suicide had threatened the state with extinction, and a system of regulation had been introduced.

Sadeur's initial enthusiasm for such a world begins to falter as he finds problems with its basic philosophical principles. Eventually, he and Suains agree to differ: "I realized that I could only scandalize and irritate the man by persisting in trying to instruct him in our beliefs," he concludes. This part of the work (chap. 6, "The Australians' Religion") was, significantly, that most mutilated in the 1692 edition. Its original meaning, a (somewhat ambiguous) Christian apologetics, was recast as an apology for the deism rising in popularity at the time (see n. 1). Confusion over these editions had hampered critical appreciation of the work.

The remainder of the narrative deals with descriptive aspects such as the Southern Land's fauna. There are few animals; this is another aspect of the environment that has been rationalized. Their policy is to eliminate such polluting obtrusions of the physical dimension. A brief section discusses the "Usefulness of the Southern Land's Resources": Europeans would benefit, Sadeur suggests, from a giant flying creature that serves them as an 'aerial car' or from a creature like a hog that can plow furrows with mechanical precision.

The description closes with a long chapter on "The Australian's Regular Wars." It is by now obvious that they do have real borders and enemies such as their neighbors in a part of the continent called Fund. These Fundians[9] are "half-men," who from time to time attack the Australians. Sadeur takes part in two such wars during his thirty-five-year stay. He describes how one of them, a campaign to destroy a colony the Fundians had established off the coast, turned into a bloody holocaust. This brings to a head the progressively dystopian tone mentioned; the "fundamental" hypocrisy of the Australians is revealed as they mercilessly butcher the Fundians. At the same time a hitherto meticulous structuring of their world in numerological terms spirals into a chaotic

135

enumeration of the casualties.[10] Eventually, the Australians win and complete the massacre by destroying the island itself.

Among the Australians' halfling enemies are what they call "sea monsters," who arrive occasionally in ships from places unknown to them. Sadeur recalls seeing the remains of ships around the coasts (it being the custom to preserve such trophies), including some he recognized as French and Portuguese. The latter bore the arms of the House of Braganza, enemies of the Villa Francas in the turbulent world of his youth. Suains recalls the arrival of that fleet (six months before that of Sadeur himself, around 1620) and the grim battle against the Europeans and their firearms. The latter had eventually been overcome and massacred in another orgy of irrational violence.

Even more deadly are the *Urgs,* giant birds that ravage the Australians, especially during their rut. Halberd and shield are little defense against these supreme representatives of the physical dimension. But by allying himself with them Sadeur eventually makes his getaway from the Southern Land (one symmetrical with his arrival). During the Fundian war he committed a sin that confirmed him as a half-man by succumbing to the charms of a Fundian girl (as well as failing to display appropriate brutality by collecting a string of Fundian ears). He was sentenced to suicide by eating Balf but ingeniously managed to delay this long enough to tame an Urg and fly out on its back.

After further adventures, he regained civilization via another "halfway house" at Madagascar — a counterpart to that at the Congo, again inspiring quasi-ethnological observations. The natives, he reports, are dirty, stupid, and vicious. But he meets there a venerable chief from an austral island, who had been captured at sea. Inventing an ad hoc language, he strikes up a friendship and, when the time comes to resume his voyage to Europe, the old man is thrown into despair at having to stay on in captivity. He has himself killed by his servants, who then ritually kill each other. Their bodies, cast into the sea, miraculously form themselves into a procession led by the chief and drift purposefully east toward their homeland. One might see here a parody of the Chinese or Japanese ethos as it was interpreted (in terms of "monopsychism" or mental unity) by European exoticism at the time.

With this allegorical vignette the story comes to a close. Its end had been related at the beginning in the editor's "Notice to the Reader." Sadeur had slipped and fallen from the gangplank while disembarking at Leghorn (Livorno) in Italy and died shortly afterward in the editor's care, bequeathing to him a manuscript written partly in the Southland and partly at Madagascar and "much stained with sea-water." The distancing effect achieved by presenting the story in this way would, apart from explaining its origin, enable Foigny to disown it when attacked by Calvinist churchmen in Geneva (on whom its satirical intentions were not lost).

Again, the story is authenticated in the "Notice to the Reader" by reference to the exploits of real explorers—in particular, to Quirós and his "discovery" of Austrialia del Espiritu Santo (see chap. 2). Foigny's work carries forward the realism of Neville, Vairasse, and others. The contradiction between the real and the hypothetical becomes a central theme and, as in the *History of the Sevarites,* "deconstructs" it as a utopia. But Vairasse achieves, as noted, a lower-level realism, a metonymic transfer from reality to irreality. With Foigny, the break is absolute: his "other world" is one of pure metaphor, a departure from the real so as to question uncritical assumptions about it. Its effect is to abstract the utopian novel from social and political concerns into the realms of pure philosophy.

Crucial here is the metaphor linking language and the sea to phenomena of travel, discovery, and culture contact. Language and the sea are analogous as media: they share a dual function of facilitation and exclusion, an ambiguity inherent in all communication whether between individuals, collectivities, states, or Old and New Worlds. Foigny uses the analogy to set up a proposition dear to seventeenth-century rationalism: the reduction, or abolition, of this binarity. Thus, a rational language complements the unknownness of the Southern Land, an effect further doubled, at the individual level, by the hermaphrodism of its inhabitants.

But he sets up this proposition of "splendid isolation" only to knock it down. It is critically dissected as the eutopia turns into dystopia, revealing such perfection to be problematical and, ultimately, impossible. What Foigny "makes known" in this way is a truth (implicit in classical utopias generally) about societies: the paradox whereby each imagines itself to be closed and "perfect" in its isolation but is historically open to a world of commerce, travel, and war. He builds this idea into a utopia and then equally systematically undermines it, confronting it and the traditional concept of society as an ideological (en)closure with a sort of global reality principle. This was the quintessential reality of

137

his time as an age of global discovery began to experience the cultural effects the latter brought with it.

Foigny expresses more succinctly than most writers the relationship between social ideology and territory or geopolitical configuration. He posits a closed, uniform society, one able to be egalitarian and fully rational (as many primitivists believed savage society to be) — an absolute society, "absolved" from the problems real ones encounter in coping with the differences within and without. Such monoculture would be possible only to the extent of its isolation from the world and from history, a scenario traditionally represented by the southern continent and the peoples who might live there. In his Southern Land, too, an internal absence of difference between individuals complements their lack of boundary as a community. As a political paradox it is analogous to hermaphrodism and the absolute individualism it signifies — a refusal of exchange and reciprocity carried to such lengths as to be physically impossible.[11]

The same paradigm informs his treatment of language. As a grammarian and linguist, he was familiar with philosophical problems in this area (his mention that Sadeur had decided to "reduce" his adventures to writing, for example, implies the classical valorization of spoken over written communication). The hero's problematical status among the Australians is reflected in linguistic distortions; thus, the "brothers" greet him as *le clé* ("the key," which, as a feminine noun, should be *la clé*). Such details prefigure the behavioral disorders that prevent his full integration and, eventually, with the revelation that his hermaphrodism is only a biographical accident and not "real" like that of his hosts, oblige him to leave.

The Australian language contrasts with other cratylist schemes in that it invests the sign-thing unity in the spatial configuration of signifiers themselves. The placement of "bits" making up a sign is harnessed to significance in a way somewhat analogous to that in dot-matrix printing or, again, to musical notation.[12] This language forms a microcosmic double of the utopia at large, the image of a configuration of language users in physical space. Here, too, uniformity is the central proposition. Through this multiple play on space Foigny was able to illustrate a rationalized existence at all levels from the individual to the global (or even cosmic).

138

A related aspect is its onomatopoeic basis. Thus, a sweet and tempting apple is *Ipm,* while a bad or unpleasant fruit is *Ird.* But the signifier "apple" has connotations in the Judeo-Christian tradition that cannot be conveyed by such a system. For the Australians fruit has a quite different significance associated with "vegetal" themes in ancient Oriental materialisms (see chap. 3). A similar impasse arises when Sadeur attempts to explain concepts such as "father" or "mother"; these are unknown to the Australians, so he has to invent an expression. After repeating it three times over, he is still not satisfied that Suains has understood.

This revelation of the limits of language doubles the society-as-exclusion theme and underlines the contrast with Vairasse's ideal language. The latter reflects the empiricist, a posteriori bias of Vairasse's utopia—its derivation from real-historical elements, whereas that of Foigny is totally abstracted from history as an a priori entity.[13] His Southland is a more radical play on boundaries, an inquiry into their role in the formation of meaning.[14] As a rhetorical device, it is closer to metaphor (a "carrying-beyond" of meaning, to find outside correspondences) than that of Vairasse, which is more akin to metonymy—a displacement of the real that never fully transgresses it.

The same paradigm (and contrast with his contemporary) is found, furthermore, in Foigny's treatment of religious ideology, to which language is profoundly linked, both as its vehicle and as its structural analogue. Paraphrasing Lacan, one might say that religion is structured like a language. Both are markers of cultural difference and are originally related to territorial configurations. Religion "binds" a community, beyond which lies the material world—one in itself universalizable and unproblematical but which becomes inflected by local difference when it is represented. This might take the form of a cosmic "scheme of things" or simply of the everyday naming of things by language, but in either case there is a passage from the physical to the metaphysical that is freighted with local difference.

Sadeur explains that religion takes two forms in Europe: a deist one claiming ancient authority and a fideist, or revealed one. The former, being more rational, finds favor with Suains. The pair discuss the materialist cosmogonies that go with deist cults, agreeing that it might in theory be possible to trace a physical principle of generation back to its source. But Suains asserts that it is impossible in practice. This view had led the Australians, about forty-five "revolutions" earlier, to suppress all speculation about a supreme being, beyond recognizing it as the "foundation of all their principles."

This exposition of skeptical, rationalist, or libertine trends of the time does not represent—as was long assumed—Foigny's own position.[15] The argument developed through Sadeur progressively rejects that philosophy in ways that its relative weakness in the 1692 edition (used by most critics until the twentieth century) has obscured. As Sadeur tries to elaborate on revealed religion, the common ground begins to give way and, with it, his admiration for the elegant rationality of the Australian system. He asks why they have no cult, no regular ceremonies, to worship their "Great Sovereign." Suains replies with the classic argument of the savage sage; he makes Sadeur admit that Europeans do not agree on the identity of this Being nor on the proper way to worship it and that this causes wars that contradict the very principle of religion.

This was a truth that could not be countered other than by a eutopian departure from reality. Although Suain's logic may be impeccable, his case is irrelevant—applicable only to a closed and timeless world that can never exist. Nor does Sadeur himself formulate an effective response. But one is implied in his further behavior and in the utopia's self-destruction. To see Foigny as a "Enlightenment man" could not be further from the truth; he actually debunks the deist position by revealing its utopian aspect.[16]

A related development concerns the inconsistency, as Suains sees it, of the concept of an afterlife. Sadeur gropes for a psychological explanation; this is not intended in any literal (physical) sense, he implies, but as a metaphor figuring the esteem or otherwise of the community one leaves behind. But Suains is unable to grasp the concept except in terms of a metempsychosis, or transmigration of souls. In subsequent dialogues Sadeur becomes increasingly confident in his rejection of the Australians' philosophy, realizing that the whole point of metaphysical truth is its inconsistency with the universal truth of the material world:

> I concluded that it would only be casting pearls before swine, to attempt such a discussion. . . . The knowledge I have acquired of this nation leads me to believe it all the more incapable of supernatural knowledge in that it considers impossible or "incomprehensible" what it cannot understand. Certainly, it is capable of a great deal; reason guides

it and would make it incomparable if joined to faith. But this same reason that raises it so far above others in natural knowledge drags it down beneath all others in that it does not know its own salvation. You could say that its science serves only to blind it.[17]

Sadeur realizes that the Australians have no concept of soul in the sense of a moral construct or projection of personal identity. An Australian is not a person in that sense but a unit in an antlike society, a mental clone. Nor do the conditions of Australian life favor the formation of such a concept; there is neither difference within (owing to sexual binarity and the kin groups it structures) nor difference without, arising from real contiguity with other cultures. They have no need of structural mechanisms beyond the instinctual level, yet they claim, paradoxically, to represent an absolute humanity.

But this becomes — by its absolution from difference, from the structuring tension of an interior and exterior — an absence of humanity. The Australians, recognizing no other dimension of existence than the physical, deny that which is specifically human. Whether as individuals or as a society, they see themselves as having absolute boundaries and assume similar boundaries between nature and culture or life and death. Hence, their existential anguish; they are unable to think in relational or relativist terms. An absolute boundary amounts to an absence of boundary; any real boundary is the site of an unresolved tension.

The postulate of a "natural society," transcending metaphysics, focused a central issue of Foigny's time — the rise of materialist ideologies, displacing the traditional authority of "revealed" truth. But his Australians so totally divorce ideology from history that they are forbidden (like Arthus's earlier hermaphrodites) to discuss the subject or the related one of cultural origins.[18] Their separation of the two dimensions seems, initially, to correspond to Sadeur's unique consciousness resulting from his checkered career, but that congruence is undermined as the austral world spirals into nationalism and war (effects Europe was experiencing with the rise of political absolutism).

The crux of the encounter occurs in chapter 5 on "The Nature and Customs of the Australians." Discussing the role of sexual binarity and whether it poses an obstacle to dialectical reason,[19] the pair reach an impasse over the definition of humanity. Suains, as mentioned, casts it in purely material terms as a physical quality, whereas Sadeur draws a distinction between the physical and ideological (or animal and human) realms and points to the arbitrary, undetermined nature of the boundary between the two. His ability to straddle the latter, no doubt, arises from having experienced with catastrophic suddenness the gamut of childhood severances. He had, for example, described Braganza troops who ambushed him on his way to Coimbra as "inhuman beasts, worse than flesh-crazed wolves." He experiences a variety of relationships between the human and animal worlds from the torpid passivity of Congolese life to the absurd activism of the Southland. Such qualities are expressed, in terms of the terraqueous physics that frames the story, by his "amphibian" relationship with the sea. Through him the sea theme, with its ramifications in terms of language and writing, is linked to dichotomies of nature and culture or culture and culture and, in general, to a controlling dichotomy between passive and active modes of relation with the Other.

At issue here is less the content or even the function of ideology than its extension — the historical givenness of boundaries and their role in grounding cultural difference. In religion, language, or customs local difference arises from the mutual exteriority of societies; social cultures grow in isolation from, and opposition to, each other (cf. chap. 1, n. 17). Religious ideology is not only about metaphysics and cosmic truth but involves sociological and even geographical factors, a fact Foigny articulates in a more profound way than others before him and links more explicitly to the formal resources of the classical utopia. Hence, too, this convergence (building on predecessors such as Lucian, Hall, and Arthus) of the austral and hermaphrodite metaphors — an antipodean physics of the body and of the world and its appearance in an era on the threshold of total geographical knowledge.

A dialectical tension is set up during Sadeur's visit that extends across various dimensions from the personal to the cultural and territorial. It is in the end Sadeur, not the Australians, who reveals himself a master of it and of the media in which it is played out. His metaphorical hermaphrodism corresponds to his superior logical faculties or, at least, to the broader experience these require. He is able to encompass two worlds in his dialogue with Suains and to reject the latter's unworldly wisdom. He reveals not so much its inconsistencies as the inevitability of rational inconsistency itself — what the Australians claim to have transcended in their cocoon world.[20]

Their undoing ultimately occurs, however, in a dimension that transcends terrestrial boundaries. The physicality they repress returns with a vengence in the air in the form of the Urgs.[21] These are the Australians' most feared enemies because they come and go in a medium from which the latter are totally debarred. Like death itself, they represent a duality no dialectician can encompass. Prefigured by the Congo's giant peacocks or eagles, they become prominent with Sadeur's entry into the Southern Land. But with his exit from it on one and the full revelation of the Australians' relationship with them, it becomes clear that the ground-air divide is an ultimate boundary (a point illustrated, too, by real modern developments in transport and warfare).

Thus, the air takes over from the sea as the medium of communication and dissolution around which the plot is woven; it represents forces the Australians are unable to master. Both in believing themselves totally rational and in imagining their country to be absolutely (un)bounded, they carried to the limit a primitive social dynamics based on exclusivity and ascetic constraint—on the extraction of ideological effects from physical givens. But raw physicality reclaims them in the end.

Again, mastery of the air corresponds to the power of writing in the realm of discourse. The heightened materiality of writing relative to the primitive word enables it to transcend the bounds of time and space and, thereby, to override and dissolve the local nature of social relationship. Such powers were also (in the form of navigational, cartographical, and ethnographic practices) the ones that, both in the story and in reality, were the undoing of austral isolation, bringing the "sea monsters" from nothern lands.

Sadeur negotiates with such powers, opting for a reality of compromise. He knew, before experiencing the Australian ethos and its deflowering—indeed, from birth—the tension of warring forces that man inhabits. He accepts the claims of the physical (especially when confronted with a Fundian girl after thirty-five years of abstinence) and returns to a world torn by conflicts: over woman's share in a "man's world," over land and the social culture it grounds, over claims to know the truth. A world that recognizes, finally, the place of death—the ultimate boundary—in life. It can be seen how acutely Foigny perceived modern trends toward physicalism and absolutism yet how skeptical he was of them from within the classical worldview that was still his.

Sadeur's arrival in the Southland was, as noted, a symbolic rebirth, one for which he had been psychologically conditioned by his early ex-periences. Cast out of an amniotic paradise, torn from the maternal bosom, set adrift in the world with neither family nor community, he straddles two dimensions of consciousness (the somatic and symbolic) from the beginning and throughout his life, rather than progressing from one to the other by a gradual repression of "original" experience. His is a world of metaphor, a metaphorical womb, the oceans its am-niotic fluid and the Southern Land the "great unknown" to which the primal passage leads. In this sense he is an avatar of the Odysseus fig-ure, an archetypal Old World man on a voyage into a modern "world of body."

Hence, his being "conceived in America and born on the ocean, a too-telling presage of what I would one day become." What he be-comes is a master of media, initially in the physical realm and, ulti-mately, in that of discourse. His hermaphrodite and amphibian qualities make him a prophet of the transport culture arising from Europe's New World expansion. His experience becomes a story of some significance, and he ends up a writer, his word a testament. In this way he achieves what the Australians fruitlessly aspired to — transcendance of one's physi-cal existence. Indeed, as a result of a further rebirth during his austral experience — into philosophical wisdom — he becomes more than a trav-eler, ambassador, or writer. He becomes a sort of messiah, bearing a response to humanity's radically changing existential reality in a global-ized world that liquidates all boundaries and ideologies — washing out the local color of signification and reducing it to the materiality of the signifier. He shows a way of meeting that destiny by negotiating with it as he does by taming an Urg.

CHAPTER TEN

The *Mighty Kingdom of Krinke Kesmes* (1708)

The hypothesis of a real castaway story from the Southland, while reaching back to the *Isle of Pines,* focuses on a Dutch work published four decades later by Hendrik Smeeks.[1] Although it has been discussed mainly as a precursor of *Robinson Crusoe,*[2] it forms an essential link in the "family"[3] of works appearing in 1668 and proliferating throughout the century of Enlightenment. It has two very distinct stylistic and narrative layers: the main story is a fully imaginary utopian novel (without much literary merit), whereas an inner story is more realistic and suggests direct or indirect experience of the events examined in chapter 7. Such disjuncture was typical of the austral works and crucial to the way they linked the hermeneutics of discovery to problems of narrative truth.

The outer story is that of Juan de Posos, an enterprising Dutchman who assumes a Spanish identity and in 1702 sails from Panama to the Philippines to make his fortune. His ship is driven by a storm onto the coast of the southern continent, and when he leads a scouting party inland, they are captured by warriors of an advanced civilization, the Kingdom of Krinke Kesmes.[4] At the city of Taloujaël, he learns about this society from its *Garbon,* or prime minister. It has restrictions on commerce, travel, and so forth, and a juridical code condensed into five laws. Emphasis is laid on two areas of policy, reflecting Dutch concerns of the day: commerce and religious sectarianism. Finally, de Posos returns to Europe a wealthy man, having been allowed to trade there briefly.

The first three chapters recount his early military career and friendship with a doctor known as "the Master," his switch to a merchant career and trips to America between 1679 and 1698, and adoption of the name of Juan de Posos (a living man). His meetings with the Master included one in 1696 in Amsterdam when he acquired information bearing on travel to the Southland; this occupies long digressions on scurvy or improvements to the Texel channel.[5] The Southland events occupy chapters 4 and 5: his hospitable reception in the kingdom, conversations with the Garbon about its history, its religious troubles, its offshore islands of Nemnan and Vonvure (anagrams of *Mannen,* men, and *Vrouwen,* women), and policies on religion and education. In chapter 6 de Posos meets a former Dutch castaway, the El-ho (Freeman), who gives him a written account of his adventures and acts as his guide in Taloujaël. Then the Garbon shows de Posos a fantastic stepped pyramid that is the focus of their laws and customs, and there is much satirical discussion of moral-philosophical issues. In chapter 8 de Posos returns to Spain via Panama and sends the Master his journal containing all this new information about the Southland.

Various elements, apart from the Southland theme itself, here recall the better-known *History of the Sevarites* and other "family" works. The Kesmian religion, for example, is a native sun cult, modified as a result of previous cultural contact. A ship had arrived around A.D. 1030, bringing Arab pilgrims, Christian slaves, Indians, and Jews. The resulting sectarian violence caused the king to banish all sects (except the Dutch Reformed one) and to forbid any further discussion of theological issues. Parallels with the founding of the Sevarite civilization are obvious.

Again, a Huguenot refugee in Holland, Simon Tyssot de Patot, would soon after imagine a southern-continent society formerly influenced by a Portuguese monk and a Christian missionary shipwrecked there. Tyssot seems to have drawn from Vairasse and Smeeks and, living at Deventer, near Smeeks's town of Zwolle, may even have known the latter and modeled his fictional doctors on him.[6] Other such figures mentioned earlier were Dr. Van der Haert, who authenticates the *Sevarites* story, or the real Wouter Schouten.

Further features common to the works of Smeeks and the others are sexual regulation[7] (thus, the islands mentioned are segregated places of education), an artificial language, and guiding principles of rationalism and religious skepticism—views for which Smeeks suffered some persecution. Here again, ironical, or even dystopian, overtones suggest that his aim was more satirical than idealist in a projective sense (de Posos, for example, portrays Europe as a model of religious toleration).

On thematic and rhetorical grounds, then, *Krinke Kesmes* can be related not only to the later Robinsonade but to the earlier cycle of austral novels. Despite its late appearance within the latter, it seems to be based on elements arising close to, or even at, a common source for the whole development—the seventeenth century Dutch disasters on the Australian coast. This hypothesis focuses on the inner story (chapter 6), that of a Dutchman who, castaway as a cabin boy during those events, had been integrated into the kingdom and is encountered there by de Posos. Internal and external evidence suggests that this may have been based on a real marooning. Such speculation is not new, but it is placed in a new and more compelling light by closer analysis, both thematic and chronological, of the austral works taken as a set. This suggests their common origin in a story which, although notorious, was suppressed.

The El-ho relates his arrival with an expedition searching for survivors from the *Vergulde Draeck:* "I was a boy of twelve and could read and write when I arrived at Batavia as a cabin boy in the Company's service in the year 1655. When I had been there three months I was ordered one day to present myself the following morning with my sea chest aboard the ship *Wakende Boey,* which was sailing for the Southland to rescue the castaways from the ship *Goude Draak,* which had been lost there, and bring them to Batavia" (161).

At the Southland he volunteered for a landing party, not out of zeal to find the survivors but to seek "refreshments" (scurvy and its prevention being, as noted, a major concern of Smeeks). He became separated from his mates, and, after some days, the ship sailed, leaving his sea chest buried on the shore marked by a note fixed to a stake. He set up camp and organized his solitary life with the benefit of tools, other goods, and a dog from a wrecked ship. These are elements of the Robinson tradition,[8] another of which is that the protagonists were humble, unheroic people.[9] Again, the El-ho's religious experience during his marooning is a theme prominent in *Robinson Crusoe* and in Foigny's *Southern Land, Known.* Another common theme (with an ancient tradition behind it) is that of giant birds: the El-ho shoots and eats such a bird, in a passage that Defoe later reproduces almost verbatim.[10] Defoe's relationship with Smeeks has been a contentious issue, however.

In any case the debate over it has tended to overlook the debt of both authors to a common source and, even more importantly, the fact-fiction problem associated with that source. Clues to the latter lie in the *Isle of Pines,*[11] which, as noted earlier, features a similar narrative disjuncture to *Krinke Kesmes.* Its inner story, told to a Dutchman visiting the Southland, is that of George Pines, who as a youth had been shipwrecked there. He, as were the El-ho (and Sadeur), had been the captain's servant. Thus, parallels between the works of Defoe and Smeeks extend to that of Neville and suggest that it was the first of the austral series—the first published work deriving from a source to which the El-ho's story is, nevertheless, closer. The latter's appearance after a delay of forty years was probably the result of VOC secrecy and embarrassment over the events in Australia. This would explain the extraordinary but short-lived interest in the *Isle of Pines,* which did much to establish marooning as a literary theme.

Further suggestive of such links are the El-ho's words when he was surrounded by local inhabitants: "Men, what country is this? and what people are you?" (187). The Dutch visitors to the Isle of Pines had similarly "asked them in our *Dutch* tongue *Wat Eylant is dit?* to which they returned this Answer in English, *That they knew not what we said.*"[12] The El-ho is adopted by these Kaskes, or Beachdwellers, and married to a young girl. But they are then attacked and massacred by the more powerful civilization of Krinke Kesmes, whom the El-ho, having been spared, joins. These are the multiple societies or layers of civilization mentioned: a "lower," ethnologically plausible one and a "higher" one that is frankly imaginary. Critics, however divergent their views on other points, have agreed that the El-ho's story is quite distinct from the rest of *Krinke Kesmes,* more lively and realistic as if based on real experience.[13]

Does, then, Smeeks's reference to the *Vergulde Draeck* searches merely reflect his readiness (like that of Defoe) to exploit the abundant adventure stories of the period? Were Defoe and later writers indebted to Smeeks or to earlier writers such as Neville? Did they all draw, directly or indirectly, on a true story?[14] And why was the realist basis of several otherwise English stories a Dutch one? These questions call for closer scrutiny of the strident claims such works made to be telling a true story.

As discussed, several rescue missions followed the loss of the *Vergulde Draeck,* but the El-ho seems to confuse them. The sudden departure he mentions was not that of the *Waeckende Boey* (an expedition launched in 1658 and planned months in advance) but that of the *Witte Valck,* which left to join the *Goede Hoop,* already at sea, on June 8, 1656, the day after the arrival at Batavia of survivors in the *Vergulde Draeck's* boat. The *Goede Hoop* lost three hands on shore in the search area plus a boat with eight men sent to look for them. One of these eleven could have been a boy who joined the *Goede Hoop* (having left Batavia in the *Witte Valck*) when the two ships met up; and who could, furthermore (as accounts of the expedition suggest), have been adopted by local inhabitants.

Apart from a chronological detail (more than three months elapsed from the end of 1655 to the *Witte Valck*'s departure from Batavia), the El-ho's story seems to fit the circumstances of the earlier expedition although referring to the better-known *Waeckende Boey* one. It suggests the experiences of someone marooned then (or, perhaps, during the latter expedition eighteen months later), who survived and returned to tell the tale. As was outlined earlier, the official records of these events leave the fate of those lost in Australia unknown. Other such strandings were known or, at least, possible,[15] and it will be recalled, too, that the ship in the *Hairy Giants* story, the *Flying Falcon,* is similar in name to the *Witte Valck.* Armed and assertive Dutch landing parties in the north of Australia had experienced violence, but such a response may not necessarily have been elicited by the presence of a few starving, unarmed men (much less a boy) on the barren west coast. Again, the effect of a two-tiered cultural encounter may reflect regular visits by Indonesians to Australia in the seventeenth century to gather trepang (*bêche-de-mer,* or sea cucumber) for the Chinese market,[16] this being, for example, a means by which castaways could have returned to civilization.

Such a story would have been classified information at the time. Smeeks could have had only oral sources for it unless he had access to the official reports and from them concocted an imaginary sequel. But this seems improbable; he more likely created a utopia out of a first-hand story, that of a youth marooned during the *Vergulde Draeck* searches and adopted by Aborigines, who later—possibly through contact with Indonesian trepangers—returned to Batavia. Smeeks's own copy of the book (in the Royal Library, The Hague, and dubbed in Buijnsters 1976 the "Handex" or hand-annotated copy) does indicate censorship on the part of the publisher, ten Hoorn, who rewrote his preface. "This preface," wrote Smeeks, "has my name printed under it, but I neither composed it, nor ever saw it before it was printed. . . . my Notice to the Reader, which I sent to Ten Hoorn to have printed for this little book, with permission to alter the style, is as follows." His own three-page address "To the Reader" is pasted in, rebutting ten Hoorn's accusation that his introduction was "the work of a child" and asserting that he had "never claimed to be a wise man."

Smeeks refers in this preface to Schouten, the VOC doctor discussed earlier: "Wouter Schouten of Haarlem states in his *Voyage to the East Indies* that while he was at Batavia the ship *Wakende Boeij* was sent from there to the Southland to get the shipwrecked crew of the *Gouden Draak* and bring them to Batavia, but found no one. . . . This demonstrable truth is no small reason for our believing the rest of the El-ho's remarkable story, and strongly attests to its veracity."[17]

On the face of it this might seem an ironical claim in the tradition of Foigny, Vairasse, Neville, or Lucian—a thinly veiled boast that he is a plagiarist and a liar. One might conclude that he had simply based his El-ho story on Schouten's account of the voyage of Abraham Leeman to Batavia in the *Waeckende Boey*'s boat. Whether or not he knew that this feat doubled that of the *Vergulde Draeck*'s second officer two years earlier, he certainly knew the similar story of Bontekoe.[18] Thus, any similarity to real events might seem to be mere coincidence, a clever manipulation of literary sources.

But Smeeks could equally well be protesting the truth of a story he knew more directly and citing Schouten as corroborating evidence. This might explain ten Hoorn's expunging of the reference to Schouten. It is further suggested when, in the same passage, Smeeks mentions that he had taken his story directly to a powerful figure who was himself interested in travel literature and in Australian exploration: "I personally delivered the propositions concerning discoveries in the interior of the Southland into the hands of Lord Burgomaster N. Witsen."[19] Moreover, the El-ho's story bears little relation to the Leeman saga; and Schouten's account of the latter is itself a garbled version when compared to Leeman's own. Schouten was clearly not the primary source for the story. As mentioned in chapter 8, too, Vairasse's work referring to the *Vergulde Draeck* events appeared in 1675, one year before that of Schouten. He was in Holland in 1672 and probably obtained then his information on the episode.[20] Both authors seem to have learned of the story in question independently of Schouten.

Such stories would have circulated in the taverns and drawing-rooms of Europe; the *Vergulde Draeck*, for example, had gone down with a rich cargo of bullion, and the *Batavia* disaster had given rise to an orgy of sex and violence. Such rumors, and the censorship that fed them, are attested from various quarters. In France, for example, Thévenot noted in his 1663 voyage collection that Governor-General Van Diemen had brought back treasure from New Holland, which was only later found to have been recovered from a ship wrecked there.[21]

No less suggestive is a chronological comparison. The eleven or twelve years that elapsed between the *Vergulde Draeck* maroonings and the appearance of *The Isle of Pines* in 1668 correspond to the period between Robinson's marooning and his finding of Friday's footprint, a development that has been linked, in turn, to the arrival in 1667 of the Dutch ship in *The Isle of Pines* (see n. 12). It might be compared with the El-ho's double return to human society: first, among the Kaskes and, second, in Krinke Kesmes. Perhaps, these are all echoes of the return, after eleven or twelve years, of a sailor marooned in 1656, bearing a story too fantastic (or from the VOC's point of view, too full of information about Australia and the events there)[22] to be published—a story, however, with irresistible notoriety and picaresque appeal. Such rumors would also, as mentioned, explain the sudden but short-lived popularity of Neville's work.[23]

Again, Vairasse's Captain Siden sails for Batavia on April 12, 1655, aboard the *Golden Dragon,* and his return about sixteen years later coincides with the author's visit to Holland when he probably learned of the Australian events. He is believed to have emigrated from France around 1665 so was probably in London, advancing in his diplomatic career and well placed to hear any such rumors, at the time of the postulated return of a castaway from the Southland.

Foigny emigrated to Switzerland in 1666 and in those years of ferment would, no doubt, also have been impressed by such a story. His hero, Sadeur, is born in 1603, reaches the Southland as a young man and spends thirty-five years there. Allowing for the adventures of his voyages there and back, this brings his return, too, toward the 1660s. Tyssot de Patot was born in 1655 and emigrated with his family to Holland in 1664. In 1667 he would have been in a place and of an age to be impressed by rumors of a Southland marooning. His hero Jacques Massé sets out in 1643, is in the Southland from 1644 to 1663, and returns to Europe after numerous adventures, which would again bring the date toward 1667. A similar chronology (1646–1671) is found in *The Hairy Giants*. Robinson Crusoe departs in 1659, and Baron Holberg's Nicolas

Klim, in *Nicolai Klimii Iter Subterraneum* (Copenhagen, 1741), in 1655. Many such works seem to refer to events of the mid-1650s and/or late-1660s, which were no longer known in detail, but the traces of which frame their narratives.

It is chronologically possible, moreover, that *Krinke Kesmes* was in one way or another autobiographical—that Smeeks was either the Master (and perhaps, too, Vairasse's Dr. Van der Haert), or even the El-ho himself—a view espoused by Hoogewerff in 1930. Aged twelve in 1655, the El-ho would have been seventy-eight in 1721, when Smeeks died at an old age. But so little is known about the latter's life that this must remain conjecture. Even his identity was, until recent research by Buijnsters, a matter of confusion;[24] he was earlier believed to be a doctor named Hendrik Smeeckes or Smekes of Oldenzeel, who in 1666 appears (aged twenty-seven) in the Amsterdam archives, but who died in 1676. This "wrong Smeeks" may have joined the VOC as a ship's doctor despite having practiced in Amsterdam (a career path not uncommon at the time). Nor was a cousin of his, a Catholic doctor living in Amsterdam, the author.

That identification fitted in with textual indications that de Posos' mentor, the Master, was a former ship's doctor living in Overijssel. He had served in a ship, the *Wapen van Essen,* that was involved in the 1672–1674 conflict with England (that in which Vairasse's Siden died). In 1930 Hoogewerff[25] further confused the issue by identifying the author with that of a popular work on piracy, *De Americaensche zeerovers,* published in 1678 by Jan ten Hoorn (Nicolaas's father). Hoogewerff saw the name of its author, O. E. Exquemelin, as an anagram of Enrique Smeex. Coincidences of style, publisher, and apparent authorship by a ship's doctor seemed to suggest that Smeeks had penned both works and had spent years among pirates. Vrijman (1932) proved that Exquemelin (from Honfleur in France) was not Hendrik Smeeckes of Oldenzeel, but the latter was not, as noted, the author of *Krinke Kesmes.* Another wrong identification, with a Henrik Smeink of Zwolle, was made by de Vries in 1958.[26]

The true Hendrik Smeeks was married in the Reformed Church of Zwolle in 1680. The couple had five children, two of whom died early, and in 1682 moved into a "dilapidated house" in the town. In 1703 they made their wills, ostensibly because of his wife's ill health (although she survived him by many years). Little else is known about him, and the register of burials in Zwolle is the only document apart from *Krinke Kesmes* identifying him as a doctor; perhaps, like the Master, he had been a ship's doctor. But obscurity turned to notoriety with the appearance of his book. Although well reviewed, it caused him trouble — first, with his editor. The accusation of "childishness" may have had some grounds, thinks Buijnsters, but the book exhibits "a certain laconic tone . . . which definitely cannot be called childish." Again, although ten Hoorn had a formal right to change the manuscript, Smeeks was probably morally justified in complaining of his interference.[27]

Further difficulties arose with the Calvinist churchmen of Zwolle who, sensitized to anything that smacked of Spinozism, condemned the book for "the stupid godlessness that emanates from it." In his defense Smeeks pointed out (like Foigny before him and Tyssot de Patot after him) that the offending opinions were not his own but those of the Southlanders; that if they "smacked of god-forsakenness and Spinozism" he, for his part, had "never read Spinoza or known him or his teachings, but had only read the arguments of Bontekoe and Overkamp against Descartes."[28] This statement was calculated to make a good impression because Descartes posed less of a threat to the Reformed faith, but even so Smeeks was excommunicated and not absolved until 1717. He (like Patot), however, could well have been acquainted with Spinoza.

Further clues to the origin and intentions of the story may lie in the relationship between the printed and Handex prefaces; in that between Smeeks and his possible alter egos, the Master and the El-ho; in the function of digressions within the narrative; and in the history of *Krinke Kesmes* criticism.

The printed preface appeals to Dutch chauvinism and commercialism. It emphasizes a continuing Spanish threat (which de Posos personifies with his dual identity) but is confident of their ability to overcome it. This realist tone is underlined by the reference to the *Vergulde Draeck* searches and by a warning not to expect a "high-flown style"; the writer was, as a sailor, not concerned with literary niceties but only with the matter itself. Smeeks's own preface differs from it (apart from referring to Schouten, as noted) in adopting a personal, almost provocative tone: "Reader, you cannot disparage this little book, because I do not care how it is received. It is all the same to me whether you believe this journey or not." Despite this pretended indifference, however, he insists on the "demonstrable truth" of the story and asserts that "I myself took part in the first journey of de Posos; the rest is his account. He has never deceived me, and why should he lie?"

The identity of de Posos is a central problem here. He had raised himself from lowly beginnings to success as a merchant (an element significant in realist terms, cf. n. 9). But he is a somewhat aloof figure, both in his dealings with the Garbon and, more notably still, with his compatriot the El-ho. His shipmates' life in the Southland does not interest him, and he remains celibate (parallels with Vairasse's Siden are again evident here). Considerable efforts are made to authenticate him in the early chapters, reaching back to the Anglo-Dutch trade wars. This effect is doubled by the Master's projective interest in the Southland and by Smeeks's claim to have taken his ideas directly to Nicolaas Witsen. The Master, an avid collector of maps and travel accounts, interests de Posos in the Southland, transferring his aspirations onto the younger man. He even presumes to correct mistakes in Dampier's or de Vlamingh's reports about Australia.[29]

De Posos's narrative, too, is notable for its patchwork effect as in the long digressions mentioned — a "baroque extravagance," notes Buijnsters (27), "that seems to mock every concept of narrative structure." He relays the Master's theories about scurvy or the Texel channel; the El-Ho's story; and the moralist "proverbs" he learns in Krinke Kesmes. These elements are variously functional: the prevention of scurvy would be of practical value in reaching the Southland, whereas the Texel channel seems a rather extraneous theme. But the El-ho's story is strikingly anomalous and inserted perfunctorily, and after about forty pages, the narrative voice suddenly reverts in the middle of a paragraph to that of de Posos. Information learned from the Garbon or other sources is juxtaposed with de Posos's own life story.

Two modes of narrative, documentary and "testamentary" (that of an absent witness), thus, hang loosely or even clumsily together in the work. This may, it is true, reflect the double aim of writing an adventure story and setting out philosophical, religious, and scientific views — a project typical of the genre. Again, the El-ho interlude could be seen as providing a dual perspective on Krinke Kesmes as a utopia. But Smeeks' more radical, textual disjuncture has led some — notably Hubbard 1921 and Hoogewerff 1930 — to assume a real biographical basis for the story, the latter speculating further, as noted, that the young Smeeks himself may have been the protagonist.

Nor can this idea be excluded, particularly in view of the little that is now known about Smeeks. He may not necessarily have gained his knowledge of seafaring matters as a ship's doctor, and because nothing is known of his earlier life, there is no reason why he could not have become a doctor after returning from a youthful adventure of the kind described. Would not marooning and prolonged self-sufficiency predispose a person to medical interests and skills?

Critics have reacted variously to this enigma. In the nineteenth century Hettner (1961) thought the 1721 German translation, *Der Holländische Robinson,* was based on a Dutch translation of *Robinson Crusoe,* but he believed that it derived from a real experience. Early bibliographers drew a somewhat confused distinction between the original and Handex prefaces and repeated the view that a true story had been used. Staverman in 1907 solved anagrams such as Kesmes or Nemnan and judged the El-ho story "slovenly and dry, like . . . a chronicle."[30] He compared it unfavorably to *Robinson Crusoe* but again remarked on its realism. Hoogewerff, too, thought in 1909 that the author had "fallen under the spell of his material . . . , for here his style becomes markedly more lively than elsewhere in the book," but, believing that Smeeks had made up the story, he focused on the work's ideological aspects.[31]

Hoogewerff and Staverman also speculated on literary sources for the work, such as the 1695 *Vermakelijke Avonturier* (Entertaining adventurer) by Nicolaas Heinsius, another doctor; the works of Neville and Vairasse; or Ibn Tophail's *Hagy ben Yaqudan,* a medieval Arabian "child of nature" story revived in the seventeenth century (cf. also n. 14). A source Smeeks acknowledges is *The Turkish Spy,* or *L'Esploratore turco* (Paris, 1684) by G.-P. Marana, an Italian living in France. This was published by Nicolaas ten Hoorn in Dutch translation two years after *Krinke Kesmes.*[32] Another acknowledged source is the Spaniard Baltasar Gracian's *Arte de prudencia* (Art of wisdom) of 1647, translated into Dutch in 1696.

In 1910 Samuel L'Honoré Naber, a maritime historian, found the work authentic enough in that respect to justify Smeeks's claim in his Handex preface, "This is the work of a seaman" (cf. n. 13). At the time this tended to reinforce the view that he had been a ship's doctor and to aggravate the related confusions of identity. Naber cast about for a key

155

to the enigma and speculated about an unnamed assistant surgeon on the *Wapen van Essen,* the ship referred to earlier.[33] He is said to have been born in Overijssel and settled in Zwolle as a physician and to have written in such a strong Overijssel dialect that his work had to be corrected by an editor.

As to possible sources for the El-ho, Naber refers to the two men marooned following the *Batavia* mutiny; to the 1701 *Nijptang* journal from de Vlamingh's expedition (the one bound with a Dutch translation of the *History of the Sevarites,* see chap. 7); to work on the Australian shipwrecks by historians such as Heeres (1899); and to Leeman's mention of losing a young sailor on the coast of Java. The latter would have had to be an oral source because, as noted earlier, the only published source at the time was Schouten, who does not mention that youth. Another theory, which Naber discussed with Hubbard did not publish, associated the El-ho with a Dutch boy named Sjouke Gabbes, who may have been left behind on the coast of Western Australia during de Vlamingh's expedition of 1696–1697. Hubbard seized on this idea, even consecrating it in the title of his book although it does not fit the facts (any more than did the name Henrich Texel given to the character in the 1721 German translation).[34] The cabin boy would by this time have been about fifty-four years old.

As did most critics, Secord[35] condemned the "Sjouke Gabbes" hypothesis, but he introduced another error by asserting that Krinke Kesmes was simply "an imaginary island in the south seas. . . . Smeeks's hero experienced his island solitude neither in 1697 nor in Australia."[36] This contradicts both explicit and implicit information in the text and the historical evidence that corroborates it. De Posos lands on a Pacific coast of the Southland (Australia), and the El-ho notes that the sun rose at sea—that he, too, was on its east coast. The *Vergulde Draeck* events, however, took place on its east coast. This contradiction may have been accidental or deliberate; perhaps the continent is supposed to have been traversed in the passage from the Kaskes to Krinke Kesmes.

Hoogewerff in 1930 responded to a theological analysis by reiterating that the main point of interest is the realism of the El-ho's story. He now considered the El-ho to be Smeeks himself, as noted, a view that Buijnsters rejects, charging that Hoogewerff had "become careless and falled victim to his own hypotheses."[37] The inference was one that has been groped for since Naber's time, at least, but cannot be proven. The subject then lapsed, yet, as Buijnsters cautions (57), "The history of *Krinke Kesmes* research resembles a comedy of errors, no less bizarre than that of the book itself or of the man at whose feet all these mistakes can be laid. Under such circumstances, no one should delude himself into thinking that the last word has been said about the Mighty Kingdom."

With this caution in mind, one can link the El-ho story, on the one hand, to a set of Southland novels as precursors of *Robinson Crusoe* and, on the other hand, to evidence that it had a factual basis. There are archival indications that a marooning may have taken place but was kept secret and literary evidence, too, that a returned castaway may have been prevented from publishing his story. Such evidence appears in Smeeks's Handex preface and, perhaps most tellingly, in the exorbitant level of public interest in Neville's work. It was, indeed, in England that the idea first became a literary theme, whereas Smeeks's version, the closest among the austral family to the original events, appeared only later— presumably, once VOC sensitivity had subsided. Although it cannot be proved that things happened this way (let alone that Smeeks was personally involved), such a hypothesis might account for numerous strange coincidences and for the extreme realism of the El-ho's narrative. It would also help to explain the sudden popularity of the austral theme from 1668. Nor would this be the first time that such a work had had to be relocated on one side or the other of the fact-fiction divide.[38]

The formative period of the Enlightenment novel of travel and utopian discovery culminates in the *Kingdom of Krinke Kesmes,* which heralds, in turn, the rise of the Robinsonade—an avatar emphasizing individual experience rather than the communal dimension in episodes of shipwreck, marooning, and culture contact. Defoe's story seems quite derivative, as would be that of Tyssot de Patot and other fallout from the original theme. The latter, whether because the events in question were forgotten or because a sort of thematic sclerosis set in, became reduced to a literary convention. But in its heyday—when VOC secrecy about events in Australia contrasted strongly with public demand for information—it embodied a historiographical problem of great significance for Enlightenment thought.

CHAPTER ELEVEN

Austral Fiction and the Rise of Realism

Documentary and Testamentary Truth

Literature based on the austral theme between 1668 and 1708 reflected not only advances in geographical knowledge but also the rise of a new kind of fiction—a quasi-documentary one that prefigured Enlightenment styles of thought more generally. Critics agree that the latter were first embodied in the novel and, by the late-eighteenth century, theorized by reference to it. Early symptoms of this process appear by 1668 in the devices used to authenticate imaginary voyages, utopias, and fictional biographies. Their relevance to wider intellectual developments has been recognized[1] but little theorized, beyond allusions to the "crisis of consciousness"[2] that set in later. But as discussed in the foregoing chapters, they can be traced to the doubt and confusion surrounding a real such adventure that seems to have occurred. That hypothesis is now set in the context of literary and aesthetic developments during the century of Enlightenment, beginning around 1668 and substantially completed one hundred years later.

Theories about the relationship between prose realism and the ideology and aesthetics of Enlightenment have tended to assume, in the absence of specific explanations, that such developments arose from a dynamics internal to the cultures concerned (mainly those of England and France, the leading powers of the day). This assumption has never been adequately demonstrated, and the evidence points rather to historical factors, in relation to which realism was more a by-product than a cause. This is an issue distinct from the more allegorical significance of exotist writing in earlier times; here, the topic comes to bear directly on problems of language and truth.

To regard the crisis of values setting in around 1680 as the cause of the literary phenomena in question is anachronistic. A literary "crisis" clearly preceded the more general one and reflected historical events in ways that can explain the sudden changes of style and rhetorical posture it brought. The broadly empiricist trend of the age was the background to a topical demand for information about New World events, one that, frustrated by secrecy or duplicity or simply by the "tyranny of distance" (Blainey), focused a wider problem of narrative truth and generated new kinds of response to it.

Pivotal to the latter was a calculated mingling of fact with fiction. It appears in that hallmark of the austral novel, the elaborate authenticating preface in which an "editor" presents the "testament" of a dead or absent author. Such devices have usually been discussed in terms of the satirical or didactic aims of the authors, and it is true that they provided a convenient means of disowning one's work, if necessary, in times of political censorship. In origin they have been thought of, if at all, as a novelistic tradition. It is necessary to review that tradition, its realist aspect, and its appropriation to political agendas in the seventeenth century, to be able to assess the impact on it of the discovery of the Southland or of the hypothetical story of marooning.

Modern realism is based on a twin doctrine, individualist and universalist, that truth is independent of cultural determination but verifiable by reference to empirical data—ultimately, to the material world. This view emerged from a split between the seventeenth-century cults of Nature and Reason. It grounded a new "idea of nature" and a literature characterized by irony and satire, a new earthiness.[3] It also brought to a head epistemological changes, part of a "vast transformation of Western civilisation since the Renaissance," notes Watt, who sees truth in its modern form as "a wholly individual matter, logically independent of the tradition of past thought, and indeed as more likely to be arrived at by a departure from it." This is a problem that "the novel raises more sharply than any other literary form [as] a set of narrative procedures . . . so commonly found together in the novel, and so rarely in other literary genres, that they may be regarded as typical of the form itself."[4] Watt locates these innovations in eighteenth-century English novels, beginning with *Robinson Crusoe*. He discusses (27–30) their use of individuating and authenticating elements (persons, events, places, language), and the wider context of Lockean empiricism, or of the economic individualism later theorized by Adam Smith.

Robinson Crusoe is generally thought to epitomize that ethos and the rise of the bourgeois or Puritan "common hero" — to be, in short, a landmark in Early Enlightenment literature and the first work of modern realism. But this view has been questioned along with a related one that French fiction was largely untouched by realist influences until Romantic times. It seems that such developments were part of a response, on both sides of the English Channel, to historical events and the changing worldview they brought. They resulted less from any internal evolution than from a coalescence of local cultures resulting from radical global movement. The literary trends manifest in *Robinson Crusoe,* but arising over the preceding half-century, were symptoms of (and factors in) that process.

As Tieje points out, Defoe and Swift have been credited with inventing a style earlier typified by Vairasse: a "forcing of credence" that departed from earlier novelistic aims (to entertain, edify, inform, depict life, or arouse emotion), "a striving towards a crude form of realism." From its roots in antiquity it was linked to travel, and "from 1579 to 1728 the *voyage imaginaire* is seldom content unless it cites the work of travellers whose accounts were admitted to be authentic." It waned between 1640 and 1670 and after 1728 — periods when the novel was attacked for a promiscuity that, it was feared, would dilute both the allegorical truth of fiction and the documentary truth of fact. But no works, as late as *Simplicissimus* (1669), featured the "startling embroideries" that became the norm around 1670.[5]

Mylne calls such devices "techniques of illusion" and traces them to earlier French developments in poetry and drama as well as in prose.[6] She shows (23f.) that older styles of novel aiming to morally "Improve" (which tended to make them a substitute for Scripture, a point also made by Willey) were eclipsed during the 1660s in France by the more popular nouvelle. It took over older devices, such as the interpolated (inner) story, but was clearly distinct and had become dominant by 1670. In England Aphra Behn led a similar trend, and the term *novel* entered common usage.

These changes occurred at a time when news (*nouvelles*) was spreading of the events in Australia. Thévenot's voyage collection, for example, containing the first accounts of them published in France, appeared in 1663 and in a definitive edition in 1672. The literary nouvelle (or novella), although of earlier vintage, clearly took on new significance in this context, its popularity coinciding, notably, with that of the imaginary voyage. Such developments generally had a New World backdrop (as can be seen, too, in the English case; thus, Aphra Behn was much influenced by her early life in Surinam), but they showed a particular interest in the Great Southland.

Tieje, however, implies in the passages mentioned that they were only an outgrowth of a seventeenth-century "struggle of the imagination against the desire for credence," one which "could not have raged without greatly affecting the entire content and structure of early fiction." Mylne, too, adopts a purely literary approach, associating the new trend with a growing separation between imaginative and literal modes of belief on the part of readers.[7] The former was labile and tended to emphasize the readerly construction of a story; whereas the latter tended to be fixed by a framework of things and events and to make the reader's response a relatively passive one.

Mylne also stresses the problem of veracity, identifying two means of inducing belief that contrasted with earlier, more naïve uses of historical material: a direct assertion that a story is true or a realism so plausible that readers will acquiesce in the untruth. Such devices were also exploited by other realist forms from around 1670: the epistolary novel and the fictional biography, or *faux mémoires,* a style later (1678–1711) dominated by Courtilz de Sandras.[8] Common to them all was the stress laid on first-person narration, the role of an eye witness: "The thoughts and feelings of the narrator tend to take on a new importance, and the way is being prepared for the subjective tone of much Romantic literature. . . . Novelists, instead of pretending to provide history itself, have turned to writing what might be considered as the raw material of history, the private source-books rather than the official compilations."[9]

They may have done so because such material was in circulation, arising from events of which hard accounts were unavailable. A "private source-book" would, notably, have been the only written source of information about the marooning in Australia of an employee of the VOC. General travel accounts were published, such as those of Bontekoe or Schouten, the latter actually referring to the circumstances of such an incident. Various evidence suggests that there was a direct account of it that remained unpublished but for which literary substitutes were elicited by a curious public.

Mylne, however, joins other critics in attributing such effects to the crisis of consciousness: it was "as a result of changing ideas and critical standards"[10] that novelists took to writing about the present or the immediate past and about common rather than great heroes. But these effects began well before the onset of the crisis around 1680; so other factors must be envisaged. One of them, noted by Mylne (24–25), is the double bind inherent in fiction's use of factual material. Events in the lives of famous people tended to be common knowledge, but it was difficult to generate belief in events and people who were purely imaginary. This dilemma was exploited as a literary technique that (although until recently disregarded by critics) was the germ of the new realism.

Its beginnings coincided, as noted, with the *Vergulde Draeck* saga,[11] which catalyzed new techniques of realist invention that went beyond the imaginary biography. Mylne does not discuss these, choosing not to deal with "satiric novels, *romans réalistes,* or, in some cases, *anti-romans.*"[12] They involved an explicitly documentary posture that confused fact with fiction—a method especially suited to events and places so remote or secret as to be practically unverifiable, such as those in seventeenth-century Australia. Sensational events that took place there were known but not their details; they were epics of heroism but involved ordinary people. These were the elements of time, place, character, and ideology that would ground a new literary style, more real to bourgeois readers and serving the cause of moral edification in new ways.

Here, then, was a real-life conundrum of documentary and testamentary truth. Did it merely elucidate the new style or actually help to engender it? Analysis suggests that it probably did both. The notoriety of the shipwrecks—and especially of a sequel involving a marooning, sojourn with locals, and miraculous return—can explain the sensation Neville's work created in 1668, and his use of the (normally didactic) pamphlet form for a story with only indirect political import corresponds to the rise of the nouvelle in France. Soon after, Vairasse based his work directly on those same events, and Smeeks's later but more explicit story evinces both a curious familiarity with them and the workings of censorship within Holland.

The rise of literary realism toward 1670 involved a radical departure from earlier styles and themes. It preceded the crisis of consciousness, rather than deriving from it. The nature and timing of events in the

Southland appears to resolve such problems and to suggest that effects have tended to be confused, in this context, with causes. This hypothesis is borne out, too, by the general relationship between empirical reality and literary or aesthetic truth at the time.

Hobson analyzes the reciprocity of fact and fiction, truth, and illusion in Enlightenment aesthetics. Her study, in terms of appearances, contrasts with those mentioned and their concern with reality. It distinguishes two basic modes of representation: *adequatio rei et intellectus,* or the adequation of thought to thing, which seeks to *simulate* objects, and *aletheia,* a sort of "revelation" that has no such interest in the empirical and that *dissimulates. Aletheia* discloses a hidden truth (that of the knowing subject), rather than the object itself. It effectively duplicates the object and (as both a false appearance and a true disclosure) admits of ambiguity, whereas *adequatio* aims to replicate the object and so must be either true or false. The play of doubles seen in various works examined here (such as that of Vairasse) fits into this schema.

The Enlightenment trend was from *aletheia* and its concern with truth to *adequatio* and its corollary, illusion. The former tended to be validated on moral or cultural grounds, the latter by reference to empirical data, to the world—a fact related, as noted, to the materialist bias of the age. Again, its rising individualism was reflected in the changing role of the subject as representation came to be cast in terms of a reality-illusion couple. Works ceased to be apprehended dually as both what appears and what lies behind it (an oscillation, revealing the contingent nature of perception, that Hobson dubs *papillotage,* or fluttering); instead, the viewer was "increasingly reduced to a single, sometimes immobile, point of view (while) the work of art, correlatively, is seen as external, as an object. . . . What had been a mediate area, a twilight zone between subject and object, is carved up into an experience seen as private and an object which is external. . . . The relation of the spectator will be reduced to that of the *voyeur,* his experience dependent on his being 'situated' by the play or painting."[13]

This trajectory, however, is discernable in the visual arts, not in the novel, which by the end of the eighteenth century was still (or rather, again) a form of *aletheia,* a more self-conscious one than classical *aletheia,* reflecting the revolution it had undergone in the meantime. As noted earlier, the alethic bearing of literature had tended to devolve onto the novel with the decline of scriptural authority; novels came to embody fundamental truths of the Age of Enlightenment. But they did so by passing (early) through an adequationist phase, manifested as the realism that became prominent around 1668. Traditional (allegorical or metaphysical) criteria of truth were then turned upside down and supplanted by empiricist ones.[14]

The novel's aberrant chronology conforms to a broader movement of ideological inversion and involution in the course of the Enlightenment; it was the age's pioneering art form. A possible reason for this was that it used a less directly material medium than the visual arts and so was less closely tied to the broad adequationist trend. Another that has been mentioned was its rhetorical kinship with documentary reporting, which placed it in a bind, a tension between truth and untruth. It had to exploit this resource of credibility but without overdoing it and ceasing to be recognizable as fiction. In relation to reality it had to remain a parasite and not turn into the host because "illusion as an aim in art is possible only when the work represents, not when it is."[15]

As it embraced these subtleties, fiction became, as noted, the object of recurrent attacks. Not only was it accused of moral laxity (for its frankness about the erotic side of life) but many feared that its aping of nonfiction would sap the ability of readers to distinguish the one from the other. But novelists exploited this confusion of codes. Increasing control over it gave rise, for example, to à clé satire alluding to real persons and affairs, a variation on the "forcing of credence" that drew further moralist fire. The novel could not be "critical" without itself becoming subject to criticism, a dilemma personified by the French novelist and critic Nicolas Lenglet Dufresnoy, who in 1734 wrote a pseudonymous defense of the genre, De l'usage des romans, then attacked it the following year in his own name. A better known such case was the novelist and historian Prévost, the author of an American utopia, Cleveland (1732).

Hobson follows other critics in stressing formal rather than historical factors in the evolution of the novel, based on the alethic and adequationist modes of truth and the different procedures they conditioned. In the latter mode, "the unreal defined as a novel is expelled," whereas in the former, "the disjunction real/unreal is made within the novel (usually as a tale within a tale) so that the novel is both true and false, real and unreal, and contains both the fictional reality and the fictional appearance—this being the structure of *aletheia*."[16] Increasing control over the novel's dilemma led to a theorizing of its parasitic relationship with history—a *mise en abyme* of the problem of narrative truth that would enable eighteenth-century novelists to intuit the drift of intellectual history before it became manifest in other areas.

The austral works began an interiorization that Hobson formulates by noting that "in purporting to be genuine, (novels) deny that they are novels. But the reflexive nature of their definitions of the 'real', made by reference to the novel as unreal, destabilises the adequation they seek to establish between text and reality. . . . It is only when the novel is claimed theoretically as fiction ('fiction is truer than truth') or when fiction as illusion is thematised, that some kind of stability is found. One may wonder why it is the novel, of all art forms, which allows the 'unreal' to define the real, and thus to reveal that even *adequatio* is only a form of likeness."[17]

This theorization of illusion, however, came later, notably with Rousseau and Diderot, from the 1760s. Writers a century earlier did not have such control, which suggests that their realist posture was more a reaction to an outside impetus, only gradually "digested" and thematized. Nor is the turn to realism around 1668 as striking in itself as the rapidity with which it occurred. Disruptive forces were clearly involved, which existing theories have not adequately explained—factors of a non-literary nature, which can be attributed only to the impact of historical events.[18] The key to the novel's aesthetic status in the Enlightenment would appear to lie in its early foray into documentary reportage at a time when circumstances provided a ready-made mix of fact and fiction.

As mentioned, biographical fiction was bound up with this problem; it, too, sought "less to simulate, to replicate, than to dissimulate. It is possible to simulate only what is clearly identifiable. But 'history' is *not* clearly identifiable in the eighteenth century."[19] The fact that analogous developments occurred at the same time there and in the imaginary voyage suggests the impact on both of a common model or, rather, that they were twin responses to the same stimulus—a story that was known by rumor but not known in factual detail. Both forms elucidate the role of the witness-narrator as a pivot between reality and literary realism.

This role had always characterized the novel and linked it to the traveler's tale, but it seems to have taken a new twist as a result of events

in Australia. New concerns to manipulate the reader and induce credence reflect the climate of thought into which a tale of marooning
would have arrived in the late 1660s. For it was then that writers began
to exploit the split between romance and history, not so much colonizing it, notes Hobson (94), as shuttling between those poles and ex-
ploiting a "framing" feature inherent in language (that expressed, e.g.,
in Magritte's paintings viewed through a painted window). Their realization that questions of truth could be applied to statement makers
as well as to their statements grounded the oscillation between truth
and untruth that Hobson calls *papillotage.*

It seems that this rhetorical tension underlying the turn to realism
and the novel's reversion to aesthetics of *aletheia* can be traced to the
vogue for *voyages imaginaires* and *faux mémoires,* the twin forms of realism characteristic of the "peculiar phase" (Tieje) beginning around
1668. Their common basis in personal experience—as conveyed by di-
aries, memoirs,[20] or even anecdotes—was particularly favored in the austral case, not only by distance or censorship but also because those
involved were "low-life" characters, whose word was a priori considered
unreliable.

In this connection, it is significant that Hobson questions the view
of Watt and others that individualism and populism were determining
factors in the rise of realism. They were not themselves theorized at
the time, she argues, and did not ground any concept of realism in the
modern sense. "Indeed, modern critics . . . have not always appreciated
how *unreal* descriptions of low life were felt to be. For at the level of
the teller of the story, there was no motive for their having been written at all."[21] A sailor's marooning in the Southland would have been
anomalous—even an anathema—to the literary canon of the 1660s. It
is difficult to see how, as a pure invention, it could have gained literary
status but easier to see how, as a true story, it would have thrown into
relief the stylistic and rhetorical effects fostered by a populist trend and
become literary, as it were, by default.

This origin of the motif outside and below literary circles may, in
addition, help to explain (together with censorship itself) the fact that
no such story has survived. Again, if the impetus derived from a "low-
life" adventure, it is reasonable to expect it (given the horror of the
low) to have been deflected in two literary directions: the imaginary
voyage or utopian novel claiming the basic plot while the hero figure

gravitated toward the old historical novel but, that genre being moribund, contributed instead to the rising popularity of *faux mémoires*. Such common (in all senses) origins might explain too why *faux mémoires* did not, any more than other forms of novel, tend toward *adequatio* nor constitute a discrete genre. Early such works, notes Hobson (89), "show little sign of technical difficulties ill-surmounted, and none at all in the constitution of an omniscient narrator. . . . The teleological explanation, according to which the novel is supposedly refining [there] its techniques of plausibility, hardly survives such an objection."

There would, of course, have been no technical obstacle to the elaboration of realist devices if these derived from real models. On the contrary, a semblance of such problems would have been generated by nonliterary factors, a highly suggestive one, for an age newly conscious of the ideological power of publicity. As Hobson shows, the *faux mémoires* were merely a variant of the modern novel in its parasitic relationship with history; a whole set of works "appears to contradict the principle of the *faux mémoires*." Defining themselves only by reference to the novel, they "cast doubt on their own status. Are they truer than a novel? Or has a fictional light been shed on an episode in history?" (98, 102). They were, it seems, a manifestation of a more general concern with narrative truth, catalyzed by events in Australia but symptomatic of a wider problem — that an old world of truths was being turned upside down.

Aspects of the Southland novel in its typical form as a voyage to a utopia can be similarly clarified. Its outer story, as a novel, did not track from *aletheia* to *adequatio*, whereas the utopian inner story did, a trend that would eventually (by the late eighteenth century, when the novel was thriving) subject the classical utopia to the same aesthetic corrosion as other art forms and, the world by then having yielded its major geographical secrets, force its switch of reference from a social exterior or "other place" to the real society within, projected into the future. Again, this reflects the fact that utopia, in "picturing" an imaginary society, was aesthetically closer to the visual arts than to its narrative vehicle, the novel.

Hence, one discerns the need for a theoretical distinction between the utopia and imaginary voyage, without losing sight of their inseparability in practice. Whereas the former was carried toward an aesthetics of adequation, the latter was in effect a memoir novel and embodied a progressively more lucid form of *aletheia*. It transcended the inner story's impossible adequation with reality, a process inscribed in the very structure of a work through rhetorical disjunctures such as the editorial preface or multiple layers of narration. The two levels of such writing would be differentially affected by the advent of empirical knowledge of the regions referred to. They were, moreover, differentially received; the fictional status of the outer story was less certain than that of the inner story because such voyages were commonplace, yet the inner story threatened "closed" horizons of truth at a deeper level. But by playing on that double fictionality, utopian novels made it into a reflection on truth itself, one that threw into relief the grounding of truth in patterns of cultural interaction.

Thus, developments from the 1660s involved fiction (by default, through its reporting of New World events) in the documentary function—that involving an adequation to objective reality. The novel's rhetorical ambivalence was carried to hyperbolic levels that would mold its subsequent evolution. Romance hitherto had only to be morally plausible, and history was present only as a stage set, but now events, places, and (especially) the word of a witness burst into prominence as aspects of a new problem of truth. Romances and the older style of "historical novel" together fell out of favor.

Crucial to these developments may have been a story, circulating sometime before 1668, of a marooning in Australia. Whether because it was mere rumor or the tale of an illiterate sailor or because censorship prevented its publication, its existence can now only be surmised. But if there were a real such inner story, secondary narrator, and so on, these devices can scarcely be considered pure novelistic inventions. Again, the story could have been a testament—either literally, because the protagonist died while returning to Europe (as in some novels) or in the sense of an excommunication, a symbolic death resulting from the disbelief of others. The culture contact it involved might help to explain, too (together with political developments in England and France), the vogue for utopias from that time. Fiction clearly responded to some such catalyst and conceived within itself a reflexive trend that would forge new rhetorical and aesthetic conventions. Interiorizing a problem of referential truth, it would generate a mode of writing close to—if not at—the heart of the new age.

Such developments can be related indirectly or, perhaps, even directly to "revelations" of the Southland. These provided models for a new literary realism in a Europe increasingly "critical" and eager for certitude. In more abstract terms they were decisive steps in the intellectual assimilation of the New World, a process of cultural coalescence that led to a crisis of values around the turn of the eighteenth century. This tension between traditional (allegorical) and modern (empiricist) modes of truth was, as a function of isolation and distance, epitomized by that between Europe and its antipodes. Unverifiable news from the latter, as an extreme case of the general problem of truth and its relativity to place, it embodied the geopolitical conditions that were fundamental vectors of such change.

The realism emerging around 1668 placed such factors in a properly global context, something the fat and fatuous novels produced up to that time had been unable to do. But the genre did not retain that role for long, tending after 1708 to become formulaic and less clearly related to real events. The catalyst for it appears, on textual, chronological, and theoretical grounds, to have been a marooning following the *Vergulde Draeck* disaster. The literary realism of the eighteenth century can be traced to reports that were sensational but unverifiable and so raised what might otherwise have remained a mere sailor's anecdote into a vibrant literary theme.

From Tropical Island to Island Continent

The austral world, from Hellenistic equatorial islands down to New Holland and Staten Landt, functioned as a trope, a symbol of social insularity. But utopias of the period 1668–1708 carried that theme to new levels of intensity. They expressed links between language, as a vehicle of truth, and the world as its context or framework. The theme came to bear on human history in the widest sense, as the articulation (into language and ideology) of a common wealth, a relationship with a territory.

Such writing was reborn in the Renaissance, conditioned (like its ancient forerunners) by a specific relationship with a social exterior— a curiosity about the wider world, aroused yet unsatisfied. Playing on the boundary between fact and fiction, it raised questions about the difference between the two. It was a "pre-lude" or "pre-text" to the resolution of Europe's distorted vision of its exterior and played on the traditional resistance to empirical information from the latter. Reference to the social world is implicit in discourse generally, and if that framework is not given, it is construed or constructed, a construction of reality linked (as sociolinguists such as Sapir, Whorf, or Berger and Luckmann have shown) to the generation of social structure itself. To it, the perception of boundaries (both ideological and territorial) is crucial.

This process is one determined by patterns of human geography, an essentially passive one, driven by factors beyond human control. An awareness of that fact seems to have been implicit in utopism, where the paradox of a nonexistent society is doubled by that of its active construction by an author or legislator. Human evolution (toward an empiricism that would banish utopia) was driven by an unconscious awareness of such factors; fictionalizing forces lurked in the background of social life, harboring doubts and anxieties that spurred on the quest for total knowledge. Despite a traditional denunciation of engagements with exotic truth as the work of "imposters," time has proved them to be the most pregnant of all discourses of discovery. They uncovered truths about truth itself and its cultural grounding—about the essential relativity of knowledge and the factors that make it so.

They led the way to a theoretical understanding of social ideology. Globalization produced the conditions for the latter and for the advent of empiricism, individualism, or realism but not these effects themselves, which were the by-products of a broader change of worldview. Indeed, Europe's initial response to the New World was to veil it with humanist illusions of universality; for example, the very term *discovery*, which originally meant to uncover or reveal, came to imply that a thing discovered has no prior existence. In political terms this attitude had effects ranging from colonialism to ethnocide, but it had deeper implications. The noumenal sought to globalize its hegemony over the phenomenal, and the knowing mind came to see itself as external to the field of worldly entities rather than as a point within it.

A mode of relating to the world was inaugurated, that would ground modern industrialism. Its dichotomizing bias, supported by educational structures that defined reality in universalist terms, was self-replicating. It is commonly assumed to have arisen spontaneously during a history conceived as a linear progression. One might ask, however, whether it was not "processed" through a confrontation of subjectivity with objectivity in exotist literature and, especially, in utopian novels. For as the exotic ceased to exist as such, and there ceased to be that screen on which to project whole (or holistic) visions of the world, the latter's description tended to become immanent and, eventually, *prescriptive* — a pretention to truth no longer aware of itself as such, "absolved" of horizons. This was the deeper absolutism in which modern political and economic trends were rooted.

The West's relationship with its exterior has evolved through cycles of rejection and guarded acceptance toward an embrace bringing a collapse of local differences. Out of a layering of collective subjectivities, objectivity was precipitated. The process brought changes of rhetorical mode, submerging older ones variously allegorical, ironical, or satirical in orientation. Old concerns with the problem of exotic truth were transcended and eventually lost to view within a new order of rationality. The possibility (and, indeed, the inevitability) of the latter was grounded by a geopolitical coalescence in which local truths or realities were assimilated to a global avatar.

It would be consciously formulated in this way at the time of the closure of the global circle (and of the demise of the classical utopia) in Kant's *Critique of Pure Reason* (1781). But it was foreshadowed in the realist trend of the Southland novels of 1668–1708. Two aspects of them reflect that awareness: the dystopian character of the alternative social worlds they portray and their obsession with veracity. By claiming to offer truth in the new empiricist key—a news report about current events—they transposed the problem of referential truth from the world into language itself. This, an opening shot in the Enlightenment war between old and new ideologies, reflected the fact that the "tropical" island of old, the trope of social insularity, was losing currency. In a global world it was being transcended, and giving way to a theoretical understanding of tropes themselves.[22]

As the southern continent was revealed to the world, it ceased to function poetically as a container of closed societies, similar to the "tropical" island—as a "continent" in (again) the etymological sense. It became *incontinent,* in that sense, when used as a setting for utopias reflecting social and political trends in Europe. This is how it appears in the dystopias of Foigny and Vairasse, which also explains, perhaps, why the theme subsequently gave rise, in *Krinke Kesmes,* to a modern form of such literature, the individualist Robinsonade.

171

CHAPTER TWELVE

The Body, the World, and the Word

Johann Reinhold Forster, reflecting on his experiences during Cook's second voyage, envisaged a "history of man in general, considered as one large body."[1] His idea was surely related to the fact that this voyage resolved the question of the southern continent. It had precedents, both recent and distant, that were rooted in perceptions of the world as a basis for society, the history of which forms part of the background to the Enlightenment. Forster's "global anthropology" appeared just as modern scientific anthropology was taking form and about one century after the austral utopias of Neville, Vairasse, Foigny, and others — works that implicitly discussed similar ideas and pioneered developments in literature, aesthetics, and social theory during the intervening period.

In those works, too, social ideals tended to be discussed in terms of the way people live as bodies. Such metaphors derived from an archaic poetics comparing collective and personal life. It was archaic, too, in a more than chronological sense. Early myths of a paradise, *isola sacra,* or earth mother, had compared collective life and its relationship with territory to one's first experiences as an infant. They were symbolic enclosures — places of immediacy, security, and unconditional relationship, as in the womb or at the breast. A society and its land (as sources of sustenance on the two levels of existence) were idealized as extensions of the maternal body.

Human society was, perhaps, originally "conceived" in this way — as a corpus of shared knowledge and beliefs, contained by the boundaries that separated it from an exterior. Its cohesion was associated with the physical integrity of a territory and especially that of an island. Such notions evolved out of primate territorial concerns and, with the rise of a political consciousness, underwrote analogies between the individual and an organ or cell of the body. With the growth of trade and sea voyaging, their residue was expressed in terms of a duality of known and unknown worlds and gave rise to the literary utopia.

The analogy with psychogenetic processes remained a dominant paradigm in the latter and can help to clarify its origin, evolution, and (with the rise of social science) its demise. On either plane the essential phenomenon is the advent of an aesthetic sophistication that "writes down" perceptions of the environment.[2] Utopia supplanted its mythic forebears as a more sophisticated way of depicting social life in terms of an ideal unity—a lost unity, analogous to that of mother and child in the splitting-off of a new personality. History eroded the closed integrity of societies; commerce and travel dissolved social boundaries and (along with demographic and technological factors) gave rise to the political state. Social structures acquired an economic rather than somatic (tribal) basis, and a realism crept into older ways of expressing social ideals. This aesthetic sophistication enabled society to represent itself not only in the sense of political representation but in literary images of its ideal integrity as a unity threatened by history.

Utopia was significant, therefore, in rhetorical rather than simply geopolitical terms; it represented an evolution in ways of conceiving the social world. This was reflected in its narrative dimension. The imaginary voyage that served it as an "envelope" played on travelers' tales and their reputation for being vague or mendacious. To report on another social world was a poetic act and, in drawing comparisons with one's own world, an impertinent or even subversive one. A voyage, real or imaginary, was also a passage between the realms of fact and fiction. It revealed not only exotic novelties but the tension within one's own culture between two drives—one inward looking and conservative, the other outgoing and progressive, a catalyst for evolution. Most seriously, it showed how closely akin the former was to fiction.

Such effects can be compared, again, to bodily processes. Truth is produced within a social context, a "closed circuit" of language; it attaches to the lining of a womblike enclosure that nurtures meanings and values. It is born where the latter opens onto the world—at the interface of fact and fiction. Exotism leavens ordinary (endotic) language by evoking a culture's self-interest in relation to its exterior. Travelers seem mendacious to the unworldly, who appear, in turn, ignorant and prejudiced. What is fact in one place is fiction in another, and an aware-

173

ness of this truth destabilizes all truth. Such awareness arose as the social body's skin was penetrated by germs of exotic knowledge carried by returning travelers; these provoked an ideological resistance comparable to the generation of antibodies in response to bacteria or to the healing effects of small doses of poison.

A similar ambivalence was inherent in exotist writing. It generated an awareness of language, which, more than merely a vehicle for literature, became its referent. Writing became aware of itself as the bearer of ideology and epitomized more general trends toward materialist, secular, or empiricist modes of experience. Utopias and imaginary voyages spoke about the world and the way culture mediates one's experience of it and showed by implication how objectivity was being precipitated out of the multiple subjectivities of societies.

Utopia was, by contrast with the universalism of the earth mother, a this-worldly reality, yet one that could not be found (nor, like its cousin the colony, founded) in the world. Existing between the ideal and the real, it embodied formal rather than empirical truths and inspired doubt rather than certitude. Images of unknown islands or continents embodied the old ideal of social insularity and its dubious status in reality, its erosion. Thus, Plato's Atlantis was both a bodily metaphor (a "matrix") and a rhetorical play in the margins of knowledge. Hellenistic works developed his model, inspired by Greek activity in the Indian Ocean and the rediscovery of archaic cultural forms in Asia (elements that fitted naturally together: sun worship with the equatorial zone, vegetalism with tropical abundance, walled cities with islands, and so on). a rebirth of commerce in the Renaissance brought such writing back into vogue and with new possibilities; More's *Utopia* recast it in a global context, and the whole world became a field for utopian play.

With this globalization came further realism, a reversion, in effect, to the old alignment on the traveler's tale. With the onset of Enlightenment, utopia merged with history, giving rise to a type of novel that would be the cutting edge of a revolution in ideas. Early Enlightenment utopias were pivotal to this turn from traditional to modern concerns and displayed elements of both. They restated primitive social ideals but with a negative twist that betrayed an ambivalence toward modern developments. Such qualities were consistent with their heritage of bodily metaphor, its evolution into literary avatars, and its underlying interest in spatial configurations. They are reflected in the narrative realism of those works and in their favorite geographical theme, the great austral unknown.

The Southland was more than a real frontier; it was the last major notional exterior, or generator, of collective difference. This symbolic significance increased as it remained (effectively) unknown right into Enlightenment times. A crisis of values that underlay the latter can be traced back to the 1660s and a shift in Europe's experience of the New World expressed in literature by themes of austral discovery. This was an old problem that had grown in notoriety with Portuguese secrecy over their activities with the fantastic claims of Quirós, and so forth. But it came to a head with the sensational Dutch disasters that inaugurated real knowledge of the continent. These joined the explorations of Tasman to inspire a new generation of exotist literature.

The latter addressed questions of geographical and cultural knowledge; it embodied trends toward objectivity and realism and a crisis of collective identity associated with them. This was a time when people's minds were divided, their feet in two worlds—one still overridden by metaphysical and ascetic distortion, the other moving toward a more direct relationship with the real. As exotism focused on real events, it shed its frankly fictional (or even monstrous) forms and became concerned with a relatively disinterested empiricism. But it did not lose its allegorical significance; indeed, it tended to take over the role of scripture as a bearer of whole images of the world, a mythos.

The utopias caught up in this change were the apogee and the swan song of the traditional genre. They marked an impending collapse of the old duality of known and unknown worlds and pioneered a realism that would flower in the Robinsonade and in eighteenth-century novels generally. In this they reflected a passage from closed to open forms of society in which holistic visions of the world were refined and split up into political, geographical, economic, and other components. It involved the progressive mediation of social life by aesthetic processes (among which, notably, was the "general equivalence" of money as a measure of value), a movement from inward reference to regimes of representation, writing down to its lowest common denominators man's relationship with the world. Utopian insularity had shown the role of boundaries in social life, but its globalization brought an abstraction (a Hegelian *Aufhebung*, or sublation) into the realm of the sign. Indeed, utopia would itself be "written down" as it was supplanted by criticism and social science.[3]

Such implications became manifest in the Southland works from 1668. Politically, too, they departed from the projective mode of earlier utopias concerned with English republicanism to address deeper problems thrown up by the rise of massified, absolutist states. Rationalism implied the idea of a rational social order (as found in early universalist myths, religions, or materialist philosophies) that could be illustrated by utopias in the southern continent. Yet it produced only dystopias: reflexive views of a writer's own society as one dogged by political or religious impostures within, rivalry and war without.

That of Vairasse is reached by a centripetal progression both to the heart of the Southland and to that of the story, but at that double center is only contradiction, paradox, and an impossible uniformity. An unwinding of its narrative and ideological structures begins once it is reached; eutopia becomes dystopia as the hero returns to the real world. Such an effect, pioneered in earlier satirical voyages to the Southland, was even more probingly exploited in the contemporary work of Foigny. Both authors handled political issues in a new way related to the "double negative" of alienation they experienced as Huguenots.

Political ideals they examine (pyramidal representation with Vairasse or "moral transparency" with Foigny) are of academic, rather than practical, interest not only today but, it is clear, for the authors themselves. A critical distance from them is implied by the narrative framework of their utopias. The voyage to the southern land created, in their works, a convergence of two dimensions—that of the world and that of the word. It revealed a social process on a deeper level. It implied, for example, that political absolutism was not an accident but the outcome of a geopolitical process, that the world's globalization might bring with that the word as a vector of social cohesion.

These were aspects of their reversion to the problem of the traveler's tale. As they focused on the problems of veracity (or "Vairasse-ity"?) thrown up by real contact with the Southern Land they engendered a deeper realism, one that went beyond politics to bear on the cultural field at large and brought a new way of theorizing culture or, rather, a very old one—for this factor was what had originally severed utopia from the earth mother and projected it into the realm of writing. It now abstracted it from positive political ideals as the age of Rationalism gave way to one of Enlightenment; the ideas "visited" in the Southland were visited ever more critically. Nor did the partial discovery of the continent known diminish its effectiveness as a literary device; it even enhanced old tensions of exotic truth and lent itself to veiled commentaries on absolutism and arbitrary power.

Such effects were also implied, as of old, by the eroticism of these works. Archaic bodily metaphors had idealized the world as a feminine, maternal, and universal one, but in reality it was one riven by social differences vested in ideologies and practices that were the masculine domain. The very phenomenon of "man" arose, as noted, from tensions of territorial difference in a collective version of Lacan's passage through the mirror stage or of the self-objectification and gender-fixing that Freud called *Spaltung* (splitting). The Same-Other split that for individuals is based on bodily identities was, in early myth, telescoped into a duality of man and earth, and utopian dualities of nation and nation or Old World and New retained this basis as a dichotomy of known (masculine) and unknown (feminine) worlds.

History, however, subjected such notions to the same "melt-down" as in the semiotic or political areas — an involutional effect that was figured by images of antipodean moral inversion or, more explicitly, hermaphrodism. Erotic themes reflected, too, an emancipation from ascetic mechanisms of integration in a "new world of body." Again, because ideology was traditionally a masculine affair and the physical side of life a feminine one, an ethos valorizing the physical over the metaphysical could be seen as reversion from "true" humanity, and this, too, was implied in the hermaphrodite dystopias of Hall, Arthus, or Foigny.

In these ways, austral works refined the utopian play on boundaries in its original, or simple, sense. They brought the various dimensions of human life together in a whole vision, one that — notwithstanding modern academic divisions of knowledge — can afford an adequately genetic perspective on human culture. Foigny's was perhaps the ultimate such work, bringing to their highest pitch early ways of writing about the conditions for culture — about the partial knowledge, or partiality of knowledge, of the world that maintained an exterior and, against it, a structure of beliefs and values within.

As those conditions shrank in scope, the old imagery built on them was intensified — squeezed out, in effect, by a writing process operating on various levels from the geographical to the scriptural. Symptomatic

177

of this crisis was the problem of news from the Southland and its dissemination (or lack of it) into the public arena. It can be traced through the works culminating in *Krinke Kesmes;* the age-old ambivalence over exotic truth came to a head as public demand for knowledge of events in Australia clashed with traditional habits of secrecy about such activities.

This theme displaced the overtly political bias of earlier seventeenth-century utopias; it brought out a deeper relationship between the world and the word. It opened a window onto the semiotic order itself, beyond any particular society and its improvement whether directly or via a utopian twin (as, for example, in the Utopia-England couple). The locus of truth was displaced into a no-man's-land between the two options as the unknown world began to acquire its own autonomous reality. All possible matrices of the word were gathered into a global one sharing a common truth problem, one that paved the way for the human sciences.

Again, as "histories of histories"[4] these works revealed a paradox whereby the word is born of locality yet evolves with it toward a global avatar. Ideologies remained in conflict in the absence of an awareness that they are all, as effects of a global configuration of societies, essentially the same. Even political theory takes as its object a social interior, one that, however, has no intrinsic being but arises in the flux of a global social history. Were it to take the latter as its object and focus on processes at the boundaries of societies, politics might have a relevance it can otherwise have only residually in the aftermath of the social closure supported by physical isolation. Such an approach becomes all the more relevant as a new order of boundary effects comes into play, arising from the impact of information technologies.

The modern disillusionment with utopian speculation (and, increasingly, with politics in general) arises from an impossible expectation that social processes can be created or controlled from within. Early utopias were often not "utopian" in that sense at all; the hero was glad to leave. Again, they have been accused of reactionary or totalitarian tendencies, whereas they portrayed such ideals only in order to negate them, putting them "under erasure" by enveloping them in a deconstructive voyage there and back. Ideals were set up propositionally in a way that the reader (like the protagonist) could take or leave.

Yet it was a device doomed to pass out of currency as the world became known; voyages would cease to discover anything, and news dispatches would supplant the traveler's tale. It found its most intense expression as a modern concept of humanity emerged, that of a social body relating in new ways to the world. Land became less a principle of social adhesion and exclusion than an object of personal ownership. Indeed, it was from a *mise en abyme* of older notions that a new kind of social universalism arose as part of a wider empiricism. A global world would reproduce the conditions that had grounded earth mother myths —that of a society bounded not by competing societies but only by the physical world. The ideal articulated by Forster, and earlier stated more poetically by Foigny, was one that primitive religions had long practiced.

To treat utopia as an avatar of archaic myths, a "losing of paradise," and a close relative of primitivism, is deplored by some.[5] So, too, may be the notion that in its most sophisticated form it was not a blithe escape into irreality but a sort of literary *Realpolitik*. It has been unduly marginalized by being assimilated to idealism of another and more recent tradition. It expressed links between society and the world—both that of its author and a wider one known (to some extent) through discovery. From its origins down to Enlightenment times, it embodied the inexorable rise of aesthetic abstraction as it focused on the body, the world, and the word itself. In it was conceived, too, a possible way of approaching the problem of social boundaries.

Notes
Bibliography
Index

Notes

1. What Was Utopia?

1. The term, Greek for "no-place," embodies a contradiction that Sir Thomas More exploited when he invented it for his eponymous work. See Marin (1984, chap. 4).

2. Louis-Sébastien Mercier's *Memoirs of the year 2500*, the first properly futurist utopia, appeared in 1772.

3. It has, however, been treated as such only sporadically. See, for example, Donaldson 1982; Gibson 1984; Spate 1987.

4. Antarctic avatars of it would, however, engage authors well into the present century. Cf. Edgar Allan Poe's *Narrative of Arthur Gordon Pym of Nantucket* (1837); V. I. Briussov's *Republic of the Southern Cross* (1907); or Howard P. Lovecraft's *To the Mountains of Madness* (1936).

5. Campbell (1988, 179).

6. Cf. Louis Marin's point that "utopia is not at the level of the concept, but . . . is a figure, a schema of the imagination" (Marin 1985, 21–22).

7. As proposed by Negley and Patrick (1952, 3) and by Cioranescu (1962, 130).

8. See Hansot (1974, chap. 1).

9. Cf. Ruyer 1950, who typecasts the utopist as a "schizoid dreamer."

10. Marin (1985, 195). Cf. ibid., 10: "When talking about the Perfect Island, the Lunar States, or the Austral Continent, utopia talks less about itself . . . than about the very possibility of uttering such a discourse, of the status and contents of its enunciating position and the formal and material rules allowing it to produce some particular expression. Utopia does not of course speak about these things as such. Rather it speaks *symbolically* of these things . . . Formal logic is its referential signified."

11. As, for example, does Mannheim (1936), in defining utopia in terms of a resistance against class ideology.

12. Suvin (1979, 7). Cf. also ibid., 22–23, 80–84.

13. See Gove (1941, 19f.).

14. Cf. Sargent (1988, xii–xiii), Davis (1981, 2–6). Raymond Trousson (1974, 367–78), noting that utopia has tended to be studied and discussed before being defined, adopts a literary approach separating ideological from novelistic aspects.

183

15. Zaganelli (1986, 21–24), who asks whether the "utopian paradigm" is a question of form or of content: "Is it a frame with well-defined formal traits, but whose constitutive elements are variables to be related to a determined culture and epoch; or are we dealing with a rigid model corresponding, from any point of view, to the model of [More's] eponymous work?" It is the former, Zaganelli concludes.

16. Bloch 1957.

17. Robert Nozick (1974, 325) raises such a concept of society but then dismisses it as an aside: "Consider the members of a basketball team, all caught up in playing basketball well. (Ignore the fact that they are trying to win, though is it an accident that such feelings often arise when some unite *against* others?)."

2. The Discovery of the Austral World

1. Cf. Bowra (1957, chap. 1); Ferguson (1975, 9, chap. 4).

2. See, in general, Warmington 1934.

3. See Hourani (1951, 6–11).

4. On Egyptian knowledge of the "Punt" route from ca. 3,000 B.C., surviving as priestly knowledge but revived by commodity demands, see Cameron (1965, 19–41); also, in general, Hollingsworth 1929.

5. See Jack-Hinton (1969, 10–23).

6. Thus, for example, an 1817 British Admiralty chart (in Stommel 1984) shows a "*Provincia Aurifera*" (Gold-bearing province) in northwest Australia.

7. Cf. Warmington (1934, 207, 248n).

8. A sense embodied in Homer's term *polytropos* at the beginning of the *Odyssey*, translated as "wiles and wanderings" by Frame (1978, ix–x).

9. Huntingford 1980 dates it ca. A.D. 95–130, others ca. A.D. 60, that is, before Marinus and Ptolemy. At the time more than 120 ships a year were active in the Eastern trade (Cameron 1965, 55).

10. Nordenskiöld (1973, 35).

11. Cf. Wright (1965, chap. 1, and 156–65).

12. On sixth-century Irish voyages to America to escape the "barbarian holocaust" pressing westward, see Cameron (1965, 68–69). On early Portuguese activities there see Bensaude 1930; on the Vikings see Cameron 1965 and Heyerdahl 1978.

13. The Hindu-related Majapahit empire in Sumatra was at its height around 1330–1400, and the spice trade was controlled at its Moluccan sources by Chinese merchants. Both were the objects of an Arab campaign resulting in their establishment in Java from 1478. See Boxer (1969, chap. 1).

14. See, for example, Cameron (1965, app. B); Boxer 1969.

15. Cf. Wright (1965, 162–63); Taylor (1968, 131); Rainaud (1893, chap. 1); Nordenskiöld (1897, 184f.).

16. Humboldt would theorize in Enlightenment times the significance to modern civilization of the grid concept; cf. McIntyre (1977, xv).

17. See Bensaude (1930, 255f.).

18. Cf. Bensaude 1912; Waters 1978; McIntyre 1977; Penrose 1967.

19. Cf. Cameron (1965, 82–95, 114–26); Heyerdahl (1978, 124–42).

20. Bensaude (1930, 280f.).

21. The globe was used to interpret Toscanelli's 1474 map on which Columbus and John II of Portugal based their plans. On Behaim (ca. 1459–1506), a pupil of the Nuremberg cosmologist and magician, Regiomontanus, see Ravenstein 1908.

22. See Nordenskiöld (1973, 9, 15, 62–66).

23. Notably, by the theologians Aurelius Macrobius and Martianus Capella.

24. See Taylor 1966. Higden believed the earth was spherical but that the antipodes were uninhabitable.

25. Nordenskiöld (1973, 100).

26. Nordenskiöld (1973, 45–48) links, for example, the 1339 "Dulcert" portolans with a 1595 Dutch nautical atlas by Barentsz and deduces that neither differed essentially from those of Marinus of Tyre. The latter were still extant in the tenth century when the Arab geographer Masudi remarked that they were "even better than those of Ptolemy."

27. Before 1509 (Nordenskiöld 1973); 1507 (McIntyre 1977, 137); or 1515 (Cameron 1965, 129). Cf. also Schilder (1976, 10). It is variously thought that the agent was Peutinger (a Lisbon-based German who may have been a spy), that João gave his information to Magellan, or that the "strait" was only the Plate estuary. The reason given for turning back (violent head winds) does, however, suggest the Cape Horn area.

28. Nordenskiöld (1973, 79).

29. Cf. McIntyre 1977; Hervé 1983; Wallis 1982; Cortesano and Teixiera da Mota 1960.

30. Cf. Dames (1967, 119–201); Cortesano (1967, lxxviii–lxxxiv); McIntyre (1977, chap. 5).

31. Not João Rodriguez Serrano, Magellan's companion during the circumnavigation; whether the two were related is not clear. Cf. Dames (1967, 1:xlvi) on this and on Abreu's links with the Serrano family; also Dalrymple (1767, 3–9, 13–24). Magellan, like Abreu, had been prominent in the Malacca siege and (according to McIntyre, after Argensola) took part in the Abreu voyage. Duarte Barbosa was Magellan's brother-in-law and captain of the *Vittoria* in the circumnavigation; he, too, had been active in the Indonesian area.

32. Fol. 39 of the nineteenth-century Count of Santarem's atlas, where it is asserted, however, that Rodriguez "made the voyage to the Moluccas in 1524–30." Cortesano and Teixiera da Mota state, moreover, (1960, 213n) that Tomé Pires was "the first to give a proper description of the Moluccas, and Rodrigues the first to represent them on a map, though neither was ever actually there." Cf. also ibid. 149–50, and Cortesano (1967, lxxix, n. 2).

33. McIntyre (1977, 81f.); others dispute this.

34. McIntyre (1977, 135f.).

35. This is the thesis of Hervé, who links it to the disappearance of the Spanish ship *San Lesmes* in a storm off Cape Horn during the Loaysa expedition. He believes she crossed the South Pacific in high latitudes, against the Roaring Forties, to "fortuitously" encounter New Zealand (cf. n. 39).

36. Cf. n. 32. McIntyre (1977, 74) suggests he was recruited before the French

expedition, Hervé (1983, 18), during it. The Parmentier brothers reached Sumatra but both died there, and the expedition returned under the command of a cartographer, Pierre Crignon, perhaps, with Alfonso's help. Cf. also Wallis 1982; Wallis (1981, 62); and Cortesano and Tiexiera da Mota (1960, 135–36, 139–40).

37. Alfonse (1559). Cortesano dates their composition ca. 1528; Musset (who edited the *Cosmographie* in 1904), ca. 1536.

38. "Java" referred loosely to major land masses in the region. Another Dieppe map of similar or slightly later date (Wallis dates it ca. 1547), the anonymous Harleian planisphere, does not join its "Australian" coasts to the southern continent but ends them in high latitudes, especially on the east coast, a fact that McIntyre associates with the wreck site mentioned.

39. Cf. n. 35, and Langdon 1975.

40. This route, too, would generate mythical or literary traditions; cf. the "lost islands" of Rica d'Oro and Rica de Plata in the vicinity of Japan (Stommel 1984); Fontenelle's late-seventeenth-century utopia *Ajao*; or part 3 of *Gulliver's Travels*.

41. Even much later geographers (De Brosses 1756, Dalrymple 1767) still believed in the existence of the continent.

42. Cf. Markham (1904, vol. 2); Kelly (1966, 1:intro., and 150f.); and Fausett 1993a (intro.).

43. Paulmier 1663. Cf. Friedrich 1967; Linon (1990, 159–68).

44. See Boxer 1965; Baker (1931, 145–77).

45. See n. 26, and Schilder (1976, 18).

46. Schilder, 50, 65. Maps sometimes covered sensitive areas (such as Australia's west coast) with a legend.

47. Hoorn was a major port and VOC chamber at the south end of the West Friesian Islands. Schouten and Le Maire, two of its most famous citizens, named Cape Horn after it. They also, in rounding the latter, proved that the land Magellan had seen to the south of his strait was not the Southland although this did not significantly affect the southern-continent myth.

48. Schilder (1976, chap. 4).

49. See McIntyre (1977, 75–77, 362–65). A 1602 map found by Dr. Mota Alves shows a route to, apparently, the Brunswick Bay area on Australia's northwest coast. Cf. also Spate (1975, 249–66); Cortesano and Teixiera da Mota (1960, 4:45); Nordenskiöld (1897, 198); Hamy 1896.

50. See Schilder (1976, 72, 76–77, 100). Schilder also discusses "Remmesen's rivier" which, together with a little-known sighting by Leeuwin at 34°S, appeared on Gerritz's maps of 1622 and 1627. Cf. n. 58.

51. English activity in the area continued until a hardening Dutch policy forced it out. The first ship wrecked on this Australian coast was the English East India Company's *Trial* at about 20°S in 1622.

52. It had been suggested six years earlier by Brouwer or, possibly, by Plancius; cf. Henderson (1982, 12–13). Whatever the case, the basic source was Portuguese; cf. Schilder (1976, 41n).

53. Cited in Schilder (1976, 91); adding that "the natives were described as pitch-black and of small stature. They were wholly naked and wore baskets or nets on their

heads (and) resembled the natives of the coast of Coromandel." The Dutchmen, concluding that they were cannibals, used guns when attacked. They also established, from a trip two miles up an estuary, a persistent legend that the interior was a vast salt lake. Another landing confirmed that the locals had "no knowledge at all of gold, silver, tin, iron, lead, and copper; even nutmegs, cloves and pepper which had been shown to them several times on the voyage made no impression on them."

54. Ibid., 94–96. Colster's findings can be inferred from later information; the area became generally known only after Tasman's voyages.

55. Ibid.

56. Major (1859, xciv–civ).

57. Editions by Jansz (1647) and Hartgers (1648), the latter with illustrations and a letter by one of the survivors, were followed by six others and a summary of the story in Thévenot (1663, 50–56). See Schilder (1976, chap. 12) and Drake-Brockman 1963.

58. Cf. n. 50. Drake-Brockman (1963, 302–4) provisionally identifies this place as Yardie Creek, at the seaward end of Exmouth Gulf, and the man as Jan Remmetszoon, a non-VOC seeker of a passage to the Pacific in 1615 or early 1616.

59. Drake-Brockman (1963, 61–62) suggests he may have been a veteran of Bontekoe's epic voyage (see chap. 6). Bontekoe's book appeared the year before the account of this incident.

60. Schilder (1976, 116).

61. See Drake-Brockman (1963, 63f. and app. 7). An orphan, Jansz was unrelated to others of that name in this history. Her servant, Zwaantie, became Jacobsz's mistress and sailed with him to Batavia. Cornelisz was a follower of Torrentius van der Beeke, an artist and ideologue who preached sexual communism and was arrested in Haarlem in 1627 for spreading Adamite and Rosicrucian ideas in Holland. (The Adamites, with their whipping orgies, flourished from the second century and in medieval times.)

62. Drake-Brockman (1963, 118), who locates (300) this marooning, the first and best-known of a series of such incidents, near the Hutt River, just north of the Abrolhos.

3. Early Austral Fiction

1. Cf. Ferguson (1975, chap. 2); Lovejoy and Boas 1935.

2. See Ferguson (1975, 10, 14–15).

3. Cf. chap. 2, n. 1. Such symbolism contrasted with a more abstract one in which the encircling Ocean provided a notional boundary enclosing the known world, an ambiguity that would remain central to classical utopism.

4. On the symbolics of utopian structures, see Marin (1984, chap. 5).

5. This relativity was at issue in humanist and Renaissance speculation about the nature, quality, and status of the primitive societies found in the New World. It appears in the works of Columbus, Martyr, Las Casas, Montaigne and others, and (obliquely) in utopian writings. Cf. Cro (1990, chap. 1).

6. Ferguson (1975, 123).

7. Cited in Warmington (1934, 133).

8. This discussion of the Hellenistic works is based on Ferguson (1975, chaps. 12, 14).

9. For example, Ecbatana (modern Hamadan) was a city with seven concentric walls representing the seven planets (as, later, in Campanella's utopia). Built around the seventh century B.C., it was sacked by Cyrus and Alexander but rebuilt in Islamic times. Other examples are Baghdad, which retained its form until the seventh century A.D., and Jerusalem. See Servier (1967, 44f).

10. See Ferguson (1975, 102–4).

11. Already in these works it can be seen how the utopia's critical function was related to the social status and function of the voyager or writer (most acutely, of the voyager *and* writer, who should in principle be disbelieved). On the sociology of scapegoating see Girard 1977.

12. Ferguson (1975, 125) detects in this work a possible knowledge of cotton, rice, or the opium poppy. Sago, a dietary staple in parts of Indonesia, was reported from medieval times at least; see Dames (1967, 201n).

13. As noted earlier, Eratosthenes used tidal data to deduce around 235 B.C. that Africa was circumnavigable. But Ferguson (125–26) dates this work ca. 250–225 B.C. and doubts that Iambulus knew of his theories or had any knowledge more precise than that acquired by a Greek visitor to India in ca. 290 B.C. "There is perhaps a vague knowlege of Ceylon . . . and the Borneo Islands, but it is certainly only vague."

14. Such themes may reflect Oriental influences, notes Ferguson (1975, 126–27) or that of the Cynics or Stoics. "It is a priori likely that a Utopian writer of this period would have been familiar with the Cynic and Stoic Utopias (and) later generations regarded Utopian writing as something of a Stoic speciality."

15. Ferguson deduces (ibid., 174) that "A fairly high proportion of Lucian's readership were familiar with Euhemerus and Iambulus."

16. Volcanoes terrified early voyagers; cf., for example, Dames (1967, 197n.); Campbell (1988, 43, 52).

17. A translation by Pierre d'Ablancourt (1654) added two apocryphal chapters to complete the story. Baudouin had also translated it into French in 1613 and Hickes into English in 1634. These were the versions available to seventeenth-century writers although many early readers used the Greek text.

18. Lactantius Firmianus (ca. 260–ca. 340) *The Divine Institutes*, 3:24; (St.) Augustine Aurelius (354–430) *The City of God*, 16:9.

19. Cf. the derivation of *paradise* itself from the Old Persian *pairi* (around) and *diz* (mold) (*Oxford Dictionary*).

20. Servier (1967, 159); cf. also ibid., 337–338; Bachelard (1942, 7–8, chap. 5); Eliade (1967, 39–72). Wunenburger (1979, 35) notes that "mythical thought has developed a cosmogony and an eschatology in which the womb is the archetype of an ideal space and time. If myths are more than merely ludic or illusory inventions of the mind, we need to elucidate their psychic archaeology by revealing the affective and intellectual forces behind this persistant, universal language of images."

21. Wunenberger (1979, 39; after Rimbaud) compares the "utopian" city of Baby-

lon to the "holy" one of Jerusalem. In his view only this discontinuity between myth and utopia, inverting older symbolic regimes, can explain the novelty of utopian writing (cf. also Dubois 1978, 212–23). Analogous to it is the friend/enemy couple, in relation to which a stranger is an ambivalent third—a "variation of the master-opposition between the inside and the outside," notes Bauman (1990, 143).

22. Campbell (1988, 19, 31).

23. Ibid. 42, noting the continued absence of an anthropological dimension. Cf. also Turner (1974, 1979).

24. Campbell (1988, 12, 67–68); noting (ibid., 8) that "a world normal at its center and monstrous at its margins is easy to see as the self-image of a culture quite literally scared of its own shadow." Bishop (1986) adopts a phenomenological approach to "liminality."

25. Cf. Olschki 1960, Said 1979. On Marco Polo's knowledge of the austral regions see Bosetti 1984; Masefield 1908.

26. Cf. chap. 5 on *The Antipodes*. In the sixteenth century Mandeville's work appeared as fact in the first editions (1582, 1589) of Hakluyt's voyage collection. Explorers such as Raleigh, Frobisher, and (apparently) Columbus, as well as cartographers such as Mercator and Ortelius, also took it on authority (Campbell 1988, 218, 126).

27. Possible historical sources for the story are examined by Slessarev 1959; cf. also Zaganelli 1986.

28. Olschki (1931, 1–14) thinks the *Letter* has a utopian or theocratic bearing. Slessarev (1959, 106n) disagrees; cf. also Helleiner (1959, 47–57). Elements of the story appear in utopias such as *Antangil* (see chap. 5).

29. See Lasky (1977, 18–27); Cohn 1957.

30. See Morton (1952, chap. 1).

31. Architectural utopias had appeared earlier: Sforzinda, named after the ruler of Milan, in the *Trattato* of Filarete (Antonio Averlino, 1400–1466), and one by Leon Battista Alberti in *De re ædificatoria* (written 1452). See Grendler 1969; Davis 1981.

32. On the geography of Utopia see Marin (1985, chaps. 2, 5); Berneri (1950, 59); More 1965.

33. Among literary sources, Peter Martyr's accounts of Cuba and the West Indies (*De Orbe Novo* 1511–1530) were influential. See Donner 1945; Campbell (1988, 215–17); Cro 1990.

34. Marin and Dagron (1971, 312–17).

35. Ibid.

36. Ibid.

37. Ibid.

38. On the policies and concepts this process involved see Shennan 1974. Central to them was a separation of abstract from personal sovereignty affecting both the status of a king's "two bodies" (physical and symbolic, see Kantorowicz [1957, 21–23]) and the middle classes with their rising individualism.

39. See Castinian (1969, 97–107) and, on Inca history, Rowe (1949, 2:143).

40. See Marin (1985, chap. 8). On linguistic aspects of More's scheme see ibid., chap. 4.

41. On Andreae's relations with Campanella, Rosicrucianism and so forth, see Hansot (1974, 79–92); Davis (1981, 73–83).

42. Cf. Pierre Bergeron's *Relation des Voyages en Tartarie* (Paris, 1634); the *Voyages Fameux* of Vincent Le Blanc; and later, Jean-Baptiste Tavernier's travels through Asia to the East Indies, edited by the Jesuit Bernier 1676. See Atkinson (1920, 108–19); Chinard (1970, 202–3); Tavernier 1968.

43. Imbroscio (1986, preface).

44. Menippus was a freed Phoenician slave who made a fortune in the Greek city of Thebes in the third century B.C. A follower of the Cynic Diogenes, he parodied (in works now lost) Homer and exotism generally, founding a style followed by Roman writers (Varro, Petronius, Seneca), by Lucian (who caricatured him as Icaromenippus), and later by humanists.

45. Frye (1966a, 309–11). Satire itself "is said to come from *satura,* or hash, and a kind of parody of form seems to run all through its tradition" (ibid., 233).

46. Campbell (1988, 123, 140).

47. A 1585 encyclopedia by Gabriel Chappuys mentions it as a real place (Campbell 1988, 213–14). Critical references to it appear in 1610 in England and 1710 on the Continent (in Leibniz's *Theodicy*). Early translations from the Latin were by Robinson (1551), Burnet (1684), and (into French) Sorbière (1643). On the growing awareness in the seventeenth century that utopian works formed a series see Benrekassa (1980, 127).

48. Campbell (1988, 221).

49. Cited in Campbell (1988, 221). Cf. chap. 4, n. 23.

50. *The anatomy of melancholy. What it is, with all the kinds, causes, symptomes, prognostickes, & several cures of it . . . philosophically, medicinally, historically, opened & cut up, with a satyricall preface* (London, 1621). See Burton 1932.

51. Frye (1966a, 311–12).

52. Davis (1981, 88); cf. generally, ibid., 86–104.

53. Burton (1932, 1:98). More ominously, perhaps, the cure involved using such places to relieve England's overpopulation (ibid., 3:246); prefiguring developments in Australia a century and a half later. He specifies, moreover, that the ideal land should be at about 45°S latitude.

4. Baroque Allegories

1. Hall 1605. Published in Latin in Frankfurt (and again in Hanau in 1607), it was translated by Hall's Cambridge colleague John Healey in 1609. That text is in Brown 1937, and a new translation is by Wands (1981).

2. Cf. Brown 1937; Wands (1981, xxv–lviii); Zucchini (1976, 248–75).

3. In a later work based on the travel theme, *Quo vadis?* (1617), Hall warns merchants "lest they go so far, that they leave God behind them" (cited in James 1982, 69).

4. Translated by John Florio in 1603. Cf. Frame 1948; Cro (1990, chap. 1).

5. He first introduced into England "genuine satire of a moral and dignified type, after the ancient Latin model of Juvenal and Persius" (Anderson 1908, x–xi; cf. also

Morley 1885, 267). Earlier Continental works of the type were Erasmus's *In Praise of Folly* (1511) and Sebastian Brandt's *Ship of Fools* (1494).

6. Brown (1937, xvii) considers Mercurius Britannicus "a combined anti-Catholic and anti-Calvinist." On other sects Hall aimed at see Brown (197f.); Lascassagne (1972, 141–56).

7. The pen name of a real theologian, Franciscus Junius. Cf. n. 14.

8. Cf. those of *Don Quixote* (1605); Ariosto's Roland (parodied in Greene's *Historie of Orlando Furioso*, 1594); Thomas Nashe's *Unfortunate Traveller* (1594); or more ribald examples in the works of Rabelais and Poggio Bracciolini. In addition, Hall followed rhetorical and aesthetic theories of Horace, Juvenal, and others and partook of the Menippean tradition discussed earlier. See Salyer (1927, 240–51); Zucchini (1976, 266–72).

9. Rabelais had made a similar suggestion for the walls of Paris (Zucchini 1976, 257).

10. A motif also central to Hall's *Characters of Virtues and Vices* (1608), inspired by Theophrastus.

11. This system is compared to Italy's being a "leg" of Europe; cf. also n. 22.

12. According to Zucchini (1976, 263n), Hall's model here was *L'ospitale de' pazzi incurabili* (Piacenza, 1586) by Tommaso Garzoni da Bagnacavallo, a satire on aristocratic greed and waste translated in 1600 as *The Hospital of Incurable Fooles*.

13. Hall (1937, 99), referring to Essex, Sussex, and Middlesex.

14. The pen name of François Brouart (1556–ca. 1629), a Huguenot who converted to Catholicism. He wrote an *Idée de la République* (1584) in imitation of *Utopia*, *De la sagesse* (1593), and (anonymously) *Le Moyen de parvenir* (1610), works that Zucchini (1976, 254n) links to the *Mundus*. On Béroalde and Arthus and their positive views on knowledge and education (particularly for women) see Zinguer (1982, 60–77). Cf. also Hall's *Virgidemiae* (1597–1598), a work along the lines of Aristophanes's *Ecclesiazusae* (Assembly of women) of ca. 393 B.C., and the popular *City of Ladies* by Christine de Pisan, translated in 1521 (Esdaile 1912, xxii).

15. He may also have been in contact with Franciscus Junius; see n. 7.

16. Cited in Slessarev (1959, 70) from an early printed version of the *Letter*.

17. Campbell (1988, 110, 154n).

18. Brown (1937, xxiii). Cf. also Wands, who anachronistically calls the continent Antarctica or the South Pole. The view that Australia had little economic value arose only later in the century; see Blainey (1985, 7).

19. Cf. Dames (1967, 175, 186, 196, 205–7). The *Books* of Duarte Barbosa and Tomé Pires discussed such questions from the early sixteenth century; those of Rebelo, Eredia, or Dutch writers, from later in that century: see chap. 2.

20. Hall observes, in the preamble, that "our Drake and our Candish" (Thomas Cavendish) and other circumnavigators had "put girdles about the whole world."

21. He is widely viewed as a sixteenth-century man—closer to More, Erasmus, or Hooker (author of *The Ecclesiastical Polity*, 1593/7) than to contemporaries such as Milton. Cf. Wands (1981, xx); McCabe 1982.

22. As noted by Dubois (1974), who adds that "Guillaume Postel, in his *Compendium*, associates the geography of Europe with the feminine form." Postel (1510–

191

1591) was interested in the question of world unity, and his works (such as *Les très merveilleuses victoires des femmes du nouveau monde*) may have influenced Hall. See Bouwsma 1957.

23. Raleigh's *Discoverie of the Large, Rich and Bewtiful Empire of Guiana, with a Relation of the Great and Golden City of Manoa (which the Spaniards call El Dorado)...* appeared in 1596. His Virginia colony was founded in 1592, and John Healey joined it in 1609 (the year his translation of the *Mundus* was published). Hall mentions as well an offshoot of the Virginia colony, a Canadian project of 1597.

24. Cf. Elaide (1978, 20–22); and chap. 3, n. 20.

25. On its editions, critical reception, and the question of its authorship, see Brown (1937, xxvii–xxx); Wands (1981, lii–liv). Gabriel Naudé mentioned it in his *Bibliographia politica* (1641), and Bayle (1697) devoted an article to Hall.

26. Hall (1669, 5–6, 63). A Land of Parrots (*psittaci* in Latin) appeared on maps of the southern continent (see plate 11). The other work mentioned is *Travels through terre australis incognita, discovering the laws, customs (...) of the south Indians; a novel. Originally in Spanish* (London, 1684).

27. Perhaps via Andreae, thinks Cioranescu (1962, 157). Hall may have influenced, too, a legal allegory, Richard Bernard's 1626 *Isle of Man... or the legall proceedings in Manshire against sinne* (Esdaile 1912, xxiii).

28. Milton feared the parodic element inherent in utopism and sought to uphold referential literality; "no man of the seventeenth century, and no great man of whatever time, was less fitted by temperament or position to appreciate *Mundus alter et idem*." (Brown 1937, xxxii). See also Frye 1966b.

29. Arthus 1605 (see bibliog., Primary Texts). References here are to the 1724 edition. See n. 30 on the date of the original.

30. Zinguer (1982, 60) notes of this "parisien né vers le milieu du seizième siècle ... d'une famille honorable" that he was a historian and translator. Zinguer gives (91–92) a bibliography of his works, and refers to René Muffat, "L'Auteur de l'Anti-Hermaphrodite, et son livre (1606)" (*Bulletin de la Société de Saintonge* 3 [1880–1882]: 418). The "Notice to the Reader" in the 1724 edition states that the work was "only" published in 1605 (perhaps implying that it circulated earlier) and that Henri IV had it read to him and thought it dangerous but did not take any action against the author.

31. Bayle (1697, 1,000). The Valois king, Henry III (son of Henri II and Catherine de Médicis), reigned 1574–1589.

32. Arthus (1724, 24).

33. "The more bizarre features of the king's personal behaviour, mixing debauchery and ostentatious religious fervour, won him few friends, while the appearance of a new group of royal favourites, the mignons, added to the factional rivalries at court" (Briggs 1977, 26).

34. Goubert (1973, 187). See also, on the sorry end to Henri's reign, Treasure (1981, 1–4).

35. Arthus (1724, 30–31, referring to second-century Roman emperors).

36. Ibid., 31–36.

37. This emphasis on freedom of the will recalls Rabelais's Abbaye de Thélème

(Abbey of the will) in *Gargantua* 57 (1532), with its motto "Fais ce que vouldras," or "Do your thing."

38. Arthus (1724, 40). The Gnostics were early Christian mystics.

39. Ibid., 45–49.

40. Ibid., 53–57.

41. Ibid., 58–61. Cf. note 14: a similarly caustic tone is evident in Béroalde de Verville's *Moyen de Parvenir* (1610).

42. Arthus (1724, 61)

43. Ibid., 63–65.

44. Ibid., 66. Solon was one of the Seven Sages of antiquity; Lycurgus, the founding lawgiver of Sparta. Plato perfected his social philosphy after attempting (unsuccessfully) to put it into practice for the Sicilian tyrant Dionysius of Syracuse.

45. Ibid., 72–75.

46. Ibid., 96–97. Cf. techniques of celestial navigation, an analogy that recalls, too, the ancient Oriental and other sources for heliocratic metaphors discussed earlier.

47. Ibid., 124.

48. Ibid., 142–43.

49. The area between Sumatra and Java is called "la Sonde" in French; this usage suggests a local or other source.

50. Arthus (1724, *Discours de Jacophile,* 169). These "reasonable animals" may be the orang-utans that were beginning to fascinate Europe by this time.

5. Utopia and Seventeenth-Century Rationalism

1. "A History of the Great and Admirable Kingdom of Antangil, Hitherto Unknown to Historians and Cosmographers, Composed of 120 Beautiful and Fertile Provinces. With Descriptions of the Latter, of its Unparalleled Order, both Civil and Military; of the Education of its Youth and of its Religion." See I.D.M.G.T. 1616 (bibliog., Primary Texts). Some editions had an imprint pasted over the original (Saumur: Thomas Portau), indicating it was published at Leyden by Jean Le Maire (Cioranescu 1963, 17–25).

2. The *I* of his initials was interchangeable with *J* in early scripts, and he has been variously identified as Jean de la Montagne, a Touraine gentleman (Lachèvre 1968, 261f.); a Saumur Protestant, Joachim du Moulin (Van Wijngaarden 1932, 22); Jean de Moncy, a Saumur schoolteacher (Cioranescu 1963); or a nobleman and soldier named Jean du Matz (Africa 1979, 277).

3. The real Jacob Cornelius Neck (see chap. 2), whose account was published in 1601. Again, a Bay of Antongil on the coast of Madagascar had recently been named after its discoverer, the Portuguese Antão Gil: cf. Van Wijngaarden (1932, 13); Cioranescu (1963, 17); and chap. 6.

4. Or Sanché (Lachèvre 1968). The original text is unclear. A possible source here is the name "Anne de Sanzay, Comte de Magnagne" added to a map of ca. 1504 by the Portuguese cartographer Pedro Reinel. It is thought that this Protestant soldier, godson of the famous duke Anne de Montmorency, used the map during a

campaign in Algeria (Cortesão and Teixiera da Mota 1960, 25; Hamy 1896, 154).

5. Possibly signifying *passion de Quir,* the passion (whether in the prosaic or the biblical sense) of Quirós, whom the French called "Quir." As outlined in chap. 1, his *Requeste* was published in 1613 and again in French in 1617. *Antangil* presumably coincided with calls for the latter edition.

6. James (1982, 66). Cf. chap. 1 on the Australian "Land of Concord" named by Hartog in this same year, 1616.

7. If, however, the (not impossible) average figure of twelve thousand per town were supposed, the total population would be 144 million—the "apocalyptic" population of Foigny's Australia in 1676.

8. Lachèvre (1968, 262) calls the system a "fiscal inquisition." Van Wijngaarden (1932, 29) thinks the author was an admirer of Sully—Maximilien de Béthune, Duc de Sully (1560–1641), the Huguenot Superintendent of Finances under Henri IV, who restored France's economy by prudent housekeeping. There was, furthermore, a real such office in government and in the VOC at the time; that of Lord Fiscal.

9. Lachèvre notes (1968, 263–64) that "the work aroused not the slightest emotion" among critics. Berneri (1950, 175) thinks it "without doubt the dullest French utopia of the seventeenth century," a view shared by Africa 1979.

10. On the troubled regency of his widow, Marie de Médici, see Treasure (1981, 97–107). Louis XIII and the Infanta, Anne of Austria, were married (both aged fifteen) in 1615.

11. "Column of faith and piety," according to Lachèvre (1968, 262). His interpretation (like that of Antangil as meaning "celestial grace") is rejected by Cioranescu (1963, 17) as "pure fantasy."

12. Slessarev 1959.

13. I.D.M.G.T. (1616, bk. 5, chap. 16).

14. Cf. Van Wijngaarden (1932, 40); Lachèvre (1968, 265).

15. Lachèvre (1968, 267). Cf. also Africa (1979, 189–93).

16. Van Wijngaarden (1932, 45); adding that the author was a "backward" thinker (*un retardataire*)—a reformist, not a revolutionary.

17. As does Lichtenberger 1895, or Van Wijngaarden 1932.

18. Van Wijngaarden (1932, 26).

19. Cf. chap. 3 and Kaufmann (1961, 65n).

20. See Kaufmann (1961, chap. 2).

21. In *a Jovial Crew* (1641), one of the last plays staged before the closure. In dedicating *The Antipodes* to the Earl of Hertford, he pleads, "If it meet with too severe construction, I hope your protection." The edition cited is that of Haaker 1966.

22. Cf. Davis 1943.

23. Terms such as *terra australis, nuper inventa sed nondum cognita* (recently discovered but not yet known) still appeared on maps at this time. The "semantic warp" undergone by this concept is discussed in chaps. 3 and 11. Cf., too, the "discovery" made by the original Peregrine, a Cynical philosopher said by Lucian to have set himself on fire at an Olympic Games, expecting those present to intervene, but none did.

24. *The Antipodes* was probably also influenced by Jonson's masque, *News from the New World Discovered in the Moon,* performed before King James in 1620. It reviews

traditions of "other worldly" satirical inversion and mentions, for example, Menippus and an Isle of Epicoenes (hermaphrodites).

25. Cited in Haaker (1966, xv). Shaw (1980, 122) notes of *The Antipodes* that "the effect is as if the audience were standing with its back to a large mirror and seeing what is reflected in it over its shoulder by using a second mirror held in the hand." Brome achieves this effect by means of a play within a play, or "byplay," a dramatic equivalent of the prose "story within a story." An actor in the play is named after this device.

26. By comparison with Jonson and other writers aiming at this effect, Brome's approach is seen as a relatively sympathetic, subtle, or seductive one; cf. Shaw (1980, 32); Kaufmann (1961, 60); Haaker (1966, xix–xx); Donaldson (1970, 97).

27. Possibly a reference to William Laud, bishop of London and archbishop of Canterbury, and a focus of Puritan moralism.

28. Cf. a real case, the philosopher Thomas Hobbes (who was about two years older than Brome).

29. Brome (1966, 15). He imagines that they have three sons who are great travelers — "that one shook the Great Turk by the beard" (ibid., 19).

30. Probably a reference to relations between Charles I and Laud.

31. Andrews (1913, 117).

32. Haaker (1966, 36).

33. Plymouth, Massachusetts, had recently been settled, and Quakers would soon leave for Pennsylvania. Brome also takes this opportunity to reject the capitalist "projects" by then in vogue as offering any moral salvation.

34. Donaldson (1970, 85–86), who sees Brome's usage of the theme as formulaic (by contrast with Jonson, for whom such devices were a secondary consideration). He emphasizes (78–86) the comic, rather than satirical, aspect of expressions such as "to act the antipodes" or medical metaphors for dramatic catharsis (boil lancing, purging, "humors" comedy, etc.). For Kaufmann, too (1961, 61), "*The Antipodes* is not quite successful, for there is an intellectual awkwardness, a loss of proper proportion that attacks Brome whenever he becomes too abstract or intellectual. He thought in terms of actable metaphors."

35. Brome (1966, 106). Cf. Ovid's Hermaphrodite, born of a possessive fusion.

36. Haaker (1966, xix–xx). Cf. also Kaufmann (1961, 66): "Our preoccupation with the obviously 'escapist' aspect of much Caroline drama has blinded us to just how socially engaged the better plays were."

37. Shaw (1980, 122).

38. Cf. the discussion of More's *Utopia* in chap. 3 (n. 36). Apart from the sources mentioned earlier, Bacon, Rabelais, and Lucian also influenced Brome (Shaw 1980, 118, 126–29).

39. Bacon (1857, 3:139–41).

40. Cf. Armytage 1961; Davis (1981, chap. 6); Tuveson 1949; Cohn 1957; Lasky 1977; Manuel and Manuel 1979.

41. See Armytage (1961, 8–12). The name "Antilia" appears in Alfonse 1559. Robert Boyle (a chemist) promoted such schemes while a related trend, Rosicrucianism, was promoted by the Platonist Robert Fludd. Anabaptists, too, proclaimed that the

Scriptures were mere allegory and spiritual perfection could be attained on earth through man's will. A Dutch offshoot was the Family of Love under David Joris; another Dutchman, Henry Niclaes, set up Familist groups in England and was immortalized by Bunyan in *Pilgrim's Progress* (1678).

42. *A Description of the famous Kingdom of Macaria; shewing its excellent Government* . . . London: Francis Constable, 1641.

43. Gott 1902. Cf. chap. 4, n. 28, on Milton's relationship with utopism. That with Puritanism, too, was increasingly problematical as he came to identify commerce as the cause of man's fallen state.

44. See Pocock 1977.

45. Both motives lingered on, however. In 1661 Hartlib, who had fostered Commonwealth utopism, declared that "of the Antilian Society the smoke is over, but the fire is not altogether extinct." A new Macaria, by the Dutch Mennonite Pieter Plockhoy, proposed a colony in Bermuda for persecuted churchmen (like himself). See Armytage (1961, 9).

46. However, similar fantasies included Madeleine de Scudéry's "Carte de Tendre" (in *Clélie,* 1654), an allegorical mapping of sentiments such as love and friendship somewhat recalling Hall's *Mundus* (see Filteau 1980), François d'Aubignac's *Relation du royaume de coquetterie* (1655), or Charles Sorel's *Description de l'isle de portraiture* (1659).

47. Cioranescu (1974, 441–48) considers its futurism more decorative than significant. A closer forerunner of futurism is Samuel Madden's *Memoirs of the 20th Century* (London, 1733).

48. Demoris (1975, 53).

49. In Godwin's *Man in the Moone* the Lunarian language is to be tonal (in Chinese fashion) and can be reduced to musical notation. See Cornelius (1965, 25–38).

50. Cited in Cornelius (1965, 34n), who notes his influence on Wilkins.

51. *Praeadamitae . . .* (1655), cited in Cornelius (1965, 66).

52. Cornelius (1965, 56n–57n).

6. Real and Imaginary Voyages

1. Bontekoe (1929, 1). The work had gone through nineteen editions by 1708, and extracts appeared in French in Thévenot (1663, 1672, 1695).

2. Geyl (Bontekoe, 1929, 5) notes that "the system of Councils, which pervaded the whole service of the Company as it did the government of the Dutch Republic, encouraged methods of deliberation and consultation rather than of command." Roland Barthes compares a ship to a society "closed without remission" — a "superlative house" (cited in Leibacher-Ouvrard [1989a, 439]).

3. Bontekoe (1929, 34). Cf. chap. 5, n. 3.

4. Ibid., 36–37. Cf. n. 19.

5. Ibid., 48. The latter detail appears in a similar incident in the *Vergulde Draeck* saga (see chap. 7).

6. Probably Engano, fifteen miles off southern Sumatra (Geyl 1929, 54n).

7. Ford (1920, 19).

8. Three separate editions by Jacob Vinckel, Amsterdam; Jacob Stichter, Amsterdam; and Joannes Naeranus, Rotterdam.

9. At least four editions. The Royal Printer, Cramoisy, printed a four-page summary translated from the Dutch and dated Amsterdam, July 19, 1668. It added details not found in other editions, such as locating the island "below the equinoctial line" (title page) or at "XXVIII or XXIX degrees of Antarctique latitude" (in the text, possibly reflecting associations with the *Batavia* disaster). Another edition was translated from the English; it has no imprint, but Ford speculates that it was printed in Amsterdam in 1668. Winter 1978 mentions another, the *Voyages du sens commun à l'isle d'Utopie* (1668); and a *Relation fidelle et véritable de la nouvelle découverte d'une quatrième isle de la Terre Australe . . . sous le nom d'Isle des Pins* (Leyden, 1668) is mentioned in Headicar and Fuller 1931.

10. Ford gives at least five 1668 editions: Frankfurt (based on the Dutch translation); Hamburg (from the English); Munich (from a French version); one in Strasbourg based on the English, Dutch, and French versions; another at Breslau, claiming to be from the English but probably closer to the Dutch; and one of uncertain origin. In addition, J. G. Schoeben's translation (Lüneburg, 1668) of Jean Mocquet's influential *Voyages en Afrique* (1616) included a somewhat free version of "the story of Joris Pines, quite notorious at Lisbon" (Ford [1920, 18]; who notes that Schoeben claimed to have met one of the Pines family, "all regarded as notable seamen," while at Lisbon en route to the West Indies).

11. Giacomo Didini, Bologna and Venice (a translation of the Cramoisy version, also dated Amsterdam, July 19, 1668).

12. Cambridge, Mass.; "probably by Marmaduke Johnson," notes Ford. The latter refutes (1920, 3–10, 20–29) an early view that the original edition had also appeared in Massachusetts. The mention "Printed by S. G." in its imprint was assumed to refer to Samuel Green, university printer at Harvard and Marmaduke Johnson's father-in-law and professional rival (a rivalry in which the American edition was embroiled), whereas the real S. G. was a London printer.

13. The position of Madagascar although Ford mentions (1920, 26–28) some islands with names similar to "Pines" southwest of Cuba and in the Darien region (which contributed to the theory of an American first edition).

14. Ford (1920, 40–41). The shock effect of the initial "news" had by then, it seems, worn off; the piece was recognized as conveying no new information about the Southland.

15. As is indicated at the end of the story, this is adjacent to St. Helena, that is, on the other side of Africa. A similar confusion and the name Del Principe itself in the outward voyage in Foigny's *La Terre Australe connue* suggest a debt to the *Isle of Pines* as do the themes of a violent storm and the "merciless element of water" that are emphasized here.

16. Cf. (chap. 10) a similar phrase in *Krinke Kesmes.*

17. This reflects libertine arguments that an appeal to biblical authority in enforcing a moral code was hypocritical, particularly in relation to incest because descent from Adam implied that incest had once been practiced. Again, a problem raised by

early contact with tribal societies was whether they should be regarded as living in pagan sin. Structures such as clan endogamy were interpreted as incest or even bestiality, yet primitivists could refute this both on the formal grounds mentioned and by showing the relative felicity of savage life.

18. Arcadian, cornucopian, or primitivist elements were often ironically intended in such works as a satire on the author's own society (cf. chap. 3). Ford (1920, 47) notes, as possible sources for Neville, Thomas Nashe's satirical play *The Isle of Dogs* (1597), for which he was imprisoned and tortured, or John Day's *Isle of Guls* (1606). Other likely influences are the works of Hall and Arthus.

19. Cf. n. 4.

20. He was seen as "a man of good parts, yet of a factious and turbulent spirit" (Ford 1920, 31). His interest in Machiavelli formed a link between English republicanism and its humanist forebears; see Davis (198) and, on Machiavelli's influence on later theorists such as Rousseau, Cro (1990, 28–30, 138–42).

21. It seems, particularly with the bowsprit episode, that Pines is an anagram for penis: a point made at the time by the anonymous M.M.G.N.S. (see n. 24). Ford (1920, 38–39) adds that "Sloetten" too "suggests a somewhat forceful English word — slut." Again, "Cornelius" may suggest a horn, whether in the anatomical sense or in that of a cornucopia (horn of plenty).

22. Cf. Aldridge (1950, 464–72); Ford (1920, 48). In this connection too, it is worth asking whether *pines* was not an anagram of *espin* or Spinoza, whose ideas of a natural basis for ethics were by this time undermining traditional theology.

23. Neville's political and literary career, indeed, resembles in some ways that of Hall (who died when Neville was thirty-six).

24. Defoe did, however, quickly produce a sequel involving women, the *Further Adventures of Robinson Crusoe*.

25. Ford (1920, 39–40), stressing the absence of "keys to a Utopian intention." Aldridge (1950, 465) calls the work "one of the most successful literary hoaxes in the English language." Apart from the thirty-odd editions already mentioned, there was a refutation by an anonymous German author, M.M.G.N.S. (Hamburg, 1668); a Bremen thesis on it (1674); Danish reeditions in ca. 1690, 1710, 1713, 1720, 1721, and 1733; a French translation by Prévost (1737); and an edition in J. C. L. Haken's collection of Robinsonades (Berlin, 1805–1808).

26. "I would apologize for taking so much time over a nine-page hoax did it not offer something positive in the history of English literature. It has long been recognized as one of the more than possible sources of Defoe's *Robinson Crusoe*" (1920, 48). But as will be argued, "Defoecentrism" has tended to distort the analysis of many earlier imaginary voyages.

27. Cf., too, later variations on the theme: in *Eutopie* (1711), by François Lefebvre, a French merchant founds a full-scale society — a Catholic theocracy — on an island in the Indian Ocean after coming to grief there with his daughter. Schnabel's *Insel Felsenburg* (1731) is populated by a single hero, and in Tiphaigne de la Roche's *Histoire des Galligènes* (1765) an island population descends from the son and daughter of a Huguenot shipwrecked there. Another example was Grivel's *Ile Inconnue, ou Mémoires*

du Chevalier de Gastines (1783). The providential bowsprit or spar forms a leitmotiv throughout this tradition.

28. Schooten 1671. 1671 is mentioned as the date of publication in the title of an edition "reprinted in the Year 1766, and Sold by J. Spilsbury, in Russel-Court, Covent-Garden." The original edition is cited here without pagination.

29. The strait discovered by Le Maire and Schouten at Cape Horn in 1616; see chap. 2.

30. Cf. (chap. 7) the *Witte Valck* (White falcon), a ship involved in the search for the *Vergulde Draeck* survivors.

31. The words *Banks, Adventure,* and *Discovery* in these passages are interesting and may be related to the fact that the imprint of the British Library copy is cropped as is elaborated below.

32. On the Patagonian giants allegedly seen or described by Olivier du Noort, Willem Schouten, Spilbergen, Drake, and others at the tip of South America, cf. Adams (1962, chap. 2); Duchet (1977, 61).

33. A breed of shaggy dog.

34. *Cassanack* may refer to cassava, a West Indian tuber made into flour and bread. Such ideas are found in utopias as early as the Hellenistic sun states discussed in chap. 3.

35. Others have explained the enigma by assuming that Drake was at the cape itself, or at the adjacent islets of Diego Ramirez. Cf. Morris (1987, 52); Stommel 1984.

7. Shipwreck and Marooning in the Southland

1. See Green (1977, 23–60) for background research by Lous Zuiderbaan de Vries; also Henderson (1982).

2. See Henderson (1982, 52). This error may have been deliberate; latitude was relatively easy to calculate, and there was plenty of time to do so (cf. n. 22).

3. Netherlands Archives, cited in translation in Green (1977, 50).

4. Ibid., 51–53; noting that these letters, written on May 5 and 7, 1656, "are the first and only mention of any written record at the time of the loss. . . . It is a pity these letters were never found again, for they would probably have given more information about the place where the ship was wrecked and what happened to the survivors in those first ten days on the Southland." They do, however, tell us that the pinnace crew left at least nine days after the shipwreck.

5. Batavia Council, cited in translation in Henderson (1982, 63).

6. Ibid. Van Riebeeck had shown similar anxieties: "As we hope not to have to doubt your zeal" (cited in translation in Green 1977, 53). Local piracy, too, may have been a threat.

7. Henderson (1982, chaps. 9, 10). Reports of the episode referred variously to "the two galliots" or "the two fluyts."

8. Ibid., 73–75; Green (1977, 54).

9. In the view of Henderson (1982, 75–83).

10. Ibid., 86. Cf. Green (1977, 57), "Strange enough it was in this period that Jonck sent the boat ashore."

11. Jonck's log, cited in translation in Henderson (1982, 86), who adds that it "did not pose the obvious question of whether this could be signals of the sixty-eight lost survivors of the *Vergulde Draeck.*" Again, men had been lost from the *Goede Hoop* a few miles to the south; even the two from the *Batavia,* marooned thirty years earlier about 120 miles to the north, could have been in the area if still alive.

12. Henderson (1982, 89), who is sceptical about these details. Aboriginals are assumed to have been, as in recent times, nomadic. But Jonck showed the "three inhabitants' houses" on his chart at 30° 25'S, adding in his journal (ibid.) that "the appearance of the inhabitants of the Southland we understand to be as follows: The men are of robust build, naked except for their genitals which are a little covered, with a crown on their heads; very black." Stone buildings were, as mentioned earlier, built on that coast during the *Batavia* episode.

13. Or, according to Henderson (1982, 95–96), twenty-two.

14. Volkersen, cited in translation in Henderson (1982, 96). Leeman himself recorded that "a pine plank 2.5 to 3 metres long had been placed upright in the ground, supported by 12 or 13 similar planks standing at an angle"; his party dug to a depth of about four feet in the spot, but found nothing (cited in Henderson 1982, 114). The pieces of a boat, notes Henderson, were probably from the *Draeck*'s second boat, which had been wrecked in the surf.

15. Volkersen's log, cited in Henderson (1982, 100). At this time, however, the *Emeloordt* was landing her boat on the coast only a few score miles to the north (cf. n. 10).

16. Volkersen prepared for the VOC a report on this island and the adjacent coast: "Description of the Southland by the Captain, Samuel Volkersen." Henderson (1982, 101–2) thinks it was probably Leeman's work. It mentions, for example, "high sand dune downs covered with grass and sand so deep that in walking one's foot is buried ankle-deep and leaves great traces behind it." (Cf. chap. 10 on the "Friday" motif in *Krinke Kesmes* and *Robinson Crusoe*; Smeeks's hero, the El-ho, is supposed to have been aboard the *Waeckende Boey*).

17. Leeman, cited in translation in Henderson (1982, 118).

18. Volkersen, cited in translation in Henderson (1982, 106–7).

19. See Henderson's reconstruction from Leeman's diary, using modern knowledge of the coast (ibid., chap. 15).

20. Such details and Leeman's leadership echo the epic voyage of Bontekoe (see chap. 6).

21. He is the only known candidate for a real basis in these events of the cabin boy in *Krinke Kesmes* (see chap. 10).

22. Cited in translation in Henderson (1982, 153–54). Green (1977, 59) notes that the outcome of this trial is unknown, but "their sentences cannot have been heavy, as before he died in October, Volkersen was still Captain of the *Waeckende Boey.*" Leeman was of English extraction; his name, van Santwits, deriving from Sandwich in Kent. Henderson speculates (109) that his family may have fled from Habsburg persecution in the Low Countries in the sixteenth century.

23. This ship spent eighteen days near Cape Naturaliste. A shore party reported seeing aboriginals wearing skins, "like the southern Africans." But "these valuable contributions were not incorporated in the maps of the following years, perhaps because of the disgrace of a skipper who marooned an officer and thirteen sailors on the Southland" (Henderson 1982, 155).

24. Cited in translation in Green (1977, 60).

25. Wouter Schouten, *Oost-indische Voyagie* . . . (Amsterdam: J. Meurs, 1676). There is no English translation; the present extract is my translation of the French version (Schouten 1708, 1:40–51). I have italicized words or phrases to emphasize Schouten's divergences from the first-hand accounts.

26. This seems to contradict the account of Leeman's landing but to conform to those from the *Goede Hoop* or the *Emeloordt*.

27. That is, neither the eleven from the *Goede Hoop* nor Leeman's fourteen; perhaps Schouten is not counting the boy referred to in n. 21. As will be seen, other literary evidence also points to the presence somewhere in these events of a castaway youth.

28. In preparing for the journey, Schouten says they stocked the boat with these and caulked it; but neither detail is mentioned by Leeman. Later, he says, "the seaslugs went bad, and there was no way of eating them: so that no sustenance remained except water." In fact, Leeman's men had food but could not eat it because of a lack of water.

29. Cf. the various accounts of the presence of aborigines.

30. The rank of second officer or understeersman was that of the unknown skipper of the *Vergulde Draeck*'s boat, not that of Leeman, who was an uppersteersman, or first officer.

31. In Leeman's account three had by now died, leaving only eleven, of whom seven could swim.

32. Mataram was the name of the town, not the title of the "emperor" (who was only a local sultan).

33. See Henderson 1982; Major 1859.

34. Henderson (1982, 170–71); noting that castaways would have gone inland to search for birds and water. The *Vergulde Draeck*'s second officer had mentioned that, as he left for Batavia, those left behind were about to do so (see n. 4).

35. Henderson (1982, 160).

36. On the 1972 excavation and reconstruction of the wreck see Henderson (1982, chaps. 20–22); and Green 1977.

37. Cf. Henderson (1986, 93–94).

38. Cited in translation in Green (1977, 51), my italics.

39. Ibid. 45–48.

40. Green (1977, 43, 48–49, 53) mentions his being signed on; being among the survivors; reaching Batavia with their letters; and being sent back with the *Witte Valck-Goede Hoop* mission. The latter was instructed to chart the coast "with particular attention . . . , so that we can use that for the benefit of the Company's Indian trade, for which purpose the aforementioned understeersman of the *Draeck* will sail thither at once."

41. In 1695 the Heren XVII wrote to Batavia, "who knows whether in those lands some of the people which have saved themselves from the *Vergulde Draeck* may not still be alive and may be found" (cited in translation in Schilder 1985, app. 5). Cf. also ibid., app. 6 (an extract from a resolution of the Amsterdam Chamber advising further Southland exploration) and 2, 57, 85.

42. *Journal of a Voyage Done by Order of the Dutch East India Company . . . to the Unknown South Land, and onward to Batavia.* See Schilder (1985, 74).

43. Grey, George. *Journals of Two Expeditions of Discovery in North-West and Western Australia . . .* Cited in McIntyre (1977, 77–81), who adds that another figure resembled "a medieval portrayal of a saint or other religious figure, complete with halo, medallion, draped garments with sleeves and armbands. Its style is almost Byzantine (and) the face is white. . . . Grey immediately thought of European contacts."

44. By Godinho de Eredia; in 1569 by Gabriel Rebelo, who had lived in the Moluccas; by Joao Alfonso, and others: see chap. 1. Uhden (1939, 10f.) mentions reports dating from the first Portuguese contacts of *homens brancos* (white men) to the south of Sumatra.

45. Schilder (1976, 129–30).

46. This expedition, in the *Heemskerck* and *Zeehaen,* is well documented. See Schilder (1976, 144f.).

47. Cited in Schilder (1976, 189n). Whether or not this referred to Tasmania or to Tasman's violent encounter at "Murderer's Bay" in New Zealand or to his reception in Tonga (cf. n. 48), its literary potential is evident.

48. Schilder (1976, 158–59, 163). A "Pacific legend" was similarly nourished by Tasman's visit to the Tonga group (earlier named the Friendly Islands by Schouten and Le Maire), where "contact with the friendly people and especially the abundance of food had a deleterious effect on discipline" (177).

49. Schilder (1976, 150). Montanus's work, *De Nieuwe en Onbekende Weereld: Of Beschryving van America en t'Zuid-land . . .* (Amsterdam: J. Meurs, 1671), was translated by J. Ogilby as *The unknown Southland in America, being the latest and most accurate description of the New World . . .* (London, 1671). Haelbos's own text is translated in Sharp (1963, 40–53).

50. Schilder (1976, 418), who quotes Goos from a 1668 English edition of his atlas: "Sith [since] the Coasts are but partly discovered, and that we have no knowledge of the inward Countreys, wee shall as yet them rest under Asia, til further discovery; and commend such a division to our posterity, if wee by our life gaine no more knowledge."

8. The *History of the Sevarites* (1675–1679)

1. Vairasse 1675. The publisher, Henry Brome, was no relation of the playwright Richard Brome.

2. Vairasse 1677. This version, earlier thought to be identical to the original (cf. Lachèvre 1968, 208), is longer and develops philosophical, linguistic, and sociological aspects. See also Cornelius (1965, 134n).

3. See Von der Mühll (1938, 256).

4. A biographical outline was published by the Huguenot Christian Thomasius (who may have known Vairasse) in *Freymüthige Vernunft und Götzmässige Gedanken über allerhand* . . . (Halle, Nov. 1689). It was referred to by the French critic Prosper Marchand in his *Dictionnaire historique* (The Hague, 1758) and later used by Georges Ascoli in "Quelques notes sur Denis Veiras d'Alais." (*Mélanges Lanson,* 1922). See Lachèvre (1968, 167f.).

5. A Catholic sect inspired by the Dutchman Jansenius and, ultimately, by St. Augustine. Their headquarters at Port-Royal near Paris brought together some of the age's most able grammarians and philosophers: Lancelot, Arnauld, and Pascal (see Marin 1975). Various aspects of Vairasse's thought can be compared (and, perhaps, even linked) to theirs.

6. It was known to Bayle, Leibniz, Locke, Montesquieu, Voltaire, Hume, Rousseau, Kant, and others; see Von der Mühll 1938. Racault (1991, 369–403) sees it as a "paradigm-text" for the subsequent literary development including the Robinsonade.

7. The real *Vergulde Draeck* departed on Oct. 4; nor does Apr. 12 correspond to any significant event in that saga.

8. The real date was Apr. 28. In Aug., however, a rescue mission likely to have generated a marooning on the Australian coast took place; see chap. 7.

9. Cf. Atkinson (1920, chap. 5); Von der Mühll 1938.

10. It also recalls the premarital inspection in More's *Utopia* or later avatars, such as the erotic schemes of Restif de la Bretonne or, in general, the contrast between Jansenist moral rigor and French mores, or between English Puritanism and Restoration licentiousness. Cf. Aldridge 1950.

11. Formerly a peninsula between two adjacent rivers, it had been severed by huge canals dug between them (in the manner of Utopus, but also recalling Paris and its Ile de la Cité). Significantly, Vairasse dedicated his French "First Part" to Riquet, the builder of the Canal du Midi and other engineering feats under Louis XIV. Apart from the prudence of associating himself with a powerful but politically anodyne figure (or the fact that Riquet was a compatriot from Languedoc), he contrives here again to blur the line between fact and fiction.

12. A satirical reference to the Sun-King, Louis XIV and, no doubt, also a pun implying a "king of vice." On the targeting of Louis XIV by utopias of this period, see Yardeni 1980; Leibacher-Ouvrard (1986, 1989).

13. Many such details were additions to the 1675 version and, suggests Atkinson (1920, 114), probably inspired by Foigny's work, which appeared between the First and Second parts.

14. Leibacher-Ouvrard (1989, 183n) associates the work's popularity with the two major influences on eighteenth-century exotism: the Chinese on social thought and the Inca on literature.

15. Thus the Giovannites, a sect based on the teachings of Giovanni, are tolerated even though they reject the official rationalism and maintain a traditional fideism. Siden compares them to Calvinists, and Von der Mühll (1938, 217–18) to the Mandaean gnostics, a Persian sect described by seventeenth-century travelers.

16. As does Atkinson (1920, 95–96).

17. At least eighty-one men could have been alive on the Australian coast by this time: two from the *Batavia,* sixty-eight from the *Vergulde Draeck,* and eleven from the *Goede Hoop.* Others may have survived the *Trial* disaster of 1622, and Portuguese had been active in the area since early in the sixteenth century. A prompt death was their most likely fate, but others such as integration with locals cannot be dismissed and at the time, certainly, could not be (cf. chaps. 7 and 10).

18. Cf. chap. 6, n. 32; chap. 4, n. 50.

19. Possibly an acquaintance of Vairasse and his source for the *Vergulde Draeck* story, notes Von der Mühll (1938, 62n). Another real person appropriated to the story (as Siden's companion Van-de-Nuits) is Pieter van Nuyts, who in 1627 was storm-driven one thousand miles across Australia's south coast.

20. Bourez notes (1984, 36) that two real Skinners could have been known, directly or indirectly, to Vairasse or, again, that Thomas Skinner and the letter may have simply been a means of referring to things that were common knowledge in Holland.

21. Von der Mühll (1938, 63n).

22. Von der Mühll (ibid.) was unable to resolve this question despite research. Van der Haert may have been a real Dutch acquaintance of Vairasse (Bourez 1984, 42), and he somewhat recalls Hendrik Haelbos, the ship's doctor on Tasman's expedition (see chap. 7) whose quasi-ethnographic account of the latter appeared in 1671, the year before Vairasse visited Holland. Suggestive too in this regard is the figure of Hendrik Smeeks, the doctor who wrote *Krinke Kesmes;* see chap. 10.

23. This was not known until 1934 when details of the "Tryal Rocks" were found in British Admiralty archives. Vairasse, however, may have had access to such information through his relations with Pepys (later head of the Admiralty) and others; he seems to have been something of a spy. Perhaps, too, the name Thomas Skinner may be associated with the fact that a boat reaching Batavia from the *Trial* was skippered by an officer named Thomas Bright. See chap. 2 and Schilder (1976, chap. 10).

24. Von der Mühll (1938, 61n) mentions another such case: around 1636 a Dutch ship was wrecked in a rocky bay on the coast of Madagascar. Its company of about five hundred built a boat in which half of them left for Batavia but soon perished. Those who stayed behind in a wooden fort were massacred except for two who joined the locals. Another possible source was John Narborough's voyage of 1669–1671. It was not published until 1694; but here again, Vairasse's official contacts may have given him inside access to such information.

25. On French perceptions of the Southland in this period see Garagnon (1982, n. 6).

26. Cf. Stafford (1984, 446): "Important linguistic developments occurred during the seventeenth and eighteenth centuries precisely because of the utilitarian requirement for an invisible or unobtrusive idiom. . . . Thus armed, writers and artists rose to meet the flood of incoming data." A later exponent of the new style was William Dampier, whose *New Voyage Round the World* (1697) went through five editions in six years and influenced Defoe, Swift, and others. See also Taylor (1938, 105); Von der Mühll (1938, 51).

27. Leguat 1708, Cf. Racault 1984; North-Coombes 1979. Leguat's text may have been retouched or plagiarized by another Huguenot, François-Maximilien Misson.

28. For example, by Atkinson (1922, 37).

29. See Cornelius (1965, 136–40); Pons 1932; Knowlson 1963, 1975. Leibacher-Ouvrard (1989, 29–37) notes the "*déterminisme pointilleux*" (punctilious determinism) of Vairasse (which, with Foigny, becomes literally "pointillist" as will be seen).

30. As mentioned earlier, Vairasse's rationalism may reflect his links with the Jansenists. The Port-Royal grammarians Lancelot and Arnauld had produced their influential *Grammaire générale et raisonnée* in 1660.

31. As Leibacher-Ouvrard notes (1989, 30).

32. Bourez (1984, 38) notes that, although the mystery has evaporated, "we can still take pleasure in the constant echoes that reality and fiction send each other. Modern criticism is interested in novelistic alchemy, the honest lie. Vairasse played that game well: between the real and the imaginary he kept his balance, sometimes with cunning and sometimes with malice, on the high wire of credibility." But has the mystery evaporated?

33. A mental process in which understanding derives from an overlaying of phenomena, revealing their common elements. Its significance for modern social history has been analyzed in particular by Michel Foucault. As noted earlier, its roots can be traced to a crisis in baroque aesthetics (cf. chap. 5, n. 48).

34. Leibacher-Ouvrard (1989, 186). Despite Vairasse's claim to originality, the seeds of this effect can be seen in More's *Utopia* as was discussed in chap. 3.

35. "Liminality" (cf. chap. 3, n. 24) is seen at various levels from the imaginary geography to the philosophical significance of discovery. The scenic and narrative progression from the margins to the center embodies a *mise en abyme* that facilitates the latter's realization on the planes of political, linguistic, and religious philosophy.

36. In 1669 Locke drew up for Shaftesbury a constitution for the colony of Carolina. Like Vairasse he had links with Holland (where he lived for five years from 1683).

37. There may be echoes in this, however, of contemporary English experience: the failure of republicanism to create an ideal commonwealth.

38. "Depuis ce tems-là quelques Personnes curieuses m'ont proposé plusieurs difficultez qu'ils pensoient y avoir trouvé; Mais comme ils n'en avoient lû que le commencement, ils ne disoient rien de solide sur ce sujet. Entre tous ceus qui s'en sont entretenus avec moy, et qui m'en ont parlé raisonnablement, un des plus savans Hommes de notre siècle, dont les Ecrits sont admirez de tous les gens habiles, tant à cause de la force de ses raisonnemens, et de la sublimité de ses pensées, que de la pureté de son style, me dit un jour, parlant de l'*Histoire des Sévarambes,* qu'il doutoit fort qu'elle fust véritable, parcequ'il ne croyoit pas qu'il y eût au Monde de si honnestes gens. En effet, si l'on considère avec soin les Mœurs, la Religion, le Gouvernement et la politesse de ces Peuples, comme toutes ces choses sont représentées dans ce Livre, on aura peine à croire qu'il y ait sur la terre une Nation si honneste et si vertueuse. Nous donnons au public le corps de cette Histoire feinte ou véritable, et nous prions le Lecteur d'excuser nos négligences et les fautes de l'impression" (Vairasse 1677, preface).

39. Lachèvre (1968, 168–71, after Ascoli).

40. Cf. Hourani (1951, 79–81). Beyond Sofala (in Mozambique) and Qanbalu (Madagascar) lay, according to legend, a Land of Waqwaq, of which two variants can be discerned: one in the region of Africa, the other in the Far East. The latter

has been identified with Sumatra (from which migrations to Madagascar took place early in the Christian era and again in the tenth century). But these identifications are conjectural; it seems at least possible that the eastern Waqwaq was Australia.

41. Ibid., 16, 98, 107. This may even have contributed to medieval associations of Solomon's Ophir with the eastern Indian Ocean (although it was more commonly linked with the western side or with India).

42. Vairasse (1787, 210).

9. Splendid Isolation: *The Southern Land, Known*

1. See the introduction to my translation of the original work (Fausett 1993a). An English translation was made in 1693, but from a bowdlerized version published in 1692 by, it is thought, the French deist François Raguenet. The history of the work has been clouded by confusion of these editions, which are quite different in philosophical orientation.

2. Foigny's geographical information was, in part, derived from two cosmographies by Gaston Jean-Baptiste, Baron de Renty (Paris, 1645, 1657). Again, a work at the center of the "Dieppe" enigma mentioned in chap. 2, Alfonse 1559, mentions a Trinity Island with quasi-magical details resembling those of Foigny although it was in the Caribbean. As noted, too, a major source for Foigny was the Hellenistic sun states.

3. A parody of the primitivism in vogue since the previous century (notably with the Spaniard Las Casas) and promoted by French missionaries in the seventeenth century. It often linked the nudity of native peoples to their supposed felicity (cf., for example, Fontenelle's *Lettre sur la nudité des sauvages,* 1690).

4. These metaphorical implications were discussed in Bayle 1697 ("Sadeur" article, 988–91; cf. also "Salmacis" and "Adam"). Literary sources for them included Plato's *Symposium* and Ovid's *Metamorphoses.* Comparable speculations of the time appeared in Thomas Browne's *Religio Medici* (London, 1635) and Antoinette Bourignon's *Le nouveau ciel et la nouvelle terre, contenant des merveilles inouies jamais vues ni declarées de personne* (Amsterdam, 1679). Cf. also Dubois (1987, 11–27).

5. Primitivism lent itself to developments in this ironical or satirical vein (as, for example, in Baron de La Hontan's *Dialogues with a Savage* of 1703). It occupied a rhetorical borderland between fact and fiction, which the utopian novel also exploited. A primitivist work that may have influenced Foigny was Juan de Palafox's *L'Indien ou portrait naturel des Indiens* (Paris, 1672), a tract against the Jesuit Reductions (a utopian or colonial regime imposed on the American Indians).

6. *Neutre* means in French both "neutral" and "neuter."

7. As mentioned in chap. 3, this was largely derived from Garcilaso de la Vega's account of the Inca religion and from reports of heliocracy or heliolatry in Asia.

8. Cf. chap. 5 and Cornelius (1965, 65–103, 112f.); Pons 1932; Knowlson 1963, 1975; Pellandra 1986; and Leibacher-Ouvrard (1989, 17–41). The idea of a *lingua humana,* or world-language, was largely inspired by the Chinese example as perceived by early Jesuit missionaries (or, for Leibniz, by his mathematical work ca. 1672–1676).

9. The name (*Fondins,* in the French) implies the fundament, or anus, and with it an "irrational" physicality.

10. See Ronzeaud (1982, 292, 301f.). This was a satire on the rise of mass warfare, particularly under Louis XIV (whose ideas of "solar" omnipotence derived in part from sources mentioned in n. 7 — a tradition that could be exploited in various ways).

11. Over the following decades an interiorization of the process of cultural dissolution, a "crisis of European consciousness" (Hazard 1953), formed a conceptual counterpart to the rise of political absolutism. It also underlay the epistemological advances later made by Kant, who theorized a process of "neutralizing" abstraction. See Marin (1985, 19–22).

12. Cf. Rousseau's fascination with written music, which also accompanied his interests in language and society.

13. See Pellandra (1986, 55–71). Leibacher-Ouvrard (1989, 31) notes that Comenius (cf. chap. 5, n. 50) had circumscribed the choices available to any creator of a new language: a radical break into artificiality, or a recasting of existing languages. Foigny opted for the first method, Vairasse the second. Cf. also Leibacher-Ouvrard, 1989, 24: the brevity of Foigny's exposition of his language shows that he knew what problems he would make for himself if he took it any further.

14. As noted, this is implicitly true of utopia in general — "formal logic is its referential signified." (Marin 1985, 10; cf. also Marin 1974, 777–82).

15. Cf. n. 1, for a fuller discussion of these problems.

16. As was observed by Patrick 1946.

17. Foigny (1993, chap 6).

18. Their annals are briefly mentioned together with a creation myth involving a primordial serpent, but these resemble more a parody of the biblical Creation than a history of origins in the modern sense.

19. "You cannot reconcile the use of reason with the exclusion of one of the sexes," insists Suains.

20. He decides, in effect, that it is "ours not to reason why; ours but to do and die" (as in the Charge of the Light Brigade, an event comparable to the Australians' wars).

21. Etymologically, the name recalls the Greek *ergon* (work) or the Latin *urgere* (to press, drive); in general, it evokes the overriding power of physical drives.

10. The *Mighty Kingdom of Krinke Kesmes* (1708)

1. Smeeks 1708. The title is translated by Hubbard (1921, xxiii) as "A Description of the Mighty Kingdom of KRINKE KESMES. Being one large, and many smaller Islands thereto belonging; Making together a part of the unknown. SOUTHLAND situated under the tropic of Capricorn. Discovered by Mr. Juan de Posos, and composed from his writings by H. Smeeks. Amsterdam, at Nicolaas ten Hoorn's, Bookseller, over the Old Gentlemen's Inn, 1708." Hubbard translated an extract from the work. My forthcoming edition of the first English translation is introduced by a fuller

version of the present study. Unless otherwise indicated, the edition cited here is Buijnsters 1976.

2. See Secord 1924; Peterson 1987; Buijnsters (1976, intro.).

3. Trousson's term (1975, 103), referring to a thematic set spanning the years 1675–1715. The present study further defines it as an austral set (exceptions are Claude Gilbert's 1700 *Histoire de Caléjava,* set in the Baltic region, and the *République des Philosophes ou Histoire des Ajaoiens,* a north Pacific utopia attributed to Fontenelle and dated in the 1690s).

4. The name is an anagram of Smeeks's own as was pointed out by Hoogewerff 1909.

5. The main thoroughfare for East Indies shipping, in the Zuider Zee. Cf. chap. 7, n. 41 on VOC speculations at the time.

6. Notably, in *Le Voyage et avantures de Jaques Massé* (ca. 1710–1717). See Rosenberg (1972b, 124n; Rosenberg 1972a, 96–102).

8. Although generally used to parody religious asceticism, this theme derived from real models, as mentioned earlier.

8. As pointed out by Hettner 1862 and others (see n. 13, 14).

9. See chap. 11. The same trend is seen in nonfictional austral voyages, notably that of Bontekoe, which Smeeks includes (170) among the effects left for the El-ho by his shipmates.

10. Cf. Hubbard (1921, xlviii); Goebel (1923, 302–13); Mulder (1923, 277–80). Secord (1924) considered *Krinke Kesmes* a "Utopia" that it was obscure in its time, a view questionable on both counts (cf. Buijnsters 1976, 51–52).

11. A point made by Hippe 1894.

12. Cited in Ford (1920, 57). Hubbard (1921, 75) regards this incident, furthermore, as corresponding to Defoe's introduction of Friday into his story.

13. Such views were expressed in Smeeks's time (see Staverman 1907, 53) and from 1892 (see Hubbard 1921, xxviii, xxix–xxx). Cf. also Hoogewerff (1909, 396–98); L'Honoré Naber (1910, 427–48); Polak (1914, 304–7).

14. Hubbard (1921, xliv) speculates on "a common source, which, unless it be Simplicissimus, is still to be discovered." This work, *Der Abenteuerlicher Simplicissimus* (Nürnberg, 1669) by Hans Jacob Christoffel von Grimmelshausen (writing as German Schleifhein von Sulsfort), was, like that of Neville the previous year, a product of the new fad for travel adventure.

15. Cf. chap. 8, n. 17. Again, survivors of the 1727 *Zeewijk* wreck in Houtman's Abrolhos found evidence of a previous European presence (albeit fairly recent). See Henderson (1982, 130–31).

16. See Henderson (1986, 30); Macknight 1976. Cf., too, local linguistic elements; thus, *poele* in "Poele Krinke Kesmes" is the Malay *pulau* (island). See Buijnsters (1976, 135n).

17. Cited in Buijnsters (1976, 265). Hoogewerff (1909) drew attention to the handwritten preface and discussed the debt to Schouten, concluding (385–92) that the cabin boy's story is textually distinct from the rest of the work and that it was the cause of both the accusation of "childishness" on the part of ten Hoorn and that of Spinozism, to be discussed.

18. See n. 9. Von der Mühll (1938, 64) speculates that "a hundred years after this catastrophe, which had evidently caused quite a stir, a man returns and relates what happened to the survivors" and adds, in a footnote (64n), "the *Golden Dragon* story is told by Wouter Schouten in his 'East-Indian Voyage' . . . and found later in a voyage, this time imaginary, by Hendrik Smeeks: 'The Mighty Kingdom of Krinke Kesmes or the Dutch Robinson' of 1708."

19. Nicolaas Witsen was mayor of Amsterdam, a VOC director and prime mover behind de Vlamingh's expedition in 1696, and the author of a work on Asia, *Nort en Oost Tartarye* (1705).

20. Cf. Von der Mühll (1938, 62n): "These slight differences between the manuscript [in the archives] and Vairasse's novel are probably due to the fact that he learnt of the story from oral sources." Some critics (cf. Winter 1978, 140–41) have assumed that Smeeks lifted the theme from Vairasse.

21. Major (1859, xcix–c); cf. chap. 7, n. 33. Major notes the skepticism with which foreign observers treated Dutch reports about the Southland: "The mystery which the Dutch make of the matter, and the difficulties they throw in the way of publishing what is known about it suggest the idea that the country is rich. But why should they show such jealousy with respect to a country which produces nothing deserving so distant a jouney?"

22. As mentioned earlier, portions are missing from the archives relating to the trials of the captains in the *Waeckende Boey* expedition. This and other elements of the story of the Dutch shipwrecks suggest possible discrepancies between the official record and the activities themselves.

23. See chap. 6. What Secord (1924, 96) calls the "unprecedented popularity" of *Robinson Crusoe* had, in fact, been preceded by that of the *Isle of Pines*.

24. Cf. Buijnsters (1976, 12–24); Rosenberg 1972a.

25. Hoogewerff (1930, 225–36).

26. Buijnsters (1976, n. 40).

27. Ibid., 19.

28. Cited in Buijnsters (1976, 22); cf. n. 17. Hubbard (1921, xxvi) notes that the Handex preface includes a note dated 1775, in a hand not Smeeks's (although signed "H. S."), which accuses him of "pernicious things concerning religion" and, specifically, of ridiculing two medical doctors, Bontekoe (not the sea captain) and Overkamp, who wrote on metaphysical topics.

29. As Buijnsters notes (1976, 25), "The most striking aspect of all is Smeeks's personal involvement with his book, which needs to be further researched." Buijnsters does not regard de Posos as a real person—unlike the Master, whom he considers (ibid., n. 51) to be an alter ego of Smeeks himself.

30. Staverman 1907, cited in translation in Hubbard (1921, xxix).

31. Hoogewerff (1909, 386–97). On approaches to the work in terms of Dutch Cartesianism see Buijnsters (1976, 56).

32. See Marana 1970. The change in translation from "Esploratore" (explorer) to "Spy" (*Espion, Spion*) may be related to the success of a work published the same year, *L'espion du Grand-Seigneur et ses Relations secrètes envoyées au divan de Constantinople,* and also recalls the activities of Vairasse and his friend Scott around this time (see chap. 8).

33. Naber (1910, 430–31). Cf. n. 29.
34. Hubbard (1921, xxxiii); cf. also Staverman 1925.
35. Secord (1924, n. 330).
36. Ibid., 96, 109.
37. Buijnsters (1976, 56).
38. Cf. the case of François Leguat, mentioned earlier.

11. Austral Fiction and the Rise of Realism

1. Cf. Tieje (1913, 213–52) and others to be discussed.
2. Cf. chap. 9, n. 11.
3. See Willey (1986, 23f.).
4. Watt (1977, 11–13, 31–32, 62). Cf. also Auerbach 1953.
5. Tieje (1913, 213–23). He correctly assessed *Simplicissimus* (see chap. 10, n. 14), but seems not to have realized that *The Isle of Pines* had begun the trend in question the year before.
6. Mylne (1965, esp. 31n).
7. Ibid., 8–10.
8. This style is also emphasized by Tieje and by Stewart 1969. Cf. also Showalter 1972.
9. Mylne (1965, 26–27). Cf. also chap. 5, n. 48.
10. Mylne (1965, 31).
11. For example Segrais, in *Nouvelles françoises* (1656, the year the *Vergulde Draeck* was wrecked) associated the genre with factual history and with the dilemma of narrative truth. For another study of the latter, see May 1963.
12. Mylne (1965, 18).
13. Hobson (1982, 43–44); adding that "only the greatest modern thinkers in aesthetics—Kant, Schiller, Hegel—relate these areas dialectically." Mylne (1965), too, discusses the trend toward readerly passivity. Cf. also chap. 5 on *The Antipodes;* these speculary alternatives are the ones that Brome has Peregrine and the Joyless couple act out.
14. As Hobson notes (1982, 89), prose fiction reflected this trend in a growing polarization of its basic elements, romance and history.
15. Ibid., 91, 11. Cf. also 82, 94: "'What is the status of what is offered in a novel?'—is it historical? and if it is not historical, is it untrue?—that is, false?" This is a problem "not so much causing us to make a mistake . . . (illusion as *adquatio*), as inducing doubt: perhaps it isn't a novel? perhaps it is more than a novel (illusion as *aletheia*)."
16. Ibid., 83; suggesting, too, that "the novel succeeds theatre, and precedes the film, as the art form felt to embody illusive appearance in its most dangerous and perhaps subversive form" (82).
17. Ibid.; adding that today, by contrast, we "neutralise this possibility of truth/falsehood by sending the novel to a critical vacuum, where we claim that the question true/false is naïve."

18. An interesting recent study on the year 1674 (Beugnot 1984) again lacks such a perspective.

19. Hobson (1982, 81).

20. Thus, for example, a pseudonymous critic (possibly Swift or Steele) observed early in the eighteenth century that "The word memoir is French for a novel." (Stewart 1969, 235).

21. Hobson (1982, 86).

22. Dumarsais-Fontanier's influential work on rhetorical figures, *Les Tropes,* appeared at this time.

12. The Body, the World, and the Word

1. "Observations," cited in Smith (1960, 64).

2. It is not possible to elaborate here on psychoanalytical theories about this process, except to note its quasi-spatial aspect (the infant becomes aware of configurations of objects and events and, by comparing them and ordering them into patterns, becomes able to objectify himself as a separate entity), and that this process, which Freud called *Bahnung* or trail blazing, is compared by him and other psychoanalysts to writing.

3. Cf., for example, Foucault (1972, chap. 10).

4. Or "stories of stories" (Hazard 1935, 33). Such works doubled, or closed off, history by describing a society whose history was contained in the description. In this way (and to the extent that the description was realistic) they exposed the fictional element in all history.

5. As Leibacher-Ouvrard notes (1989, 439).

Bibliography

Primary Texts

Alfonse (Alphonse) de Saintonge, Jean. 1559. *Voyages avantureux*. Poitiers: Jan Marnef.

Arias, Juan Luis. 1859. *A Memorial addressed to his Catholic Majesty Philip the Third, King of Spain, Respecting the Exploration, Colonization and Conversion of the Southern Land*. Translated by R. H. Major. [In Major 1859; see Secondary Texts.]

Arthus (Artus), Thomas, Sieur d'Embry. 1605. *Description de l'Isle des Hermaphrodites nouvellement découverte, contenant les Moeurs, les Coutumes & les Ordonnances des Habitants de cette Isle, comme aussi le Discours de Jacophile à Limne, avec quelques autres pièces curieuses. Pour servir de Supplément au Journal de Henri III*. N.p., ca. 1605 (National Union Catalogue) or 1605 (British Library Catalogue, noting a possible 1610 edition). A 1724 reedition has the imprint "Cologne: for the Heirs of Herman Demen" but was published in Brussels.

Bacon, Sir Francis. 1857. *The Works of Francis Bacon*. edited by J. Spedding, R. Ellis, and D. Heath. 14 vols. London, 1858–1874.

Beschryving van't onbekende Zuyd-land. 1701. (Description of the unknown Southland). Amsterdam.

Bontekoe, Willem Ysbrantsz. 1929. *Memorable Description of the East Indian Voyage, 1618–25*. Translated by C. B. Bodde-Hodgkinson and P. Geyl. Edited by Pieter Geyl. New York: McBride.

Brome, Richard. 1966. *The Antipodes*. Edited and with an introduction by Ann Haaker. Lincoln: Univ. of Nebraska Press.

Burton, Robert. 1932. *The Anatomy of Melancholy (1621)*. 3 vols. London: Dent.

Callander, John. 1768. *Terra Australis Cognita: Or, Voyages to the Terra Australis, or Southern Hemisphere during the Sixteenth, Seventeenth, and Eighteenth Centuries*. 3 vols. Edinburgh, 1766–1768.

Cavendish, Margaret. 1666. *The Description of a New World, Called the Blazing World*. Pt. 4 of *Observations upon Experimental Philosophy)*. London: Maxwell.

Dalrymple, Alexander. 1767. *An Account of the Discoveries made in the south Pacifick Ocean, previous to 1764*. Pt. 1. London: Author.

De Brosses, Charles. 1756. *Histoire des Navigations aux Terres Australes*. 2 vols. Paris: Durand.

De Bry, J. T., and J. I. De Bry. 1628. *Indiae Orientalis Historia*. 6 vols. Frankfurt am Main, 1598–1628.

Foigny, Gabriel de. 1676. *La Terre Australe connue: C'est à dire, La Description de ce paysinconnue jusqu'ici, de ses moeurs & de ses coûtumes. Par Mr. Sadeur. Avec les avantures qui le conduisirent en ce Continent, & les particularitez du sejour qu'il y fit durant trente-cinq ans & plus, & de son retour. Reduites & mises en lumiere par les soins & la conduite de G. de F.* Vannes, par Jaques Verneuil, rue S. Gilles. [The true place of publication was Geneva. The text is reproduced in Lachèvre 1968, Ronzeaud 1990, and Trousson 1981 (facsimile ed.).]

———. 1993. *The Southern Land, Known*. Edited, translated and with an introduction by D. Fausett. Syracuse: Syracuse Univ. Press.

Garnier, Charles-Georges-Thomas, ed. *Voyages imaginaires, songes, visions et romans cabalistiques*. 39 vols. Amsterdam and Paris, 1787–1789.

Gott, Samuel. 1902. *Nova Solyma, the ideal city; Or, Jerusalem regained, an anonymous romance written in the time of Charles I, now first drawn from obscurity and attributed to the illustrious John Milton*. Translated, edited, and with an introduction by W. Begley. 2 vols. London: J. Murray.

Hall, Joseph [pseud., Mercurius Britannicus]. 1605. *Mundus alter et idem, sive Terra Australis antehac semper incognita, longis itineribus peregrini Academici nuperrime lustrata*. Frankfurt am Main: for Ascanius de Rinialme.

———. 1609. *The Discovery of a New World or a Description of the South Indies hitherto unknowne*. Translated by John Healey. London: For E. Blount and W. Barrett.

———. 1669. *Psittacorum regio. The Land of Parrots: Or, the She-Lands. With a Description of other adjacent Countries, in the Dominions of the Prince de l'Amour, not hitherto found in any Geographical Map. By one of the late most reputed Wits*. London. [Plagiarized from Hall 1609; author catalogued as "Psittaci" in British Library.]

———. 1908. *Mun'us alter et idem*. [Abridged]. Edited and with an introduction by H. J. Anderson. London: Bell.

———. 1937. *The Discovery of a New World (Mundus alter et idem)*. Translated by John Healey. Edited and with an introduction by Huntington Brown. Cambridge, Mass.: Harvard Univ. Press.

———. 1968. *Mundus alter et idem*. [Facsimile ed.] Amsterdam: Theatrum Orbis Terrarum.

———. 1981. *Another World and Yet the Same: Bishop Joseph Hall's Mundus alter et idem.* Translated and edited by John Millar Wands. New Haven: Yale Univ. Press.

Harrington, James. 1656. *The common-wealth of Oceana.* London: J. Streater for Livewell Chapman.

I.D.M.G.T. 1616. *Histoire du grand et admirable royaume d'antangil. Incogneu jusques à present à tous les Historiens et Cosmographes: composé de six vingts Provinces très-belles et très-fertiles. Avec la description d'icelui, et de sa police nom-pareille, tant civile que militaire. De l'instruction de la jeunesse. Et de la religion. Le tout compris en cinq livres.* Saumur: Thomas Portau for I.D.M.G.T.

Leguat, François. 1708. *Le Voyage et Avantures de François Leguat, & de ses Compagnons, En Deux Isles Desertes des Indes Orientales.* London: David Mortier.

Lucian. 1820. *Lucian of Samosata, from the Greek.* Translated and edited by William Tooke. 2 vols. London.

Marana, Giovanni Paolo. 1970. *Letters Writ by a Turkish Spy.* Edited by Arthur J. Weitzman. London: Routledge and Kegan Paul.

More, Thomas. 1965. *Utopia.* Edited by E. Surtz and J. H. Hexter. New Haven, Conn.: Yale Univ. Press.

Neville, Henry. 1668a. *The Isle of Pines, or, A late Discovery of a fourth Island in Terra Australis Incognita. Being A True Relation of certain English persons, who in the dayes of Queen Elizabeth, making a Voyage to the East India, were cast away, and wracked upon the Island near to the Coast of Terra Australis, Incognita, and all drowned, except one Man and four Women, whereof one was a Negro. And now lately Anno Dom. 1667. a Dutch Ship driven by foul weather there, by chance have found their Posterity (speaking good English) to amount to ten or twelve thousand persons, as they suppose. The whole Relation follows, written, and left by the Man himself a little before his death, and declared to the Dutch by his Grandchild.* London, Printed by S. G. for Allen Banks and Charles Harper at the Flower-deluice near Cripplegate Church. [Original nine-page pamphlet, published June 27].

———. 1668b. *The Isle of Pines of A late Discovery of a fourth Island near Terra Australis, Incognita. By Henry Cornelius Van Sloetten. Wherein is contained, A true Relation of certain English persons, who in Queen Elizabeth's time, making a Voyage to the East Indies were cast away, and wracked near to the Coast of Terra Australis, Incognita, and all drowned, except one Man and four Women. And now lately Anno Dom. 1667 a Dutch Ship making a Voyage to the East Indies, driven by foul weather there by chance have found their Posterity, (speaking good English) to amount (as they suppose) to ten or twelve thousand persons. The whole Relation (written and left by the Man himself a little before his death, and delivered to the Dutch by his Grandchild) Is here annexed with the Longitude and Latitude of the Island, the scituation and felicity thereof, with other matter observ-*

215

able. Licensed July 27, 1668. London, for Allen Banks and Charles Harper next door to the three Squerrills in Fleet-street, over against St. Dunstans Church. [Quarto ed. of 1668a and 1668c with definitive title. Reproduced in Ford 1920; see Secondary Texts.]

————. 1668c. *A New and further Discovery of The Isle of Pines In A Letter from Cornelius Van Sloetton a Dutchman (who first discovered the same in the year, 1667) to a Friend of his in London. With a Relation of his voyage to the East Indies. Wherein Is declared how he happened to come thither, the Scituation of the Country, the temperature of the Climate, the manners and conditions of the people that inhabit it; their Laws, Ordinances, and Ceremonies, and their way of Marrying, Burying, & c. the Longitude and Latitude of the Island, the pleasantness and felicity thereof, with other matters of concern. Licensed according to Order.* London. [July 1668, sequel to Neville 1668a].

————. 1737. *La Découverte d'une île inconnue ou les aventures de Georges Pinès. Le Pour et le Contre* Vol. 13. Paris.

Paulmier de Courtonne, Jean 1663. *Memoirs touchant l'établissement d'une mission chrestienne dans le troisième monde, autrement appellé la Terre australe, Méridionale, Antarctique et Inconnuë. Presentez à Nostre S. Pere le Pape Alexandre VII. Par un Ecclesiastique Originaire de cette mesme Terre.* Paris: Cramoisy. [Published anonymously.]

Quirós (Queiros, Quir), Pedro Fernandez de. 1617a. "Copie de la requeste présentée au Roy d'Espagne par le capitaine Ferdinand de Quir, sur la descouverte de la cinquiesme partie du monde appelée Terre Australe incogneue et des grandes richesses et fertilité d'icelle." In *Mercure de France*. Paris.

————. 1617b: *Terre Australis incognita, or a new Southerne Discovery*. London.

Rotz [Ross, Rose), John. 1981. *His Boke of Idrography.* Edited and with an introduction by Helen Wallis. London: Roxburghe Club.

Schooten, Henry [pseud.]. 1671. *The hairy-giants, or, A description of two islands in the South Sea called by the name of Benganga and Coma, discovered by Henry Schooten of Harlem in a voyage began January 1669, and finished October 1671: also a perfect account of the religion, government and commodities of those islands, together with the customs and manners of the inhabitants . . . : likewise a description of the compass and situation of those islands, with their longitude and latitude: whereunto is annexed an appendix for the instruction of mariners. Written in Dutch by Henry Schooten; and now Englished by P. M., Gent.* London: A. Maxwell, for John Watson.

Schouten, Wouter. 1708. *Voïage de Gautier Schouten aux Indes Orientales, Commencé l'An 1658 & fini l'An 1665. Traduit du Hollandois. Où l'on void plusieurs Descriptions de Païs, Roïaumes, Isles & Villes, Siéges, Combats sur terre & sur mer, Coutumes, Maniéres, Réligions de divers Peuples, Animaux, Plantes, Fruits, & autres Curiositez naturelles.* 2 vols. Amsterdam: Pierre Mortier.

Smeeks 1708: Smeeks, Hendrik. *Beschryvinge van het magtig Koningryk Krinke Kesmes, Ontdekt door den Heer Juan de Posos, en uit deszelfs Schriften te zamen gestelt door Hendrik Smeeks.* Amsterdam: N. ten Hoorn. [Text reproduced in Buijnsters 1976; see Secondary Texts.]

Tavernier, Jean-Baptiste. 1968. *Travels in the Mogul Empire.* Edited by A. Constable. Translated by I. Brock. Delhi: Chand.

Thévenot, Melchisedech. ed. 1663. *Relation de divers voyages curieux qui n'ont point esté publiés et qu'on a traduites ou tirées des originauz des voyageurs françois, espagnols, allemands, portugois, hollandois, persans, arabes, etc.* 4 vols. Paris: Jacques Langlois.

————. 1672. *Relation de divers voyages curieux.* Paris: Durand. [Definitive ed.; reedited Paris: Thomas Moette, 1696].

Tyssot de Patot, Simon. 1710. *Voyages et avantures de Jaques Massé.* Bordeaux: Chez Jaques L'Aveugle. [Facsimile ed.: see Trousson 1979 in Secondary Texts.]

Vairasse (Veiras) d'Alais, Denis. 1675. *The History of the Sevarites or Sevarambi a nation inhabiting a part of the third continent, commonly called Terrae Australes Incognitae. With an Account of their admirable Government, Religion, Customs, and Language. Written by one Captain Siden.* London: for Henry Brome.

————. 1677. *L'Histoire des Sévarambes, peuples qui habitent une partie du troisième Continent, communément appellé la terre australe. Contenant un compte exact du Gouvernement, des Moeurs, de la Religion et du langage de cette Nation, jusques aujourd'hui inconnuë aux Peuples de l'Europe. Traduit de l'anglais.* Part 1, vol. 2. Paris: Claude Barbin.

————1678. *L'Histoire des Sévarambes . . .* Part 1, vol. 1. Paris: Author, Theodore Girard, and Estienne Michalet.

————. 1679a. *Conclusion de l'Histoire des Sévarambes, peuples qui habitent une partie du troisième Continent, communément appellé la terre Australe. Contenant un conte exact du Gouvernement des Moeurs, de la Religion, et du langage de cette Nation, jusques aujourd'hui inconnuë aux Peuples de l'Europe.* Part 2, vol. 3. Paris: Author and Estienne Michalet. [Text reproduced in Garnier 1789, vol. 5.]

————. 1679b. *The History of the Sevarites.* [Ed. of Vairasse 1675 plus "A further Account of their Government, Religion, Customs, and Language. The Second Part more wonderful and delightful than the First."]

Secondary Texts

Adams, Percy G. 1962. *Travelers and Travel Liars, 1660–1800.* Berkeley: Univ. of California Press.

————. 1983. *Travel Literature and the Evolution of the Novel.* Lexington: Univ. Press of Kentucky.

Africa, Christine. 1979. *Utopias in France, 1616–1789.* Ann Arbor, Mich.: University Microfilms.

Aldridge, A. Owen. 1950. "Polygamy in Early Fiction: Henry Neville and Denis Veiras." *Publications of the Modern Language Association of America* 65: 464–72.

Amherst, Lord, and B. Thompson. 1901. *The Discovery of the Solomon Islands by Alvaro de Mendaña in 1568.* 2 vols. London: Hakluyt Society.

Andrews, Clarence Edward. 1913. *Richard Brome: A Study of his Life and Works.* New York: Holt.

Armytage, Walter. 1961. *Heavens Below. Utopian Experiments in England, 1560–1960.* London: Routledge and Kegan Paul.

Atkinson, Geoffroy. 1920. *The Extraordinary Voyage in French Literature before 1700.* New York: Columbia Univ. Press.

————. 1922. *The Extraordinary Voyage in French Literature from 1700 to 1720.* Paris: Champion.

————. 1924. *Les Relations de voyages du XVIIe siècle et l'évolution des idées.* Paris: Champion.

Auerbach, Erich. 1953. *Mimesis: The Representation of Reality in Western Literature.* Translated by W. Trask. Princeton: Princeton Univ. Press.

Bachelard, Gaston. 1942. *L'Eau et les rêves.* Paris: Corti.

Baker, J. N. L. 1931. *A History of Geographical Discovery.* London: Harrap.

Bauman, Zygmunt. 1990. "Modernity and Ambivalence." *Theory, Culture and Society* 7: 143–69.

Baxter, Christopher R. 1968. "Problems of the Religious Wars." In *French Literature and its Background.* Vol. 1, *The Sixteenth Century,* edited by J. Cruickshank. London: Oxford Univ. Press.

Bayle, Pierre. 1697. *Dictionnaire historique et critique.* 2 vols. Rotterdam: Reinier Leers.

Beaglehole, J. C. 1934. *The Exploration of the Pacific.* London: Black.

Benrekassa, Georges. 1980. *Le Concentrique et l'excentrique: Marges des Lumières.* Paris: Payot.

Bensaude, Joachim. 1912. *L'Astronomie nautique du Portugal à l'époque des découvertes maritimes.* Bern: Dreschel.

————. 1930. *Lacunes et surprises de l'histoire des découvertes maritimes.* Coimbra: Presses Universitaires de Coïmbre.

Berneri, Marie-Louise. 1950. *Journey Through Utopia.* London: Routledge and Kegan Paul.

Beugnot, Bernard, ed. 1984. *Voyages: Récits et imaginaire. Papers in Seventeenth-Century Literature* 16.

Bishop, Norma J. 1986. *Liminal Space in Travellers' Tales: Historical and Fictional Passages.* Ph.D. diss., Pennsylvania State Univ.

Blainey, Geoffrey N. 1985. *The Tyranny of Distance.* Melbourne: Sun Books.

Bloch, Ernst. 1957. *Das Prinzip Hoffnung.* 2 vols. Frankfurt am Main: Suhrkamp.

Bosetti, Gilbert. 1984. "Marco Polo et l'horizon austral de l'océan indien." In *Le Voyage austral,* edited by Chocheyras, 8–21. Grenoble: ELLUG (Université des Langues et Lettres de Grenoble).

Bourez, Marie-Thérèse. 1984. "La Terre australe inconnue et l'*Histoire des Sévarambes* (1677) de Denis Veiras." In *Le Voyage austral,* edited by Chocheyras, 22–43. Grenoble: ELLUG (Université des Langues et Lettres de Grenoble).

Bouwsma, William James. 1957. *Concordia Mundi. The Thought and Career of Guillaume Postel.* Cambridge, Mass.: Harvard Univ. Press.

Bowra, Cecil Maurice. 1957. *The Greek Experience.* Cleveland, Ohio: World Publishing.

Boxer, Christopher R. 1965. *The Dutch Seaborne Empire, 1600–1800.* London: Hutchinson.

———. 1969. *The Portuguese Seaborne Empire, 1415–1825.* London: Hutchinson.

Briggs, Robin. 1977. *Early Modern France, 1560–1715.* Oxford: Oxford Univ. Press.

Brown, Huntingdon, ed. 1937. Hall, Joseph. *The Discovery of a New World (Mundus alter et idem).* Translated by John Healey. [See Hall 1937 in Primary Texts.]

Buijnsters, P. J., ed. 1976. Smeeks, Hendrik. *Beschryvinge van het magtig Koningryk Krinke Kesmes.* Zutphen: Thieme.

Cameron, Ian. 1965. *Lodestone and Evening Star. The Seamen Who Mapped the World.* London: Hodder and Stoughton.

Campbell, Mary B. 1988. *The Witness and the Other World. Exotic European Travel Writing, 400–1600.* Ithaca: Cornell Univ. Press.

Castinian, Donald G. 1969. *El Inca Garcilaso de la Vega.* New York: Twayne.

Chinard, Gilbert. 1970. *L'Amérique et le rêve exotique dans la littérature française.* Geneva: Slatkine Reprints. [Orig. Paris: Hachette, 1913.]

Chocheyras, Jacques, ed. 1984. *Le Voyage austral.* Grenoble: ELLUG (Université des Langues et Lettres de Grenoble).

Cioranescu, Alexandre. 1962. *L'avenir du passé: Utopie et littérature.* Paris: Gallimard.

———. 1963. "Le *Royaume d'Antangil* et son auteur." *Studi francesi* 28:17–25.

———. 1974. "Epigone, le premier roman de l'avenir." *Revue des Sciences Humaines* 155:441–48.

Cobo, Bernabe. 1979. *History of the Inca Empire,* edited and translated by R. Hamilton. Introduction by J. Rowe. Austin: Univ. of Texas Press.

Cohn, Norman. 1957. *The Pursuit of the Millennium.* Fairlawn, N.J.: Essential Books.

Cornelius, Paul. 1965. *Language in Seventeenth and Early Eighteenth Century Imaginary Voyages.* Geneva: Droz.

Cortesão, Armando, trans. and ed. 1967. *The "Suma Oriental" of Tomé Pires . . . and the Book of Francisco Rodriguez, "Rutter of a Voyage in the Red Sea . . . in the East before 1515."* Nendeln, Liechtenstein: Kraus Reprints.

Cortesão, Armando, and Avelino Teixeira da Mota. 1960. *Portugaliae Monumenta Cartographica.* Lisbon.

Cro, Stelio. 1990. *The Noble Savage: Allegory of Freedom.* Waterloo, Ontario: Wilfred Laurier Univ. Press.

Dames, Mansell Longworth. 1967. *The Book of Duarte Barbosa* (ca. A.D. 1518). 2 vols. Nendeln, Liechtenstein: Kraus Reprints.

Davis, James Colin. 1981. *Utopia and the Ideal Society: A Study of English Utopian Writing 1516–1700.* Cambridge: Cambridge Univ. Press.

Davis, Joseph Lee. 1943. "Richard Brome's Neglected Contribution to Comic Theory." *Studies in Philology* 9:520–28.

Delcourt, Marie. 1958. *Hermaphrodite. Mythes et rites de la bissexualité dans l'antiquité classique.* Paris: Presses Universitaires de France.

Demoris, René. 1975. *Le Roman à la première personne.* Paris: Armand Colin.

Donaldson, Ian. 1970. *The World Upside-Down. Comedy from Jonson to Fielding.* Oxford: Clarendon.

———, ed. 1982: *Australia and the European Imagination.* Canberra: Australian National Univ.

Donner, H. W. 1945. *Introduction to Utopia.* London: Sidgwick and Jackson.

Drake-Brockman, Henrietta. 1963. *Voyage to Disaster. The Life of Francisco Pelsaert. Covering his Indian report to the Dutch East India Company and the wreck of the ship* Batavia *of western Australia together with the full text of his journals concerning the rescue voyages, the mutiny on the Abrolhos-Islands and the subsequent trials of the Mutineers.* London: Angus and Robertson.

Duchet, Michèle. 1977. *Anthropologie et histoire au siècle des Lumières.* Paris: Flammarion.

Dubois, Claude-Gilbert. 1974. "Une Architexture fixionelle." *Revue des Sciences Humaines* 155:449–72.

———. 1978. "Urbi et orbis. Le discours de la ville dans la production utopique de la Renaissance." *Le Discours utopique. Colloque de Cérisy,* 212–23. Paris: Union Générale d'Editions.

———. 1987. "L'Hermaphrodite." *Cahiers de Littérature du XVIIe siècle* 9:11–27.

Eliade, Mircea. 1967. *Myths, Dreams, and Mysteries. The Encounter between Contemporary Faiths and Archaic Realities.* Translated by P. Mairet. New York: Harper Torchbooks.

———. 1971. *The Myth of the Eternal Return. or, Cosmos and History.* Translated by W. Trask. Princeton: Princeton Univ. Press.

————. 1978. *A History of Religious Ideas*. Vol. 1, *From the Stone Age to the Eleusinian Mysteries*. Chicago: Univ. of Chicago Press.

Esdaile, Arundle James Kennedy. 1912. *A List of Printed English Tales and Prose Romances before 1740*. London: Bibliographical Society.

Fausett, David J. 1988. *Amnioticon: Histoire de l'utopie 'australe'*. Ph.D. diss., Ecole des Hautes Etudes en Sciences Sociales, Paris.

————. 1990. "Pour une histoire de l'imaginaire austral: De l'ailleurs fictif au territoire d'exploration." *Ailleurs imaginés*. Edited by J. -M. Racault. Paris: Didier (Cahiers CRLH-CIRAOI) 6:169–81.

————, trans. and ed. 1993. Foigny, Gabriel de. *The Southern Land, Known*. Syracuse: Syracuse Univ. Press.

Ferguson 1975: Ferguson, John. *Utopias of the Classical World*. London: Thames and Hudson; Ithaca: Cornell Univ. Press.

Filteau, Claude. 1980. "Tendre: la Clélie de Madeleine de Scudéry." *Cartes et Figures de la Terre*. Paris: Centre Georges Pompidou.

Ford, Worthington Chauncey, ed. 1920. *The Isle of Pines*. Boston: Club of Odd Volumes. [See Neville 1668b in Primary Texts.]

Foucault, Michel. 1972. *The Order of Things: An Archeology of the Human Sciences*. New York: Pantheon.

Frame, Donald M., trans. and ed. 1948. *The Complete Essays of Montaigne*. Stanford: Stanford Univ. Press.

Frame, Douglas. 1978. *The Myth of Return in Early Greek Epic*. New Haven, Conn.: Yale Univ. Press.

Friedrich, Werner P. 1967. "The Image of Australia in French Literature from the 17th to the 20th Centuries." *Mélanges offertes à M. Brahmer*. Warsaw.

Frye, Northrop. 1966a. *Anatomy of Criticism*. New York: Atheneum.

————. 1966b. "Varieties of Literary Utopias." In *Utopias and Utopian Thought*, edited by F. Manuel. Cambridge, Mass.: Riverside.

Garagnon, Jean. 1982. "French Imaginary Voyages to the Austral Lands in the Seventeenth and Eighteenth Centuries." In *Australia and the European Imagination*, edited by Ian Donaldson, 87–107. Canberra: Australian National Univ., 1982.

Gibson, Ross. 1984. *The Diminishing Paradise: Changing Literary Perceptions of Australia*. Sydney: Angus and Robertson.

Girard, René. 1977. *Violence and the Sacred*. Translated by P. Gregory. Baltimore: Johns Hopkins Univ. Press.

Goebel, Julius. 1923. "The Dutch Source of *Robinson Crusoe*." *Journal of English and Germanic Philology* 21, no. 2:302–13.

Goubert, Pierre. 1973. *The Ancien Régime: French Society 1600–1750*. Translated by S. Cox. London: Weidenfeld and Nicolson.

Gove, Philip Babcock. 1941. *The Imaginary Voyage in Prose Fiction: A History of its Criticism.* New York: Columbia Univ. Press.

Green, Jeremy N. 1977. *The VOC Jacht Vergulde Draeck.* London: British Archaeological Reports.

Grendler, Paul. 1969. *Critics of the Italian World (1530–1560).* Madison: Univ. of Wisconsin Press.

Haaker, Ann. ed. 1966. *The Antipodes.* Lincoln: Univ. of Nebraska Press. [See Brome 1640, Primary Texts.]

Hamy, E. 1896. *Etudes historiques et géographiques.* Paris.

Hansot, Elisabeth. 1974. *Perfection and Progress: Two Modes of Utopian Thought.* Cambridge, Mass.: M.I.T. Press.

Hazard, Paul. 1935. *La Crise de la conscience européenne.* Paris: Boivin.

———. 1953. *The European Mind, 1685–1710.* translated by J. Lewis May. London: Hollis and Carter.

Headicar, B. M., and C. Fuller. 1931. *London Bibliography of the Social Sciences.* London: London School of Economics.

Heeres, J. E. 1899. *The Part Borne by the Dutch in the Discovery of Australia, 1606–1765.* London: Lucaz.

Helleiner, Karl F. 1959. "Prester John's Letter: A Medieval Utopia." *Phoenix. Journal of the Classical Association of Canada* 13:47–57.

Henderson, Graeme. 1986. *Maritime Archeology in Australia.* Perth: Univ. of Western Australia Press.

Henderson, James A. 1982. *Marooned: The wreck of the* Vergulde Draek *and the abandonment and escape from the Southland of Abraham Leeman in 1658.* Perth: St. George Books.

Hervé, Roger. 1982. *La Découverte fortuite de l'Australie et de la Nouvelle-Zélande par les navigateurs portugais et espagnols entre 1521 et 1528. Résultats de la critique des cartes dieppoises et documents apparentés.* Paris: Bibliothèque Nationale.

———. 1983. *The Chance Discovery of Australia and New Zealand (1521–1528).* Translated by J. Dunmore. Palmerston North, New Zealand: Dunmore Press.

Hettner, Hermann. 1961. *Geschischte der deutschen Literatur im achtzehnten Jahrhundert.* Revised by Gotthard Erler. 2 vols. Berlin: Aufbau-Verlag.

Heyerdahl, Thor. 1978. *Early Man and the Ocean.* London: Allen and Unwin.

Hippe, Max. 1894. "Eine vor-Defoe'sche englische Robinsonade." *Englische Studien* 19:66–104.

Hobson, Marian. 1982. *The Object of Art. The Theory of Illusion in Eighteenth Century France.* Cambridge: Cambridge Univ. Press.

Hollingsworth, Lawrence William. 1929. *A Short History of the East Coast of Africa.* London: Macmillan.

Hoogewerff, Godefridus Joannes. 1909. "Een Nederlandsche bron van den Robinson Crusoe." *Onze Eeuw: Maandschrift voor staatkunde, letteren, wetenschap en kunst* (Haarlem: F. Bohn). 9:396–98.

———. 1930. "Hendrik Smeeks, geschiedschrijver der boekaniers." *Tijdschrift voor Geschiedenis* 45:225–36.

Hourani, George Fadlo. 1951. *Arab Seafaring in the Indian Ocean in Ancient and Early Medieval Times.* Princeton: Princeton Univ. Pres.

Hubbard, Lucius L. 1921. *A Dutch Source for Robinson Crusoe: The Narrative of the El-Ho "Sjouke Gabbes" (also known as Henrich Texel). An Episode from the Description of the Mighty Kingdom of Krinke Kesmes, etc., by Hendrik Smeeks, 1708. Translated from the Dutch and compared with the story of Robinson Crusoe.* Ann Arbor: George Wahr.

Huntingford, G. W. B., trans. and ed. 1980. *The Periplus of the Erythraean Sea.* Hakluyt Society, 2d ser., no. 151. London: British Library.

Imbroscio, Carmelina, ed. 1986. *Requiem pour l'utopie? Tendances autodestructives du paradigme utopique,* with an introduction by R. Trousson. Pisa: Goliardica; Paris: Nizet.

Jack-Hinton, Colin. 1969. *The Search for the Islands of Solomon, 1567–1838.* Oxford: Clarendon.

James, W. Trevor. 1982. "Nostalgia for Paradise: Terra Australis in the Seventeenth Century." In *Australia and the European Imagination,* edited by Ian Donaldson, 59–85. Canberra: Australian National Univ., 1982.

Johnson, J. W. 1982. "The Utopian Impulse and Southern Lands." In *Australia and the European Imagination,* edited by Ian Donaldson, 41–58. Canberra: Australian National Univ., 1982.

Kamenka, Eugene, ed. 1987. *Utopias.* Canberra: Australian National Univ.

Kantorowicz, E. H. 1957. *The King's Two Bodies.* Princeton: Princeton Univ. Press.

Kaufmann, R. J. 1961. *Richard Brome, Caroline Playwright.* New York: Columbia Univ. Press.

Kelly, Celsus, ed. 1966. *La Austrialia del Espiritu Santo. The Journal of Fray Martín Munilla O.F.M., and other documents relating to the Voyage of Pedro Fernández Quirós to the South Sea (1605–1606) and the Franciscan Missionary Plan (1617–1627),* with an introduction by G. S. Parkinson. 2 vols. Cambridge: Cambridge Univ. Press, for Hakluyt Society.

Kippenberg, August. 1892. *Robinson in Deutschland bis zur Insel Felsenburg (1731–43).* Hannover: Goedel.

Knowlson, J. R. 1963. "The Ideal Languages of Veiras, Foigny and Tyssot." *Journal of the History of Ideas* (April–June): 269–78.

———. 1975. *Universal Language Schemes in England and France, 1600–1800.* Toronto: Univ. of Toronto Press.

Kuon, Peter. 1986. *Utopischer Entwurf und fiktionale Vermittlung: Studien zum*

Gattungswandel der literarischen Utopie zwischen Humanismus und Frühaufklärung. Heidelberg: Carl Winter.

———. 1987. "L'Utopie entre 'mythe' et 'Lumières': La *Terre Australe connue de Gabriel de Foigny et l'Histoire des Sévarambes* de Denis Veiras." *Papers in French Seventeenth Century Literature* 14:253–72.

Lachèvre, Frédéric. 1968. *Les Successeurs de Cyrano de Bergerac.* Vol. 12 of *Le Libertinage au XVII siècle.* Geneva: Slatkine [orig. ed. 1922].

Langdon, Robert. 1975. *The Lost Caravel.* Sydney: Pacific.

Lascassagne, Claude. 1972. "La Satire religieuse dans *Mundus alter et idem* de Joseph Hall." *Recherches Anglaises et Nord-américaines* 2:141–56.

Lasky, Melvin J. 1977. *Utopia and Revolution.* Chicago: Univ. of Chicago Press.

Lehnert, Max. 1920. "Der Böhmische Robinson sowie der Holländische Robinson." In *Robinsonaden: Eine Sammlung.* Band 5. Charlottenburg: Raben.

Leibacher-Ouvrard, Lise. 1986. "Souvages et Utopies (1676–1715): L'exotisme-alibi." *French Literature Series* 13:1–12.

———. 1989. *Libertinage et utopies sous le règne de Louis XIV.* Geneva: Droz.

Levin, Harry. 1969. *The Myth of the Golden Age in the Renaissance.* Bloomington: Indiana University Press.

Lichtenberger, André. 1895. *Le Socialisme au dix-huitième siècle.* Paris: Alcan.

L'Honoré Naber, Samuel P. 1910. "Nog Eens de Nederlandsche Bron van den Robinson Crusoe." *Onze Eeuw* 10, no. 1 (Mar.): 427–48.

Linon, Sophy-Jenny. 1990. "Contraintes et enjeux idéologiques d'une topographie imaginaire: Les terres australes inconnues d'Etienne de Flacourt (1661) et de l'abbé Jean Paulmier (1663)." *Ailleurs imaginés.* Paris: Didier (Cahiers CRLH-CIRAOI) 6:159–68.

Lovejoy, Arthur Oncken. 1964. *The Great Chain of Being: A Study of the History of an Idea.* Cambridge, Mass.: Harvard Univ. Press.

Lovejoy, Arthur Oncken, and George Boas. 1935. *A Documentary History of Primitivism and Related Ideas in Antiquity.* Baltimore, Md.: Johns Hopkins Univ. Press.

McCabe, Richard. 1982. *Joseph Hall. A Study in Satire and Meditation.* Oxford: Clarendon.

McIntyre, Kenneth Gordon. 1977. *The Secret Discovery of Australia: Portuguese Ventures 200 Years before Cook.* Medindie, Australia: Souvenir Press.

Macknight, Charles G. 1976. *The Voyage to Marege'.* Carlton, Australia: Melbourne Univ. Press.

Major, Richard Henry. 1859. *Early Voyages to Terra Australis, now called Australia.* London: Hakluyt Society.

Mannheim, Karl. 1936. *Ideology and Utopia.* Translated by L. Wirth and E. Shils. New York: Harcourt, Brace, and World.

224

Manuel, Frank E. 1966. *Utopias and Utopian Thought.* Cambridge, Mass.: Riverside.

Manuel, Frank E., and Fritzie P. Manuel. 1979. *Utopian Thought in the Western World.* Cambridge, Mass.: Harvard Univ. Press, Belknap.

Marin, Louis. 1974. "The Frame of the Painting or the Semiotic Functions of Boundaries in the Representative Process." *A Semiotic Landscape/Panorama sémiotique,* edited by Seymour Chatman, Umberto Eco, and Jean-Marie Klinkenberg. The Hague: Mouton.

————. 1975. *La Critique du discours. Sur la "Logique de Port-Royal" et les "Pensées" de Pascal.* Paris: Minuit.

————. 1985. *Utopics. Spatial Plays.* Translated by R. Vollrath. Atlantic City, N.J.: Macmillan Humanities Press.

Marin, Louis, and G. Dagron. 1971. "Histoire et utopie." *Annales E.S.C.* 26 (Mar.–Apr.): 312–17.

Markham, Clements. 1904. *The Voyages of Pedro Fernandez de Queiros, 1595–1606.* 2 vols. London: Hakluyt Society.

Martin, Henri-Jean, and Roger Chartier. 1984. *Histoire de l'édition française.* Paris: Promodis.

Masefield, John Edward. 1908. *The Travels of Marco Polo, the Venetian.* London: Dent Everyman.

May, Georges. 1963. *Le Dilemme du roman au XVIII siècle.* New Haven: Yale Univ. Press; Paris: Presses Universitaires de France.

Morgan, Arthur E. 1946. *Nowhere was Somewhere: How History Makes Utopias and How Utopias Make History.* Chapel Hill: Univ. of North Carolina Press.

Morris, Roger. 1987. *Pacific Sail: Four Centuries of Western Ships in the Pacific.* Auckland, New Zealand: Bateman.

Morton, Arthur L. 1952. *The English Utopia.* London: Lawrence and Wishart.

Mulder, Arnold. 1923. "Was *Robinson Crusoe* Written by a Hollander?" *Outlook* 135(October): 277–80.

Mylne, Vivienne G. 1965. *The Eighteenth Century French Novel: Techniques of Illusion.* Manchester: Manchester Univ. Press.

Negley, Glenn. 1977. *Utopian Literature. A Bibliography, with a Supplementary List of Works Influential in Utopian Thought.* Lawrence: Univ. of Kansas Press.

Nordenskiöld, Adolf Eric. 1897. *Periplus. An Essay on the Early History of Charts and Sailing Directions.* Translated by F. Bather. Stockholm: Norstedt.

————. 1973. *Facsimile-Atlas to the History of Early Cartography, with Reproductions of the Most Important Maps Published in the XVth and XVIth Centuries.* New York: Dover Reprints [orig. ed. 1889].

North-Coombes, Alfred. 1979. *The Vindication of François Leguat.* Port Louis, Mauritius.

Nozick, Robert. 1974. *Anarchy, State, and Utopia.* Oxford: Basil Blackwell.

Olschki, Leonardo. 1931. "Der Brief des Presbyters Johannes." *Historische Zeitschrift* 144:1–14.

———. 1960. *Marco Polo's Asia.* Translated by J. Scott. Berkeley: Univ. of California Press.

Patrick, J. Max. 1946. "A Consideration of de Foigny's *Terre Australe connue.*" *Publications of the Modern Language Association of America* 61:739–51.

Pellandra, Carla. 1986. "Transparences trompeuses: Les cosmogonies linguistiques de Foigny et de Veiras." In *Requiem pour l'utopie?* edited by Carmelina Imbroscio, 55–71. Pisa: Goliardica; Paris: Nizet.

Penrose, Boies, 1967. *Travel and Discovery in the Renaissance.* Cambridge, Mass.: Harvard Univ. Press.

Peterson, Spiro. 1987. *Writings about Daniel Defoe, 1731–1924.* Boston: G. K. Hall.

Pocock, J. G. A., ed. 1977. *The Political Works of James Harrington.* Cambridge: Cambridge Univ. Press.

Polak, Leon. 1914. "Vordefoe'che Robinsonaden in den Niederlanden." *Germanisch-Romanisches Monatschrift* 6:304–7.

Pons, Etienne. 1932. "Les Langues imaginaires dans le voyage utopique." *Revue de Littérature Comparée* 12:501–32.

Racault, Jean-Michel, ed. 1984. *Aventures aux Mascareignes.* Paris: La Découverte.

———. 1991: *L'Utopie narrative en France et en Angleterre de l'âge classique aux Lumières (1675–1761): Etude de forme et signification.* Oxford: Voltaire Foundation.

Rainaud, Armand. 1893. *Le Continent austral: Hypothèses et découvertes.* Paris: Armand Colin.

Ravenstein, Ernest George. 1908. *Martin Behaim, His Life and His Globe.* London: G. Philip.

Ronzeaud, Pierre. 1982. *L'Utopie hermaphrodite. La Terre Australe connue (1676) de Gabriel de Foigny.* Marseille: C.M.R.

Rosenberg, Aubrey. 1972a. "Hendrik Smeeks and Simon Tyssot de Patot— Were they friends?" *Verslagen en Medeleelingen van de Vereeniging tot beoefening van Overijsselsch Regt in Geschiedenis* 87:96–102.

———. 1972b. *Tyssot de Patot and His Work (1655–1738).* The Hague: Martinus Nijhoff.

Rowe, John H. 1949. "Inca Culture at the Time of the Spanish Conquest." In *Handbook of the South American Indians* Vol. 2. Washington, D.C.: Bureau of American Ethnology.

Ruyer, Raymond. 1950. *L'Utopie et les utopies.* Paris: Presses Universitaires de France.

Said, Edward. 1979. *Orientalism.* New York: Vintage.

Salyer, Sandford M. 1927. "Renaissance Influences in Hall's *Mundus alter et idem.*" *Philological Quarterly* 6 (October): 324f.

Sargent, Lyman Tower. 1988. *British and American Utopian Literature 1516–1985: An Annotated Chronological Bibliography.* New York: Garland.

Schilder, Gunter. 1976. *Australia Unveiled.* Translated by O. Richter. Amsterdam: Theatrum Orbis Terrarum.

———. 1985. *Voyage to the Great South Land. Willem de Vlamingh, 1696–7.* Sydney: Royal Australian Historical Society.

Scholte, J. H. 1930. "Die Insel der Früchtbarkeit." *Zeitschrift für Bücherfreunde* 22:49–55.

Secord, Arthur Wellesley. 1924. *Studies in the Narrative Method of Defoe.* Urbana: Univ. of Illinois Press.

Servier, Jean. 1967. *Histoire de l'utopie.* Paris: Gallimard.

Sharp, Andrew. 1963. *The Discovery of Australia.* Oxford: Clarendon.

Shaw, Catherine. 1980. *Richard Brome.* Boston: Twayne.

Shennan, J. H. 1974. *The Origins of the Modern European State, 1450–1725.* London: Hutchinson.

Showalter, English. 1972. *The Evolution of the French Novel, 1641–1782.* Princeton: Princeton Univ. Press.

Slessarev, Vsevolod. 1959. *Prester John. The Letter and the Legend.* Minneapolis: Univ. of Minnesota Press.

Smith, Bernard. 1960. *European Vision and the South Pacific, 1768–1850: A Study in the History of Art and Ideas.* Oxford: Clarendon.

Spate, O. H. K. 1957. "Terra Australis—Cognita?" *Historical Studies* 8, no. 29:1–19.

———. 1975. "Manuel Godinho de Eredia." In *Let Me Enjoy: Essays, Partly Geographical,* 249–66. Canberra: Australian National University.

———. 1979. *The Pacific since Magellan.* Vol. 1, *The Spanish Lake.* Canberra: Australian National Univ.

———. 1987. "The Pacific: Home of the Utopia." In *Utopias,* edited by Eugene Kamenka. Canberra: Australian National Univ.

Stafford, Barbara Maria. 1984. *Voyage into Substance.* Cambridge, Mass.: M.I.T. Press.

Staverman, W. H. 1907. *Robinson Crusoe in Nederland.* Ph.D. diss., Univ. of Groningen, the Netherlands.

———. 1925. "Een nederlandse bron van de Robinson Crusoe." *De Nieuwe Taalgids* 19:206–7.

Stewart, Philip R. 1967. *Imitation and Illusion in the French Memoir-Novel, 1700–1750: The Art of Make-Believe.* New Haven: Yale Univ. Press.

Stommel, Henry. 1984. *Lost Islands. The Story of Islands That Have Vanished from Nautical Charts.* Vancouver: Univ. of British Columbia Press.

Suvin, Darko. 1979. *Metamorphoses of Science Fiction: On the Poetics of a Literary Genre.* New Haven: Yale Univ. Press.

Taylor, Alan Cary. 1938. *Le Président de Brosses et l'Australie*. Paris: Armand Colin.

Taylor, E. G. R. 1968. *Tudor Geography, 1485–1583*. New York: Octagon.

Taylor, John. 1966. *The Universal Chronical of Ranulf Higden*. Oxford: Clarendon.

Tieje, Arthur Jerrold. 1913. "Realism in Pre-Richardsonian Fiction." *Publications of the Modern Language Association of America* 28:213–52.

Treasure, G. G. R. 1981. *Seventeenth Century France*. London: John Murray.

Trousson, Raymond. 1974. "Utopie et roman utopique." *Revue des Sciences Humaines* 155:367–78.

————. 1975. *Voyages aux pays de nulle part. Histoire littéraire de la pensée utopique*. Brussels: Editions de l'Université de Bruxelles.

————, ed. 1979. Simon Tyssot de Patot. *Voyages et avantures de Jaques Massé*. [Facsimile ed.] Geneva: Slatkine Reprints.

————, ed. 1981. Gabriel de Foigny. *La Terre Australe connue*. [Facsimile ed.] Geneva: Slatkine Reprints.

Turner, Victor. 1974. *Dramas, Fields and Metaphors*. Ithaca: Cornell Univ. Press.

————. 1979. *Process, Performance and Pilgrimage*. New Delhi: Concept.

Tuveson, Ernest Lee. 1949. *Millenium and Utopia: A Study in the Background of the Idea of Progress*. Berkeley: Univ. of California Press.

Van Wijngaarden, Nicolaas. 1932. *Les Odysées philosophiques en France avant 1789*. Haarlem: Vijlbrief.

Vernière, Paul. 1954. *Spinoza et la pensée française avant la Révolution*. 2 vols. Paris: Presses Universitaires de France.

Von der Mühll, Emanuel. 1938. *Denis Veiras et son Histoire des Sévarambes, 1677–79*. Paris: Droz.

Wallis, Helen. 1982. "The Enigma of Java-la-Grande." In *Australia and the European Imagination*, edited by Ian Donaldson, 1–40. Canberra: Australian National Univ.

————. ed. 1981. Rotz, John. *His Boke of Idrography*. London: Roxburghe Club.

Wands, John Millar. trans., and ed. 1981. Joseph Hall. *Another World and yet the Same: Bishop Joseph Hall's Mundus alter et idem*. New Haven: Yale Univ. Press.

Warmington, Eric Herbert. 1934. *Greek Geography*. London: Dent.

Waters, D. W. 1978. *Science and the Techniques of Navigation in the Renaissance*. Greenwich: National Maritime Museum.

Watt, Ian. 1977. *The Rise of the Novel, Studies in Defoe, Richardson and Fielding*. Harmondsworth, England: Penguin.

Willey, Basil. 1986. *The Eighteenth Century Background*. London: Routledge and Kegan Paul.

Winter, Michael. 1978. *Compendium Utopiarum*. Stuttgart: Metzler.

Wright, John Kirtland. 1965. *The Geographical Lore of the Time of the Crusades.* New York: American Geographical Society.

Wunenberger, Jean-Jacques. 1979. *L'Utopie, ou la crise de l'imaginaire.* Paris: Delarge.

Yardeni, Miriam. 1980. *Utopie et révolte sous Louis XIV.* Paris: Nizet.

Zaganelli, Gioia. 1986. "Contradiction et conciliation en utopie: La lettre du 'Prêtre Jean'." In *Requiem pour l'utopie?* edited by Ian Imbroscio, 19–34. Pisa: Goliardica; Paris, Nizet.

Zinguer, Ilana. 1982. *Misères et grandeur de la femme au siezième siècle.* Geneva: Slatkine.

Zucchini, Giampaolo. 1976. "Utopia e Satira nel *Mundus alter et idem* di Joseph Hall." *Il Pensiero Politico* 9, no. 2–3: 248–75.

Index

WRITING THE NEW WORLD
was composed in 12 on 13 Bembo on Digital Compugraphic equipment
by Metricomp;
printed by sheet-fed offset on 50-pound, acid-free Natural Hi Bulk,
Smyth-sewn and bound over binder's boards in Holliston Roxite B,
and notch bound with paper covers printed in 2 colors
by Braun-Brumfield, Inc.;
and published by
Syracuse University Press
Syracuse, New York 13244-5160